The Erotic in the Literature of Medieval Britain

This volume examines the erotic in the literature of medieval Britain, primarily in Middle English, but also in Latin, Welsh and Old French. Seeking to discover the nature of the erotic in the literature of the period and how the eroticism of the Middle Ages differs from modern erotics, the contributors address a wide range of topics, including the Wife of Bath's opinions on marital eroticism, the role of clothing and nudity, the tension between eroticism and transgression, the creation of the early modern world in Petrarch's romantic lyrics, the interplay between religion and the erotic, and the hedonistic horrors of the cannibalistic Giant of Mont St Michel.

Dr AMANDA HOPKINS teaches at the University of Warwick in the department of English and Comparative Literary Studies and the department of French.
Dr CORY JAMES RUSHTON is assistant professor of English at St. Francis Xavier University, Nova Scotia, Canada.

The Erotic in the
Literature of Medieval Britain

Edited by
Amanda Hopkins
Cory James Rushton

D. S. BREWER

© Contributors 2007

All Rights Reserved. Except as permitted under current legislation no part of this work may be photocopied, stored in a retrieval system, published, performed in public, adapted, broadcast, transmitted, recorded or reproduced in any form or by any means, without the prior permission of the copyright owner

First published 2007
D. S. Brewer, Cambridge
Paperback edition 2016

ISBN 978 1 84384 119 7 hardback
ISBN 978 1 84384 443 3 paperback

D. S. Brewer is an imprint of Boydell & Brewer Ltd
PO Box 9, Woodbridge, Suffolk IP12 3DF, UK
and of Boydell & Brewer Inc.
668 Mt Hope Avenue, Rochester, NY 14620–2731, USA
website: www.boydellandbrewer.com

The publisher has no responsibility for the continued existence or accuracy of URLs for external or third-party internet websites referred to in this book, and does not guarantee that any content on such websites is, or will remain, accurate or appropriate

A CIP catalogue record for this book is available from the British Library

This publication is printed on acid-free paper

Typeset by Pru Harrison, Hacheston, Suffolk

Contents

Foreword A. C. GRAND	xiii
List of Contributors	vii
List of Abbreviations	xi
Introduction: The Revel, the Melodye and the Bisynesse of Solas CORY J. RUSHTON and AMANDA HOPKINS	1
'So wel koude he me glose': The Wife of Bath and the Eroticism of Touch SUE NIEBRZYDOWSKI	18
The Lady's Man: Gawain as Lover in Middle English Literature CORY J. RUSHTON	27
Erotic Magic: The Enchantress in Middle English Romance CORINNE SAUNDERS	38
'wordy vnthur wede': Clothing, Nakedness and the Erotic in some Romances of Medieval Britain AMANDA HOPKINS	53
'Some Like it Hot': The Medieval Eroticism of Heat ROBERT ALLEN ROUSE	71
How's Your Father? Sex and the Adolescent Girl in *Sir Degarré* MARGARET ROBSON	82
The Female 'Jewish' Libido in Medieval Culture ANTHONY BALE	94
Eros and Error: Gross Sexual Transgression in the *Fourth Branch* of the *Mabinogi* MICHAEL CICHON	105
Perverse and Contrary Deeds: The Giant of Mont Saint Michel and the Alliterative *Morte Arthure* THOMAS H. CROFTS	116
Her Desire and His: Letters between Fifteenth-century Lovers KRISTINA HILDEBRAND	132

Sex in the Sight of God: Theology and the Erotic in Peter of Blois'   142
  'Grates ago veneri'
  SIMON MEECHAM-JONES

A Fine and Private Place   155
  JANE BLISS

Erotic Historiography: Writing the Self and History in Twelfth-century   164
  Romance and the Renaissance
  ALEX DAVIS

Index   177

Contributors

Anthony Bale is Lecturer in Medieval Literature at Birkbeck College, University of London, and previously held teaching positions at Oxford and Tel Aviv. He has recently completed a monograph on representations of Judaism in medieval England, *The Jew in the Medieval Book: English Antisemitisms 1300–1500* (2006) and is now working on Lydgate and his audiences.

Jane Bliss completed her Ph.D. thesis on 'Naming and Namelessness in Medieval English and French Romance' in 2004. Her article 'Prophecy in the *Morte Darthur*' appeared in *Arthuriana* (Spring 2003), and her piece on 'Generydes' has been published in *Notes and Queries* (March 2006). She is currently working on a book on Medieval Romance, an article about Saint Vignalis, and Anglo-Norman translations.

Michael Cichon is Assistant Professor and Head, Department of English, St Thomas More College at the University of Saskatchewan, where he teaches English and Classical, Medieval and Renaissance Studies.

Thomas H. Crofts is Assistant Professor of English at East Tennessee State University, where he teaches medieval literature, Latin and Old English. His book *Fifteenth-century Malory: The Social Reading of Romance in Late Medieval English* appeared in 2006.

Alex Davis is a Lecturer in English at the University of St Andrews. He is the author of *Chivalry and Romance in the English Renaissance* (2003), and is currently working on a study of Renaissance historical fiction.

Kristina Hildebrand teaches in English at Halmstad University College. Her primary research interests are Arthurian studies and gender studies. She is the author of *The Female Reader at the Round Table: Religion and Women in Three Contemporary Arthurian Texts* (2001).

Amanda Hopkins holds an honorary teaching fellowship in the Department of English and Comparative Literary Studies at Warwick University, and also teaches in the French department. Recent publications include *Melion and Biclarel: Two Old French Werwolf Lays* (2005), an edition and translation for the Liverpool Online Series; *Melion* is also due to be published in a book of the anonymous Old French lays (forthcoming 2007). Her main scholarly interests are the Breton Lay, and the erotic, sex and sexuality in literature.

Simon Meecham-Jones is an affiliated lecturer for the English Faculty at Cambridge, and an examiner for Medieval Latin. He has published on Chaucer, Gower, twelfth-century Latin lyrics and the eighteenth-century editing of Medieval Romance. He is preparing a book on the representation of the natural world in Chaucer, and co-edited, with Ruth Kennedy, *Writers of the Reign of Henry II* (2006) and they are currently editing *Medieval English Literary Culture and the Welsh Nation*.

Sue Niebrzydowski lectures in the School of English the University of Wales, Bangor. Research interests are in gender and sexuality in the later Middle Ages. She has published articles on Chaucerian women and medieval drama, and a monograph, *Bonoure and Buxum: A Study of Wives in Late Medieval English Literature* (2006).

Margaret Robson has published articles on medieval romance and Arthurian literature. She has taught at a number of universities in the UK and the Republic of Ireland and is currently Lecturer in Medieval Literature at the National University of Ireland, Maynooth.

Robert Allen Rouse has taught medieval literature at Durham and Nottingham, and is currently Assistant Professor in Medieval English Literature at the University of British Columbia. His publications include *The Idea of Anglo-Saxon England in Middle English Romance* (2005) and *The Medieval Quest for Arthur* (2005, with Cory Rushton).

Cory James Rushton is assistant professor of English at St Francis Xavier University in Antigonish, Canada, and previously taught at Malaspina University-College, also in Canada, and the University of Bristol, UK. He has published on Thomas Malory and various aspects of the Arthurian legend, and is currently working on the development of the legend between the end of the medieval period and the Victorian revival. He is also beginning work on the application of disability theory to the literature of the English Middle Ages, an area which shares thematic borders with the erotic and the ethnic. He will be co-editing *A Companion to Popular Romance* for Boydell.

Corinne Saunders is Reader in the Department of English Studies at the University of Durham. She is the author of *The Forest of Medieval Romance* (1993) and *Rape and Ravishment in the Literature of Medieval England* (2001). She has edited *Chaucer*, Blackwell Guides to Criticism (2001); *A Companion to Romance: From Classical to Contemporary* (2004); *Cultural Encounters in Medieval Romance* (2005); *A Concise Companion to Chaucer* (2006); (with Françoise le Saux and Neil Thomas) *Writing War: Medieval Literary Responses* (2004); (with Jane Macnaughton) *Madness and Creativity in Literature and Culture* (2005); and (with David Fuller) *Pearl: A Modernised Version by Victor Watts* (2005). She is English editor of the journal *Medium Ævum*.

Abbreviations

EETS ES	Early English Text Society, Extra Series
EETS OS	Early English Text Society, Original Series
ELS	English Literatry Studies
EMETS	Exeter Medieval English Texts and Studies
MED	*The Middle English Dictionary*
MLQ	*Modern Language Quarterly*
MRTS	Medieval and Renaissance Texts and Studies
NM	*Neuphilologische Mitteilungen*
OED	*The Oxford English Dictionary*
PMLA	*Publications of the Modern Language Association of America*
SELIM	The Spanish Society for Medieval English Language and Literature
TEAMS	The Consortium for the Teaching of the Middle Ages
TEAMS METS	TEAMS Middle English Texts Series

Editorial Note

This collection examines literature from various parts of the area now incorporated into the United Kingdom, comprising modern England, Wales and Scotland. For ease of reference, and in accordance with medieval usage by authors throughout the period covered, from Geoffrey of Monmough (c. 1138) to the *Gawain*-Poet (c. 1400) and William Dunbar (c. 1505), the term 'Britain' has been adopted in this volume.

Foreword

Having been present at the inception of this project, it is a particular pleasure to see it realised. It arose, as all Arthurian projects should, at a round table, in good company: in this case, in the bar, at the 2002 International Arthurian Congress, in Bangor, Wales. The group assembled, with the exception of the present writer, could all be termed 'Young Arthurians' and they mooted the idea of a collection of essays, with a working title not fit to print in a scholarly work, which this volume exemplifies. It is a tribute to all the contributors, and not least to the editors, that the concept survived not only to the light of the following day but to that of many more, with the result you have before you. To those editors, Amanda Hopkins and Cory Rushton, I offer congratulations and thanks for inviting me to contribute these few remarks.

A. C. Grand

Introduction:
The Revel, the Melodye and the Bisynesse of Solas

CORY J. RUSHTON and AMANDA HOPKINS

The Background: Sexuality in the European Middle Ages

'... "da mihi castitatem et continentiam, sed noli modo".'[1]

AN INDIVIDUAL'S sexual behaviour in the Middle Ages was not a personal matter. The twin powers of state and Church attempted to control every aspect of people's lives, and sexual behaviour was no exception: as Ruth Mazo Karras observes, 'One's choice of sexual partner affected one's family and the inheritance of property. One's choice of sexual act affected the social order and therefore was of concern to the entire community'.[2] The Church promoted chastity,[3] and considered virginity to be the superior sexual state for men and women.[4] Women were considered a disruptive influence and sexually predatory by both Church and state;[5] clerical and secular misogyny were widespread;[6] and in

---

1 ' "give me chastity and self-control, but not yet" ' (St Augustine of Hippo, *Confessiones*, 8.7.17, from the version at *The Latin Library* (ed. anon., [n.d.], stable URL: <http://www.thelatinlbrary.com/augustine/conf8.shtml>), translation ours).
2 *Sexuality in Medieval Europe: Doing Unto Others* (New York and London, 2005), p. 22. Requirements of state and Church were often in opposition, as can be seen in the Church's support of consensual marriage, which challenged the dynastic and economic priorities of the aristocracy (see, for example, Jeffrey Richards, *Sex, Dissidence and Damnation: Minority Groups in the Middle Ages* (London and New York, 1991), pp. 24–5).
3 Although Karras observes that 'the fact that chastity is so remarkable in saints' lives would seem to indicate that it was not expected in normal people's behaviour' (*Sexuality*, p. 26).
4 See, for example, Pierre J. Payer, *The Bridling of Desire: Views of Sex in the Later Middle Ages* (Toronto, Buffalo and London, 1993), p. 18. This view is contested hotly by Chaucer's Dame Alisoun (*The Wife of Bath's Prologue*, in *The Canterbury Tales*, ed. Larry D. Benson, *The Riverside Chaucer*, 3rd edn (Oxford, 1987), 62–146. All subsequent citations to Chaucer's works refer to this edition). Her arguments on sexuality demonstrate that in the Middle Ages virginity, as Simon Gaunt notes, was considered 'a form of sexuality as much as monogamy or promiscuity' (*Gender and Genre in Medieval French Literature* (Cambridge, 1995), p. 186). Women were classified by marital (and thus sexual) status in registers and other official documents (Shulamith Shahar, *The Fourth Estate. A History of Women in the Middle Ages* (1983; London, 1991), p. 5 et passim).
5 See, for example Carla Casagrande, 'The Protected Woman', trans. Clarissa Botsford, *A History of Women in the West. II: Silences of the Middle Ages*, ed. Christiane Klapisch-Zuber (Cambridge, MA, and London, 1992), pp. 70–104, esp. pp. 86–91. The character of Dame Alisoun illustrates this vividly.

Footnote 6 appears on page 2

noble households the number of female inhabitants was kept to a minimum, their movements restricted: in aristocratic records, 'courtesy and household books indicate a hostility towards the presence of any unnecessary women'.[7] While the secular patriarchy was obsessed with the purity and continuation of bloodlines and the avoidance of female sexual incontinence,[8] the Church was deeply concerned with the details of sexual behaviour in terms of specific activities and relative morality, the latter usually assessed on the basis of male sexual response.[9]

Acceptable sexual practices were debated by canonists (celibate and, at least hypothetically, chaste men[10]) and defined in canon law as the Church attempted to regulate every aspect of human sexual behaviour.[11] In fourteenth-century canon law, four reasons for coitus are documented: (1) procreation; (2) payment of the 'marital debt'; (3) the avoidance of fornication; (4) the satisfaction of lust;[12] the

---

[6] See, for example, R. Howard Bloch, 'Medieval Misogyny', *Misogyny, Misandry, Misanthropy*, ed. R. Howard Bloch and Francis Ferguson (Berkeley, Los Angeles and London, 1989), pp. 1–24, and Bloch's monograph, *Medieval Misogyny and the Invention of Western Romantic Love* (Chicago and London, 1991).

[7] Roberta Gilchrist, 'Medieval Bodies in the Material World: Gender, Stigma and the Body', *Framing Medieval Bodies*, ed. Sarah Kay and Miri Rubin (Manchester, 1994), pp. 43–61 (p. 59). Gilchrist notes that such households were 'for all intents and purposes male. The masculine character was reflected in the small number of women in aristocratic households; for instance, in the fifteenth-century household of the Earl of Northumberland there were nine women and 166 men. This proportion includes servants of the household who would have been predominantly male, with only a small number of female launderers, chamberers and nursery servants' (p. 51). Women of higher status often had their own separate households within the castle or palace: 'increasing status seems to be accompanied by greater segregation of women's quarters, so that residences of the highest saw a duplication of households for male and female members of the castle. This tendency towards female segregation is apparent even where women appear to have been active in commissioning their quarters' (p. 53).

[8] See, for example, Silvana Vecchio, 'The Good Wife', trans. Clarissa Botsford, *A History of Women*, ed. Klapisch-Zuber, pp. 105–35, esp. p. 115.

[9] Payer, *Bridling*, p. 6. This was not always echoed in secular law: for example, medical belief stated that female secretions necessary to achieve pregnancy resulted from pleasure, so that a woman who became pregnant as the result of rape was deemed to have enjoyed the act and probably to have encouraged her rapist (Shahar, *Fourth Estate*, p. 17).

[10] The literature of the period offers much evidence to suggest that chastity was not universally practised by the clergy, such as Chaucer's *Shipman's Tale*, and this is supported by historical records. For example, in an examination of legal documents from the Paris area in the fourteenth and fifteenth centuries, Kathryn Gravdal finds evidence of gang rape perpetrated by students: 'These collective rapes seem to have been youthful sprees. Patterns in the records indicate, however, that when young clerics eventually became priests and rectors, they continued to practice sexual abuse and these constituted the second largest group of rapists brought to trial in the Cerisy court. . . . This finding corresponds to the figures Hanawalt and Carter have established for the clergy in thirteenth- and fourteenth-century England, where clerics constituted the largest group to stand trial for rape in the secular courts. The power and prestige of their office may have led them to commit sexual abuses with a certain regularity' (*Ravishing Maidens: Writing Rape in Medieval French Literature and Law* (Philadelphia, 1991), pp. 126–7, citing Barbara A. Hanawalt, *Crime and Conflict in English Communities 1300–1348* (Cambridge, 1979), and John Marshall Carter, *Rape in Medieval England: An Historical and Sociological Study* (Lanham, MD, 1985)).

[11] Vaginal copulation, performed in what later became known as the missionary position, was the single permissible method of coitus (Payer, *Bridling*, p. 76). Intercourse was forbidden on days of feast and fast (of which there were 273 in the seventh century, although the number had decreased to 140 by the sixteenth century); intercourse was also prohibited during Advent and Lent, on Sundays, and, following Old Testament prohibitions, during menstruation, pregnancy, nursing and for 40 days postpartum (Richards, *Sex, Dissidence*, p. 29).

[12] Payer, *Bridling*, p. 62, cf. pp. 18–19.

first two were allowed some degree of moral legitimacy, but the others 'posed problems that were never satisfactorily resolved in the Middle Ages'.[13] Even in specifically procreative intercourse, sexual pleasure was deemed sinful by some authorities,[14] although 'The mainstream view remained the one expressed in the thirteenth century by St Thomas Aquinas and St Albertus Magnus, that sex had an integral part to play in marriage for the prescribed purposes so long as it was not "excessive".'[15]

Clerical attitudes towards marriage and other sacraments gradually became more stringent in the Middle Ages,[16] and the Fourth Lateran Council of 1215 decreed that communicants must make confession at least once a year.[17] Penitentials were composed and circulated for the guidance of confessors,[18] providing a framework by which priests could discover what sins had been committed and impose the appropriate penances.[19] The Church was aware that confession could be problematic: the confessor was required to ascertain precisely what sins had been committed by asking questions, but without providing suggestions for new and exciting (but, of course, prohibited) forms of sexual activity.[20] James A. Brundage notes that 'Sexual offenses constituted the largest single category of behavior that the penitentials treated'.[21] In giving 'central prominence to sexual offenses, . . . they implicitly told both confessor and penitent that sexual purity was the key element in Christian morality'.[22]

---

[13] Payer, *Bridling*, p. 62.
[14] Shahar, *Fourth Estate*, p. 69.
[15] Richards, *Sex, Dissidence*, p. 27.
[16] Richards, *Sex, Dissidence*, pp. 10–11, 24–5.
[17] Richards, *Sex, Dissidence*, p. 7.
[18] James A. Brundage, *Law, Sex and Christian Society in Medieval Europe* (Chicago and London, 1987), pp. 152–69.
[19] See, for example, Pierre J. Payer, *Sex and the Penitentials: The Development of a Sexual Code, 950 to 1150* (Toronto, 1984); Brundage, *Law, Sex*, pp. 152–175 *et passim*. Penance comprised fasting (a diet of bread and water) and sexual abstinence on the fast days of Christmas, Easter and Pentecost, as well as on Wednesday, Friday and Saturday each week, in addition to the generally prohibited times already in place (Richards, *Sex, Dissidence*, p. 28; see pp. 29–30 for a summary of sins and typical penances (based on Burchard of Worms' *Decretum*, c. 1008–13). Duration varied from a few days for a minor sin, such as masturbation practised by a male to three years for dorsal and rear-entry intercourse, seven years for anal intercourse and fifteen years for the habitual practice of the most serious sins, such as incest, sodomy and bestiality. Penances for comparable female transgressions tended to be more severe, for example, one year for masturbation using a dildo).
[20] Payer, *Bridling*, p. 77.
[21] *Law, Sex*, p. 153. Notwithstanding Brundage's carefully phrased theoretical question, ' "How much did medieval canon lawyers – professionally, of course – think about sex?" ' ('Sex and Canon Law: A Statistical Analysis of Samples of Canon and Civil Law', *Sexual Practices and the Medieval Church*, ed. Vern L. Bullough and James Brundage [sic] (Buffalo, NY, 1982), pp. 89–101 (p. 89)), the longevity of the debate and the stringency of the extensive prohibitions seem to validate Leo Bersani's view that 'the most rigidly moralistic dicta about sex hide smoldering volcanoes of repressed sexual desire' ('Is the Rectum a Grave?' *October* 43, AIDS: Cultural Analysis/Cultural Activism (Winter, 1987), pp. 197–222 (p. 198)).
[22] Brundage, *Law, Sex*, p. 174. Karras supplies a caveat, observing that the handbooks do 'not tell us much about how the offenses were perceived by the laity at large' (*Sexuality*, p. 20).

The Erotic in Medieval Literature

erotic
A. adj. Of or pertaining to the passion of love; concerned with or treating of love; amatory...
B. n. a. An erotic or amatory poem. b. ... A 'doctrine' or 'science' of love.[23]

The opening pages of Karras' monograph describe a polarised representation of sexuality in medieval Europe by contrasting stark condemnation in clerical writing with the sexual playfulness of the fabliau.[24] Despite the explicit, frequently obscene, activities and language found in fabliaux,[25] literary censorship was not unknown in the Middle Ages, and some scholarly texts dealing with biological sexuality were censored: Danielle Jacquart and Claude Thomasset note that some Arabic works proved problematic since they combined 'poetry and didacticism' and displayed an understanding of the erotic stimulation of the imagination.[26] In the secular world, even literature that appeared to champion romantic love (if stopping short of physical sexuality) was, in fact, an instrument by which sexuality was regulated: the values of the literary construct of courtly love were one way in which the state attempted to govern the sexual behaviour of the young aristocracy.[27]

---

[23] *OED*, 2nd edn (1989), online (stable URL: <www.dictionary.oed.com>).
[24] *Sexuality*, pp. 1–3.
[25] See, for example, John Hines, *The Fabliau in English*, Longman Medieval and Renaissance Library (Harlow, 1993), pp. 1–33, esp. pp. 20–1.
[26] *Sexuality and Medicine in the Middle Ages*, trans. Matthew Adamson (Cambridge, 1988), p. 3. In 'The Nature of Woman' (trans. Arthur Goldhammer, *A History of Women*, ed. Klapisch-Zuber, pp. 43–69), Thomasset explains the problem: 'Arab civilization being polygamous, men needed to understand their bodies, and women were encourage to explore pleasure for themselves.' The *Canon Medicinae* of Avicenna [Abu Ali al-Husain ibn Abdallah ibn Sina], for example, 'asserted a right to [sexual] pleasure' (p. 63), and 'alludes to caressing the breasts as a preliminary to love-making' (p. 47). More practical texts were not censored: Thomasset notes that, in some western texts, 'Intercourse was considered necessary to maintain the body's equilibrium. Trotula insisted that sexual abstinence led to serious problems in women... By the end of the thirteenth century the body had asserted its rights. A treatise was even published on the art of love, or, more precisely, on sexual positions': twenty-four positions 'described in a dry, technical manner' are included in *Speculum al foderi* (*The Mirror of Coitus*), which was 'a far cry from the single position recommended by the Church and advocated by the doctors' (p. 64. Thomasset's assessment of the text's style is apparently based on second-hand evidence, since he states that it is unedited and cites G. Beaujouan's description of the manuscript ('Manuscrits médicaux du Moyen Age conservés en Espagne', *Mélanges de la Casa de Velazquez* 8 (1972), p. 173); but see *The Text and Concordances of Biblioteca Nacional Manuscript 3356: Speculum al foderi*, ed. Michael R. Solomon, Medieval Spanish Medical Text Series (Madison, 1986), and *The Mirror of Coitus: A Translation and Edition of the Fifteenth-century Speculum al foderi*, ed. and trans. Michael Solomon, Medieval Spanish Medical Texts Series (Madison, 1990)).
[27] Georges Duby comments that works of courtly love 'beguiled their audience and therefore exerted some influence on the way people lived. Hagiographic literature was also intended to influence behaviour. The chansons and romances, like the lives of saints, dramatised exemplary lives so that they might be imitated. Although their heroes embodied to perfection certain virtues, they were not supposed to be inimitable' ('The Courtly Model', trans. Arthur Goldhammer, *A History of Women*, ed. Klapisch-Zuber, pp. 250–69 (p. 255)). Within the concept of courtly love, Duby writes, the lord's wife held the role of primary educator, 'at the heart of an instructional system designed to discipline male sexual activity, prevent excesses of masculine brutality, and pacify – civilize – the most violent segment of a society undergoing widespread

Yet, as surviving literature demonstrates, even the chastity or virginity of incumbents of enclosed communities did not preclude the use of explicitly erotic terminology in response to the divine, sometimes modelled on the Song of Songs.[28] Such a response was not automatically considered problematic because, as Karras observes, 'for many medieval thinkers the erotic, to the extent it overlapped with the spiritual, was opposed to the carnal'.[29] She also notes the dangers inherent in applying the term 'erotic' to medieval texts:

> One way of determining whether it distorts the medieval past for us to label discourses as 'erotic' is by asking whether anyone at the time did so. In fact, medieval sources not infrequently express concern over this.[30]

Here, Karras is considering only religious works, more particularly those recounting visions,[31] but her acknowledgement of the dangers of anachronistic interpretations and terminology reflects issues relevant to the wider subject of this volume. How can modern readers identify, analyse, appreciate the erotic in medieval literature? What response did medieval authors hope to provoke in their contemporary audience? What are the differences, and what is the relationship, between the sexual and the erotic?[32] Between the erotic and the pornographic — and is such a distinction applicable to medieval works?[33] How is the modern reader to interpret the dynamic between the erotic and the transgressive in texts produced by a culture in which all sexual activity was (supposedly) regulated, and sexual desire was, of its very nature, transgressive? Should personal literature not

---

and rapid change' (p. 261). Yet the educative process clearly differentiated between classes: the model of courtly love could 'influence the attitude of certain men toward *certain* women, for the same class division that existed between men carried over to women. Thus "ladies" (*dames*) and "maidens" (*pucelles*) were sharply distinguished from peasant women (*vilaines*), whom the men of the court could treat as brutally as they pleased' (p. 256, Duby's emphasis).

[28] See, for example, Karras, *Sexuality*, pp. 54–7. As Brundage observes, 'the Song of Songs vividly celebrates the joy and pleasure of marital sex and demonstrates that marital eroticism was no stranger [to] Israel' (*Law, Sex*, p. 52); the text has occasionally been subject to censorship (Vern L. Bullough and Bonnie Bullough, *Sexual Attitudes: Myths and Realities* (New York, 1995), p. 184), and certainly some medieval interpreters found its erotics disquieting or perplexing (see for example Mary Dove, 'Sex, Allegory and Censorship: A Reconsideration of Medieval Commentaries on the Song Of Songs' (*Literature and Theology* 10:4 (1996), pp. 317–28. On erotic discourse in monastic commentaries on the text, see Denys Turner, *Eros and Allegory: Medieval Exegesis of the Song of Songs*, Cistercian Studies Series 156 (Kalamazoo, 1995)). Secular authors also used the text as a model: Chaucer, for example, echoes the Song of Songs in Januarie's words to his wife (*The Merchant's Tale*, 2143–6; see Helen Cooper, *The Canterbury Tales*, Oxford Guides to Chaucer, 2nd edn (Oxford, 1996), pp. 210–11).

[29] *Sexuality*, p. 57.

[30] *Sexuality*, p. 57.

[31] See, for example, Julian of Norwich, *A Revelation of Love*, ed. Marion Glasscoe, EMETS (Exeter, 1986), and the assessment of its erotics by Gillian T. W. Ahlgren ('Julian of Norwich's Theology of Eros', *Spiritus* 5 (2005), pp. 37–53).

[32] Karras defines the scholarly use of the term 'sexuality' as referring 'to the whole realm of human erotic experience' (*Sexuality*, p. 5).

[33] Bullough and Bullough note that 'The difficulty in distinguishing obscenity from pornography stems from the fact that what is sexually suggestive – erotic if you will – to one person is sexually repulsive or filthy to another' (*Sexual Attitudes*, p. 183). Yet the issue of anachronism is both conceptual – 'When we look at the past, however, it is not always clear that what we think of as either pornographic or obscene was regarded in the same way by the people of the time' (p. 184, a comment equally applicable to 'erotic') – and semantic, since the term 'pornography', in the sense used today, was coined only in 1857 (*OED.*, loc. cit.).

intended for a public readership, such as letters, be examined using different criteria from works, such as romances and religious texts, created for publication? How far does the cultural context signify – is there a peculiarly medieval British approach to the erotic, clearly distinct from a continental attitude?

The Erotic in the Literature of Medieval Britain:[34] Critical Context

eroticism
1. Erotic spirit or character; also, the use of erotic or sexually arousing imagery in literature or art. 2. Med. and Psychol. A condition or state of sexual excitement or desire; a tendency to become sexually aroused, usu. by some specified stimulus ...[35]

In 1996, Vern L. Bullough argued in a collection of essays concerning medieval sexuality that scholars had traditionally avoided the topic of sex through 'fear, both personal and generalized': nobody wanted to be accused of perversion, 'a label that would make it difficult for one to get an academic position or, if one already had such a job, would lessen one's chances of getting tenure'.[36] The anecdotal evidence Bullough gathers is convincing, although looking back on the era he is discussing, little convincing should be required. Today, as Bullough notes, scholars working in almost any discipline can regularly engage in sexual topics as diverse as homosexuality, cross-dressing and sadomasochism.[37] The essays that follow Bullough's in the collection explore a variety of sexual practices and themes. However, only one deals with textual eroticism as, first and foremost, fantasy: Andrew Taylor writes that his 'topic is the distinctly sexual pleasure of fantasizing on a text, whether in compulsive, solitary rereading of certain passages as a sexual substitute or when two people read together as a form of flirtation or seduction, as in Paolo and Francesca's [sic] notorious reading of the story of Lancelot'.[38]

Taylor's essay is penultimate in the collection, and has been preceded by articles that query sexuality in terms of power or difference; only Taylor talks about the pleasure to be found in reading about sex, whether alone or in company. It may now be easier to 'get an academic position' despite, perhaps even by, writing about sex, but scholars may have somehow forgotten that other kinds of positions should be involved in a thorough exploration of the erotic. Taylor's subject may

---

[34] The present collection examines material from England, Wales and Scotland, and the terms Britain and British here identify the island as a whole in accordance with the practice of medieval authors, such as Geoffrey of Monmouth (c. 1138), the *Gawain*-Poet (c. 1400) and William Dunbar (c. 1505).

[35] OED (loc. cit.).

[36] 'Sex in History: A Redux', in *Desire and Discipline: Sex and Sexuality in the Premodern West*, ed. Jacqueline Murray and Konrad Eisenbichler (Toronto, 1996), pp. 3–22 (p. 3).

[37] Bullough refers to Joyce E. Salisbury's text, *Medieval Sexuality: A Research Guide* (New York, 1990), a thorough bibliography of previous work on the subject, mostly from the two decades prior to publication. Salisbury notes that her text is focused on the history of sexuality (p. xvii), and observes: 'Medievalists are relatively new to the field of the history of sexuality.... This is probably due to the number of and accessibility of sources' (p. xix).

[38] Andrew Taylor, 'Reading the Dirty Bits', *Desire*, ed. Murray and Eisenbichler, pp. 280–95 (p. 280).

still be one that troubles the wider academy: if people are taking 'compulsive, solitary' pleasure in a text, their hands might be too busy to engage in serious scholarship. The old distinction is still there – a kind of (solitary) perversion to be avoided is still present – but the borders, by and large, have shifted from silence to the safer ground of gender studies, with its cool politics and engaged social activism. Susan Crane has argued that the 'first way of conceiving gender is to contrast it to sex': 'Sexuality, broadly understood as the generation, expression, and organization of desire, is the ongoing behaviour that informs gendered identities.'[39] As important as the study of historical gender identity is, it is regrettable that the 'desire' that is the root of gender has been downplayed.

The problem is made more acute by the differences between modern and past sexualities, which Taylor himself notes in relation to E. Talbot Donaldson's famous reading of *The Merchant's Tale*. Because May is a young woman, and 'pretty young girls . . . will always warm the masculine heart',[40] Donaldson can offer 'a carnal continuity' between the past and the present, and between Chaucer and his (male and educated) readers.[41] Our innate knowledge of what is erotic cannot be shared by everyone in our own time, much less shared across vast stretches of geography and chronology. The challenge, writes Karma Lochrie, is to avoid 'presentism' without 'forfeiting the tools of contemporary theories of sexuality'.[42] It may be that Jeffrey J. Cohen is right that through 'reversing time's arrow' and looking for continuities between present and past sexualities, we might be able to see 'enduring but historically specific' manifestations of sexual practice, here masochism (of which more anon).[43] Anthony Giddens is correct in stating that 'plastic sexuality', an eroticism freed from reproduction and the threat of reproduction, has always been a feature of narrative;[44] the modern question of why neither Guenevere nor Isolde falls pregnant is not a terribly important one for romanciers. None of this obscures, or should obscure, some fundamental differences between how sexuality is seen today and how it was seen in the past.

Medieval England appears to be a particular problem for the historian of sexuality: as Bernard O'Donoghue notes, the language itself seems uncomfortable with sex, 'the unease of English with both the terms and the concepts of European love-poetry' prompting a necessary evaluation of the English concept 'of love itself'.[45] The English recalcitrance about sex can be illustrated by a story about

---

39 Susan Crane, *Gender and Romance in Chaucer's* Canterbury Tales (Princeton, 1994), pp. 5–6.
40 Donaldson, *Speaking of Chaucer* (London, 1970), p. 49.
41 Taylor, 'Reading', p. 282.
42 Karma Lochrie et al., 'Introduction', *Constructing Medieval Sexuality*, ed. Karma Lochrie, Peggy McCracken, and James A. Schultz (Minneapolis, 1997), pp. ix–xviii (p. ix).
43 Jeffrey J. Cohen, 'Masoch/Lancelotism', *Medieval Identity Machines* (Minneapolis, 2003), pp. 78–115 (p. 79). Cohen's attempt (pp. 84–5) to 'take Lancelot seriously' through the performance of a 'resexualization' of Chrétien's text, which ignores the interpretative judgements of both Dante (Lancelot 'condemned in advance to the . . . Inferno') and Malory (Lancelot as saint), shares a concern with the eroticism of the text with the current project.
44 *The Transformation of Intimacy: Sexuality, Love and Eroticism in Modern Societies* (Stanford, 1992), p. 2.
45 'Love and Marriage', *Chaucer: An Oxford Guide*, ed. Steve Ellis (Oxford, 2005), pp. 239–52 (p. 240). Meanwhile, Chaucer's contemporaries – female as well as male – in Wales were embracing the erotic uninhibitedly, in language both practical and metaphorical; see, for example, 'Cywydd y gal' (Poem of the Penis) by Dafydd ap Gwilym (ed. and trans. James Doan, 'An

Henry VI, a notoriously spiritual (some might say prudish) monarch. John Blacman, Henry's priest, approvingly relates how Henry storms from the room when a courtier presents him with a spectacle composed of bare-breasted women dancing: Henry is too pure to enjoy such a lascivious spectacle.[46] The puritanical streak shown by the king and his biographer (even if the court's centre does not quite accord with the tone of the court itself) seems to be echoed throughout medieval English society: if there is sexuality present in medieval literature, goes the argument, it isn't happening in England. The French romances that once celebrated adulterous love now end in translated narratives extolling politically advantageous marriage, or in Thomas Malory's uptight insistence that love was defined differently in those days. What, exactly, it is about the dancers' nudity that bothers Henry cannot be stated with certainty; if it is indeed the sexual nature of the nudity rather than that of the dance, this too reminds us that the Middle Ages is a long period in which sexual mores (like everything else) can change. Thomas Chestre may not think of breasts as inherently erotic;[47] a century later, Henry may well testify to their increasing eroticisation, an observation interesting because it might pinpoint precisely when this one aspect of modern, heterosexual eroticism began to take shape.

Much of this, of course, can be blamed on Michel Foucault. Murray and Eisenbichler cite Foucault's *History of Sexuality* as their starting point for the collection mentioned above; Foucault's 'relative neglect of the long period separating antiquity and modernity and ... cavalier and unsupported generalizations about this complex and rich society' has long been a site of contention for medievalists tired of their academic marginalisation in this and other areas.[48] Foucault's 'conceptual framework' – that sexuality was inextricably linked with 'social and historical specificity',[49] that power dictated sexualities as it dictated almost everything else in a given society – is one of the foundations upon which gender studies has been built. Judith Butler argues that there 'is no recourse to a "person", a "sex", or a "sexuality" that escapes the matrix of power and discursive relations that effectively produce and regulate the intelligibility of those concepts for us'.[50] True, but for most people the regulation of the intelligibility of their arousal is not very problematic; that must be doubly true for historical epochs in which people did not have access to this type of framework, even if they were interested in a framework at all. As Leo Bersani notes, 'Desire is polarized between lack and possession; the *activity* of desire is what moves the subject from the one to the other'.[51] The Wife of Bath knew this:

Unedited Welsh Poem from Peniarth 49: Cywydd y Gal' (*Comitatus: A Journal of Medieval and Renaissance Studies* 7 (1976), pp. 15–26), and Gwerful Mechain's 'Cywydd y Cedor' (Ode to the Pubic Hair), a title evincing a coyness absent from the text, the persona's praise of her genitalia (ed. and trans. Dafydd Johnston, *Canu Maswedd Yr Oesoedd Canol/Medieval Welsh Erotic Poetry* (1991; Cardiff, 1999), pp. 41–3).

[46] Edmund King, *Medieval England* (Stroud, 2005), pp. 249–50.
[47] For a discussion of this issue, see Robert Rouse's essay in this volume.
[48] Jacqueline Murray, 'Introduction', *Desire*, ed. Murray and Eisenbichler, pp. ix–xxviiii (p. x).
[49] Murray, 'Introduction', p. x.
[50] Judith Butler, *Gender Trouble: Feminism and the Subversion of Identity* (New York and London, 1971), p. 32.
[51] Leo Bersani, 'Society and Sexuality', *Critical Inquiry* 26:4 (Summer, 2000), pp. 641–56 (pp. 647–8).

> Wayte what thing we may nat lightly have,
> Thereafter wol we crie al day and crave.
> Forbede us thing, and that desiren we...
> (*The Wife of Bath's Prologue*, 517–19)

Bersani has written extensively on the need to stop 'accepting, even finding new ways to defend, our culture's lies about sexuality'.[52] These 'lies' constitute what Bersani calls 'the *redemptive reinvention of sex*', which is really about 'tenderness and love' and not penetration and power.[53] The widespread acceptance that sexual aggression, including at its extreme the crime of rape, is about power and not sex is a modern phenomenon (the reinvention of sex), a deliberate and necessary attempt to break the ancient links between sex, violence, weaponry and aggression.[54]

The medieval mind solves this problem in a different way; for them the question of rape was not a matter for the reinvention of sex, but a property issue. Rape itself was still seen as a possible consequence of erotic feeling, of lust, on the part of the man. As Evelyn Burge Vitz has argued, 'Medieval poets ... often dealt lightly with the entire array of human suffering: war, grievous loss, humiliation, castration and impotence, sickness and death, like rape all grave, essentially serious', and she asks: 'If people laughed at everything, why should rape have been exempt?'[55] While Vitz acknowledges that 'it is not possible to prove conclusively that some women in the past took pleasure in the idea of forced sex', she does point to a long tradition of writings by women for women (lasting until the nineteenth century and beyond) of literary ravishment.[56] Even if Bersani's iconoclastic argument is not taken in its entirety, it still reminds us that the broken link between sex and violent eroticism remains very much a possibility for the medieval mind, one for which many of the essays in this collection find evidence. Rape is one extreme on a spectrum of possible responses to desire; personally traumatic and socially disruptive as it is, rape was not separated from desire as it is today.

Sexuality, transparently and biologically, has something to do with desire. Any reading of sexualities that eclipses their innate eroticism to at least some of the people, some of the time, is not necessarily wrong, but it is necessarily incomplete. Bersani believes that 'Phallocentrism is ... above all the denial of the *value* of powerlessness in both men and women', and that sexuality 'may be a tautology for masochism'; further, it is 'perhaps primarily *the degeneration of the sexual into a relationship that condemns sexuality to becoming a struggle for power*':

---

[52] 'Rectum', p. 222.
[53] 'Rectum', pp. 214–15 (Bersani's emphasis).
[54] Richard Dyer, 'Male Sexuality in the Media', *The Sexuality of Men*, ed. Andy Metcalf and Martin Humphries (London and Sydney, 1985), pp. 28–43 (p. 32); the classic but controversial discussions of the inextricable link between male sexuality and violence are Andrea Dworkin, *Pornography: Men Possessing Women* (London, 1981) and *Intercourse* (New York, 1987); Catherine MacKinnon, *Feminism Unmodified: Discourses on Life and Law* (Cambridge, MA, and London, 1987); and Susan Brownmiller, *Against our Will: Men, Women and Rape* (London, 1977). Bersani makes extensive use of Dworkin and MacKinnon in 'Rectum'.
[55] 'Rereading Rape in Medieval Literature: Literary, Historical, and Theoretical Reflections', *The Romanic Review* 88:1 (1997), pp. 1–26 (pp. 3–4).
[56] 'Rereading Rape', pp. 8–12 (p. 8).

> As soon as persons are posited, the war begins. It is the self that swells with excitement at the idea of being on top, the self that makes of the inevitable play of thrusts and relinquishment in sex an argument for the natural authority of one sex over the other.[57]

The Wife of Bath's relationship with her husbands, especially the last two, is one of 'inevitable play of thrusts and relinquishment', and Bersani's theory of powerlessness and masochism might explain the problematic ending of her tale; it is an exchange of power configured differently from modern relationship negotiations because it does not hide from certain human sexual truths. Bersani's insistence on the attraction and necessity of powerlessness, of submission, is echoed in many medieval texts, as many of the essays in this collection show.

The Wife of Bath is, of course, a fiction; moreover, she is a fiction created by a male author, and thus her opinions of female sexuality are, at best, mediated by a male gaze. Still, of the major Middle English authors, only Chaucer is routinely allowed some genuinely erotic feeling, even after Carolyn Dinshaw's influential interpretation of Chaucer's 'sexual poetics' as an attempt to control the female body analogous to the scribe's control of his manuscript, an interpretative move recently described as tenuous by Alcuin Blamires.[58] In fact, Chaucer provides the title for the current introduction, derived from two lyrical phrases that apply to Nicholas' and Alison's illicit love-making while the bells of the church ring out over town (*The Merchant's Tale*, 3652–6). In a tale that hardly condones the lecherous behaviour of Nicholas, however, Chaucer's sudden lyricism has been taken to be at least mildly parodic.[59] Other instances of the sexual act in Chaucer are overtly subversive or at least mildly violent, different in tone, but perhaps not intent, from Donaldson's textual girl-watching, 'a form of iconolagnia, a sexual penetration of the kind our culture alternately glamorizes and condemns'.[60]

In a recent examination of Chaucer's erotics, specifically in *The Canterbury Tales*, W. W. Allman and D. Thomas Hanks remind us that Chaucer was actually accused of participation in 'a violent, or at the very least a potentially violent, act against a woman' – an act that has always troubled Chaucerians, especially those committed to 'the genteel view' that Chaucer (specifically through the Franklin) celebrated a kind of mutuality within marriage, a theory first proposed by Kittredge.[61] Allman

---

57 'Rectum', pp. 217–18 (Bersani's emphasis).
58 Carolyn Dinshaw, *Chaucer's Sexual Poetics* (Madison, 1989); Alcuin Blamires, 'Sexuality', *Chaucer*, ed. Ellis, pp. 208–23 (p. 208).
59 See, for example, Katherine Zieman, 'Chaucer's Voys', *Representations* 60 (Autumn 1997), pp. 70–91 (p. 79). Bersani argues, in the context of gay male camp, that 'Parody is an erotic turn-off, and all gay men know this' ('Rectum', p. 208); in a culture that gives us the fabliau, however, parody may carry an erotic *frisson*.
60 Taylor, 'Reading', p. 281. Taylor reminds us that the male gaze begins with the desire to watch beautiful women, a conscious desire rooted in the erotic; that the gaze also, perhaps inherently, acts as a gender-based control mechanism does not invalidate the intended meaning.
61 W. W. Allman and D. Thomas Hanks, Jr, 'Rough Love: Notes Towards an Erotics of the *Canterbury Tales*', *Chaucer Review* 38:1 (2003), pp. 36–65 (pp. 36–7); George Lyman Kittredge, 'Chaucer's Discussion of Marriage', *Modern Philology* 9 (1911–12), pp. 435–67. For the infamous case of Cecily Chaumpaigne, see two articles by Christopher Cannon: '*Raptus* in the Chaumpaigne Release and a Newly Discovered Document concerning the Life of Geoffrey Chaucer', *Speculum* 68 (1993), pp. 74–94, and 'Chaucer and Rape: Uncertainty's Certainties', *Studies in the Age of Chaucer* 22 (2000), pp. 67–92. An earlier, but useful, look at the case in light of modern feminist

and Hanks find that Chaucerians 'have averted their gaze or become distracted with their notes when Chaucer's characters leap into bed', an observation supported in this volume, and they reveal that the love-making that is thus ignored is often not genteel at all: it consists of the imagery of 'cutting, stabbing, bleeding and dying'.[62] The close association of 'piercing and cutting' imagery with the language of love in *The Knight's Tale* only begins to scratch the surface of Chaucer's violent sexual imagery: the authors remind us that, although Nicholas receives the red-hot poker, Absolon meant that 'violent penetration' for Alisoun:

> Perhaps one could argue that the climactic violence involving a hot coulter in the *Miller's Tale* is dissociated from the earlier erotic love of Alisoun and Nicholas. However, as both Martin Blum and David Lorenzo Boyd have recently argued, *hende* Nicholas becomes feminized by the final actions of the tale as he first puts himself in the position of receiving a kiss from a man, then suffers penetration with a hot coulter in a parody of homosexual rape.[63]

Subsequent tales (those of the Reeve and Chaucer's *Thopas* among them) continually evoke the dual meanings of *priken*: 'to cut, pierce, or spur' and 'to have sexual intercourse with'; and the Merchant's Januarie insists that married sexuality is a man's 'owene knyf' by which he cannot be harmed (*The Merchant's Tale*, 1840). Januarie pities May, forced to endure what he sees as his 'sharp and keene' lust (*The Merchant's Tale*, 1759).[64] Januarie is also, of course, an object of ridicule, as are other lovers in *The Canterbury Tales*, hinting at the possibility that 'an anti-erotics emerges amidst the lineaments of the erotic'.[65]

This should not surprise us in an author whose society also links the sacred with the violent through hagiographic accounts of martyrdom;[66] Allman and Hanks believe that 'the English canon's favorite "wayside drama" has this specific, jaundiced bodily economy of the erotic: males pierce; women bleed'.[67] That female martyrs experienced the same tortures as their male counterparts, but with the addition of specifically sexual humiliations and mutilations, strongly implies that female martyr stories were meant to be 'experienced as erotic'.[68] Robert Mills,

---

theory is Carolyn Dinshaw, 'Rivalry, Rape and Manhood: Gower and Chaucer', *Chaucer and Gower: Difference, Mutuality, Exchange*, ed. R. F. Yeager, ELS Monographs 51 (Victoria, 1991), pp. 130–52.

62 Allman and Hanks, 'Rough Love', pp. 38–9.
63 Allman and Hanks, 'Rough Love', p. 42, citing Martin Blum, 'Negotiating Masculinities: Erotic Triangles in the *Miller's Tale*', *Masculinities in Chaucer*, ed. Peter G. Beidler (Cambridge, 1998), pp. 37–52, esp. 47–9, and David Lorenzo Boyd, 'Seeking "Goddes Pryvetee": Sodomy, Quitting, and Desire in *The Miller's Tale*', *Words and Works: Studies in Medieval English Language and Literature in Honour of Fred C. Robinson*, ed. Peter S. Baker and Nicholas Howe (Toronto, 1998), pp. 243–60, esp. pp. 252–3.
64 Allman and Hanks, 'Rough Love', pp. 40–50.
65 Allman and Hanks, 'Rough Love', p. 57.
66 Jocelyn Wogan-Browne [previously Price] notes the stylisation of the violence in Middle English lives of virgin-martyrs ('The Virgin's Tale', *Feminist Readings in Middle English Literature: The Wife of Bath and All Her Sect*, ed. Ruth Evans and Lesley Johnson (London and New York, 1994), pp. 165–94 (p. 175)).
67 Allman and Hanks, 'Rough Love', p. 53.
68 Clarissa W. Atkinson, *Mystic and Pilgrim: The 'Book' and the World of Margery Kempe* (Ithaca and London, 1983), p. 189; cf. Brigitte Cazelles, *The Lady as Saint* (Philadelphia, 1991), pp. 69–74. Simon Gaunt observes: 'That hagiographical texts about female virgins were written primarily

echoing Bersani, argues that 'inactivity – passivity even – can communicate power in the space of medieval religious representation'.[69] Mills also believes, as Cohen does, that the continuities between past and present might be found in unlikely places:

> Pain, freely embraced by the masochist, generates pleasure and orgasmic release; martyrs welcome suffering as a means of escaping earthly sin and recovering eternal life. The crucial difference between martyrs and masochists is that saints adopt transcendence, rather than eroticism, as a way of handling suffering. At the same time, if we explain away these understandings of pain as the product of a failed or archaic culture (the Middle Ages) or of sexual pathology (notions of masochism as negative or dualistic), we risk ignoring the potential 'vibrations' between medieval and modern in certain encounters with pain.[70]

The potentially intoxicating links between religious devotion, sexuality and power (or the lack of power) spills over into the secular world:[71] Brigitte Cazelles draws a comparison between the female saint and the romance heroine, finding that the main difference between them is the tyrannical nature of the latter.[72] This at least opens up the possibility that the humiliations visited upon the imperious ladies of romance carry an erotic charge: Guinevere abducted or brought to the stake in her smock; Isolde handed over to the lepers to be punished by rape – lepers being both physically disgusting and riddled with a disease thought to have its origins in the sin of lust.

The medieval text sometimes seems to flirt with a dichotomous, almost Sadean, sense of virtue punished and vice rewarded: in *Beves of Hamtoun*, Goldborough is to marry a kitchen knave (think of Lynette's reaction to Gareth in Malory) while Beves's mother enjoys the obedient attentions of her lover.[73] Medieval literature

---

in the interests of men, and not of women, is also evident from the overt denigration of female sexuality and femininity inherent in the view of virginity they perpetuate and from the rampant violence and brutality inflicted on women's bodies in so many saints' lives' (*Gender*, p. 196, cf. p. 188); citing Gravdal (*Ravishing Maidens*, pp. 24–5), he continues: 'Hagiographical texts about women are deeply voyeuristic, dressing up in a pious framework the most horrific attacks on women, which the women in question are portrayed as welcoming. Certain scenes, when abstracted from their context, have much in common with modern pornography depicting bondage and mutilation' (p. 197). Both critics identify a male appreciation of such texts, but neither Gaunt nor Gravdal engages with the possibility that a female audience might be stimulated by hagiography's erotics of sadomasochism, and Wogan-Browne, noting the development of an extensive female audience for saints' lives in Anglo-Norman and Middle English in the twelfth and thirteenth centuries, with an emphasis on stories of virgin martyrs ('Saints' Lives and the Female Reader', *Forum for Modern Language Studies* 27:4 (1991), pp. 314–32 (pp. 314–15)), dismisses it: 'This diet of licensed "body-ripping" seems on the face of it scarcely sustaining literature, even allowing for the possibility of an audience colluding with its own worst interests . . . Moreover, masochistic or fantasising identification is precisely what good saints' lives are theoretically bound to avoid . . .' (p. 315).

69 *Suspended Animation: Pain, Pleasure and Punishment in Medieval Culture* (London, 2005), p. 119.
70 Mills, *Suspended Animation*, p. 175. He continues by noting that 'within the sphere of medieval devotion, religious sublimation and carnal desire can become powerfully entwined' (p. 176).
71 Richards notes that in the period 1050–1200, depictions of Christ on the cross, which had previously focused on triumph and radiance, became darker, concentrating instead on suffering and pain (*Sex, Dissidence*, p. 7).
72 *Lady as Saint*, pp. 43–5.
73 Noël James Menuge, *Medieval English Wardship in Romance and Law* (Cambridge, 2001), pp. 109–11.

always, ultimately, seems to refuse to countenance de Sade's vision, a vision that made him notorious in his time and our own. Yet the number of medieval heroines who suffer various forms of sexual humiliation (Griselda, Emaré, the Duchess of Brittany), an erotic type still mined by the erotic fiction and pornography descended from de Sade's lurid novels, should lead us to question whether medieval readers were entirely innocent, feeling only outraged sympathy for the victims of male lust, especially when many of those readers were themselves male. The feeling is not necessarily exclusively male, either: Heloise evokes the erotics of humiliation when she characterises her desire for Abelard as completely subservient to his own,

> Nichil umquam (Deus scit) in te nisi te requisivi: te pure, non tua concupiscens. Non matrimonii federa, non dotes aliquas expectavi, non denique meas voluptates aut voluntates, sed tuas, sicut ipse nosti, adimplere studui. Et si uxoris nomen sanctius ac validius videretur, dulcius mihi semper extitit amice vocabulum aut, si non indigneris, concubine vel scorti . . .
>
> (I wanted simply you, nothing of yours. I looked for no marriage-bond, no marriage portion, and it was not my own pleasures and wishes I sought to gratify, as you well know, but yours. The name of wife may seem more sacred or more binding, but sweeter for me will always be the word mistress, or, if you will permit me, that of concubine or whore.)[74]

her evocation of herself as whore echoed more genteelly elsewhere by the Maiden of Astolat, confronted by the fact that Lancelot does not love her (638/17-22).[75]

If Chaucer often presents male sexuality as inherently but not necessarily problematically violent, it is perhaps because he views sexuality as itself 'an external force', the 'uncontrollability of sexual arousal' itself seen as an aggressive aspect of humanity's sinful nature.[76] Modern readers are not surprised to find that the devil is sometimes responsible for involuntary, especially nocturnal, sexual fantasising:[77] Gregory the Great argued that 'the devil is . . . permitted to fill the minds of the saints with filthy thoughts in sleep', to which the only remedy was to raise 'the mind to higher things'[78] (perhaps gender studies, in a modern context). This is potentially a radical reinterpretation of Butler's 'matrix of power and discursive relations' – this is sin and its consequence, but also temptation and its pleasures.

---

74 'Heloysae Epistola ad Abelardum', *Epistolae Abaelardi e Heloysae*, from the online version at *The Latin Library* (ed. anon., [n.d.], stable URL: <http://www.thelatinlibrary.com/abelard.epistola.html>); trans. Betty Radice, *The Letters of Abelard and Heloise* (Harmondsworth, 1974), Letter 1, p. 113. On Heloise, see C. Stephen Jaeger, *Ennobling Love: In Search of a Lost Sensibility* (Pittsburgh, 1999), p. 167.
75 For ease of reference, citations of Malory refer to the single-volume text, *Malory: Works*, ed. Eugène Vinaver (Oxford, 1971).
76 Blamires, 'Sexuality', pp. 209–21.
77 The devil is also implicated in female mystical writing: Karras notes that 'Jean Gerson, in the early fifteenth century, wrote extensively of the need to discern whether women's visions were really divine or were sent by the devil. If from the devil, the purpose of the visions may be to lead people into carnal temptation' (*Sexuality*, p. 57).
78 Dyan Elliot, 'Pollution, Illusion, and Masculine Disarray: Nocturnal Emissions and the Sexuality of the Clergy', *Constructing Medieval Sexuality*, ed. Lochrie et al., pp. 1–23 (p. 1). See also Vitz, 'Rereading Rape', p. 16.

The medieval mind remembers that sex, at least for some people on some occasions, is supposed to be fun. That is precisely why it is so dangerous.

Medieval sexuality was also seen as inherently one of debt, what the individual owed rather than primarily what he or she could expect, the result of St Paul's influential discussion of marital relations: this, too, had an effect on the medieval erotic, perhaps best illustrated by the commercial foreplay of husband and wife at the conclusion of Chaucer's *Shipman's Tale*, when the errant wife makes a direct and playful link between financial debt and sexual pleasure:

> 'For I wol paye yow wel and redily
> Fro day to day, and if so be I faille,
> I am youre wyf; score it upon my taille,
> And I shal paye as soone as ever I may.' (414–17)

The pun on 'taille', meaning both a stick on which notches were used to record debts and the wife's genitalia, is driven home by the Shipman when he facetiously prays that 'God us sende/ Taillynge ynough unto oure lyves ende' (433–4).[79] This happy acceptance, tongue-in-cheek though it is, nonetheless indicates a sexualised interest in the metaphor itself, the inherent subordination of the debtee to the debtor, which goes well beyond the physical act and potentially speaks to a structural and otherwise unexplained fantasy: the pleasure both partners could potentially take in the negotiated exchange of sexual power. This debt could be depicted in a darker fashion, especially when the man becomes the object of commercial exchange, as when Gawain is reduced to an object during the temptation scenes in *Sir Gawain and the Green Knight*.[80] That exchange traditionally only works in certain directions. Women can withhold their bodies, but men find ways to gain access that involve money, seduction or force: sexuality, particularly male sexuality, has long been linked with violence and aggression.

The Erotic in the Literature of Medieval Britain: New Approaches

> Many people have sex in mind a great deal of the time.[81]

Medieval sexuality, as reflected in extant texts, is predominantly a masculine sexuality, which we should expect to see reflected in literary, historical and theological documents. This reflection will not be limited to overtly erotic, even pornographic, representations of the sexual act, but will necessarily include texts in which sexuality and the erotic are influencing other discussions: this is sexuality as the 'kernal of individual personality which leaves its signature on other, nonsexual

---

79 Albert H. Silverman, 'Sex and Money in Chaucer's "Shipman's Tale" ', *Philological Quarterly* 32 (1953), pp. 329–36.
80 Sheila Fisher, 'Taken Men and Token Women in Sir Gawain and the Green Knight', *Seeking the Woman in Late Medieval and Renaissance Writings: Essays in Feminist Contextual Criticism*, ed. Sheila Fisher and Janet E. Halley (Knoxville, 1989), pp. 71–105.
81 *Ever Since Adam and Eve: The Evolution of Human Sexuality*, ed. Malcolm Potts and Roger Short (Cambridge, 1999; repr. 2000), p. 1.

behavior'.[82] Where the current collection seeks to differ from recent scholarship on sexuality and gender is in its insistence on the subject of erotic pleasure, and its identification of a deliberate erotics in texts produced in medieval Britain. The collection explores its topic by looking at a wide range of texts, predominantly in Middle English, although reference is made to Anglo-Norman or Old French verse originating in Britain, and there are essays that explore the erotic in Latin and Welsh texts.

The collection opens with an examination of the Wife of Bath's discussion of the importance of eroticism in marriage: in the context of medieval clerical and medical texts, Sue Niebrzydowski explores Dame Alisoun's reminiscences of the degrees of sexual satisfaction in her marriages in comparison with the experiences of other women in *The Canterbury Tales*. Dame Alisoun, of course, chooses to recount a romance, and the popularity of this genre in the Middle Ages is reflected in this volume, with Middle English romances and lays well represented: Corinne Saunders, Amanda Hopkins, Robert Allen Rouse, Margaret Robson and Cory James Rushton all take close looks at narratives and characters that have traditionally be seen as concerned with love, if not eroticism.

Hopkins and Rouse, in particular, question whether the boundaries of the erotic have enjoyed any degree of stability from the Middle Ages to our own time: both find that nudity meant very little in a medieval context. Rather, for Hopkins the titillating quality in descriptions of female characters is located in what they wear, not in the manner with which they undress: sumptuousness and wealth play a stronger role than the vulnerability and openness of nudity. Similarly, Rouse discovers that the self-unveiling of Triamour in Chestre's *Sir Launfal* is not the prime indicator of her attractiveness; it is not that she takes her clothes off that matters, but that it is summer heat that prompts her to do so. It is all about the weather.

For Rushton and Robson context remains paramount. Gawain, long known to traditional criticism as the oversexed playboy of Arthur's court, fulfils the role of male sexual adventurer in tandem with his more overt function as Arthur's lieutenant, the only figure capable of cementing bonds between men. Both these functions depend on his pursuit of erotic possibilities, placing him within a tradition of male escapism intimately connected with the erotic. Robson's fairy knight, a troubling figure at best, represents a dangerous and possibly transgressive eroticism that colours *Sir Degarré*'s portrayal of adolescent, female sexuality.

The border between the forbidden and the erotic is of particular interest. Saunders examines the close ties between eroticism and magic through the figure of the sorceress, a doubly transgressive figure who threatens patriarchal constructs and yet remains enticing for both writers and readers. Anthony Bale makes a similar case for the Jewish woman, for much of England's history a type no more real than the sorceress after Edward I expelled all Jews from his kingdom. Bale explores the treatment of the female Jewish libido in Middle English and Scottish texts, focusing on narratives that describe Jewish daughters seduced by Christian men. The Jewish woman's libido and her erotic, transgressive attraction are a given

---

[82] Nancy Partner, 'No Sex, No Gender', *Speculum* 68 (1993), pp. 419–43 (p. 425).

in such texts, and the act of intercourse, publicised by a variety of means, is used to humiliate both the Jewess and her people; Jewesses' bodies thus become 'a site of competing jurisdictions, Christian and Jewish, with the rivalry between men articulated through controlling the Jewess'.

Michael Cichon explores more troubling sexualities: the treatment of the erotic in 'Math ap Mathonwy', from the *Fourth Branch* of the Middle Welsh prose *Mabinogi*. Cichon reads the tale's transgressive erotic possibilities (seduction, rape, sexual transformations of both gender and species) in the context of surviving Welsh codes and laws, and defines the text as primarily serving to demonstrate the problematic nature of lust itself for any given society. As Cichon suggests, the erotic stories remain erotic despite their social purpose, and are perhaps all the more effective as didactic tools for their indulgence. Thomas H. Crofts explores a more extreme transgression, arguing that the Giant of Mont Saint Michel of Arthurian legend testifies to a gluttonous sexuality that links excessive consumption with violence, making clear disturbing links between victims who are both sexual targets and food. Crofts' challenging coda argues that this dark vein within medieval eroticism still exists in some form today, comparing twenty-first century headlines with the *Alliterative Morte*'s obsession with military conflict.

Extant private correspondence of the Middle Ages also reveals a vein of eroticism: Kristina Hildebrand examines expressions of erotic affection in the private letters of the Paston, Stonor and Plumpton families, identifying, in letters between spouses or prospective spouses, an articulation of desire differentiated by gender, and revealing an awareness of the erotics of gendered roles of dominance and submission.

Other contributors have examined the treatment of the erotic in spiritual texts. In the context of other clerically produced, erotically charged works, Simon Meecham-Jones examines the purpose, effect and survival of the explicitly erotic Arundel lyrics, in particular the 'Grates ago veneri' attributed to Peter of Blois. Jane Bliss explores the sexual proscriptions of the *Ancrene Wisse*, whose author, like a confessor, is caught in the dilemma of needing to explain subtly the very sexual sins he wishes to discourage. Given the anchoress' circumstances, forbidding heterosexual eroticism would appear redundant, but Bliss examines a number of hints in the text that seem, through their own terminology or by reference to other texts, to be proscribing lesbianism.

Alex Davis closes with an investigation of the links between the erotic and traditional historiography regarding period division. Petrarch's 'discovery of the individual' through his lust for Laura has been seen as the moment when the Middle Ages gives way to the modern world; his erotic confusion leads to a fractured self, a self divided both internally and from its collective context. Despite its extraordinary persistence in academia, Davis suggests (as does this volume as a whole) that the erotic cannot stand as a marker of historical change: attempts to push the birth of individual consciousness back to the twelfth-century renaissance merely rehearses the same essential problems. The erotic has always been with us, and the people of the Middle Ages felt its sting as much as we do; this volume reveals many facets of the medieval erotic which prove just that.

*

The people of medieval Britain engaged in eroticism as individuals and couples, eroticism unique to each of them: they flirted, fantasised and sometimes erotically read non-erotic texts (just as their modern descendants do). When the idea for this book was first proposed at the Bangor International Arthurian Conference in 2002, it was more or less a jest. As the conversation continued, however, those participating saw an obvious gap between the assertion on the one hand that medieval Britain was devoid of any interest in the erotic, and on the other the growth of an academic cottage industry dedicated to gender issues rooted in an understanding of medieval sexuality that often seemed assumed rather than understood. The fact that the volume has actually happened is perhaps a warning about taking received wisdom too much to heart.

'So wel koude he me glose':
The Wife of Bath and the Eroticism of Touch

SUE NIEBRZYDOWSKI

NO DISCUSSION of eroticism in late medieval literature would be complete without consideration of the Wife of Bath, who readily embraces the subject of sex. Her comparison of sex with her first three husbands with that with her fifth, Jankyn, in which she identifies a difference not just in the quantity but in the quality, is especially memorable. Although he demanded payment of the marital debt less frequently than his predecessors, Jankyn is the one of whom the Wife of Bath admits, 'I loved hym best'.[1] Her discussion of her sex life reverberates in a culture in which the pursuit of *eros* or passionate, sensual love was disapproved of by the Church. This essay explores what the Wife of Bath reveals about the importance of eroticism within the marriage bed, and examines the definition of its most satisfying expression suggested in her fond memory of how Jankyn 'so wel koude ... me glose' (Prologue to *The Wife of Bath's Tale*, 509).

According to the Church, sex, lawful only within marriage, was not simply a matter of anywhere, anytime.[2] If when one had it was important, why one had it was crucial, and pleasure was not an approved motivation. To have intercourse to procreate and/or pay the marital debt was sinless; to have coitus to avoid sexual incontinence was a venial sin while it was a mortal sin to have sex for pleasure.[3] Experimentation with erotic sexual positions was discouraged. Canon lawyers defined the natural and moral fashion in which intercourse should take place as the missionary position since, as explained by Albertus Magnus (1200–80),

---

[1] Geoffrey Chaucer, *The Canterbury Tales*, ed. Larry, D. Benson, *The Riverside Chaucer*, 3rd edn (Oxford, 1987), Prologue to *The Wife of Bath's Tale*, line 513. All quotations from Chaucer are taken from this edition.
[2] Pierre J. Payer, *The Bridling of Desire: Views of Sex in the Later Middle Ages* (Toronto, Buffalo and London, 1993), pp. 98–9.
[3] James Brundage credits canonist Raymon de Penyafort (1175/80–1275) with writing the definitive medieval pronouncement on marital coitus. In 1230 Raymon began a collection of extant decretals about marriage at the direction of Pope Gregory IX (Brundage, *Medieval Canon Law* (London and New York, 1995), p. 222). In the *Summa* 4.2.8 (479), Raymon refines Lawrence of Spain's (d. 1248) four sinless acts of marital coitus by synthesising them with Huguccio of Pisa's (d. 1210) view of coitus as inherently sinful. Raymond concludes that 'In primo et secundo casu nullum est peccatum, in tertio veniale, in quarto mortale' (H. A. Kelly, *Love and Marriage in the Age of Chaucer* (Ithaca, NY, 1975), p. 257, n. 39).

'Nature teaches that the proper manner is that the woman be on her back with the man lying on her stomach'.[4] Oral and anal sex and coitus with the woman on top were prohibited because these positions were believed to impede conception.[5] The frequency and quality of intercourse were also a matter for thought. Instead of giving way to one's passion, according to Thomas Aquinas (d. 1274) in the *Summa Theologiae*, sexual activity should be moderated in frequency by the requirements of conservation of the species, and governed in its nature by reason through the operation of the virtue of temperance.[6] Kissing and touching were considered particularly problematic as they led to intercourse that was not the rationally governed desire to procreate endorsed by the Church. The prose sermon collection *Jacob's Well* warned that kissing and touching permitted the slime of evil to enter one's body:

> Whanne þou felyst or towchyst with mowth in kyssyng, wyth hand in gropyng, & wyth ony membre of þi body in towchyng þat steryn þe to synne & luste, þanne entreth be þe gate of þi felyng in-to þi pytt þe watyr & wose of wykkydnesse.[7]

John Myrc's *Instructions for Parish Priests* required a priest to ask any man during confession if he had committed lechery by 'Clyppynge, or kyssynge, or towchynge of lyth [the body], that thy flesch was styred with?'[8] Dan Michel's *Ayenbite of Inwyt* (1340) explained how lechery resulted from a chain reaction: foolish looking led to foolish speech, 'efterward ine fole takinges [touching]. Efterwarde in fole kessinges' leading to foolish action or intercourse itself.[9]

Medical and scientific discourse expressed a different attitude toward sexual pleasure because it was believed that a woman's satisfaction was important in aiding conception. Thomas Laqueur demonstrates how, from Aristotle (384–322 BC) and Galen (129–c. 216? AD), the Middle Ages inherited a one-sex model of humanity that understood women's anatomy as an inverted and inferior form of men's.[10] This is illustrated in the description of the womb in Lanfrank's *Science of Cirurgie* (1296): 'þe maris [womb] in a womman is maad nervous & is schape as it were a ȝerde [penis] þat were turned aȝenheer'.[11] To this body of classical knowledge the Middle Ages contributed interest in and discussion of sexual pleasure.[12] It was believed that, during intercourse, both men and women emitted seed that united to form an embryo –

---

4 Albertus Magnus, *Commentarii in IV Sententiarum (Dist. XXIII–L)* in *Opera Omnia*, ed. S. C. A. Borgnet, vol. 27 (Paris, 1894), 30.263. See translation in Payer, *The Bridling of Desire*, p. 219, n. 66.
5 Payer, *The Bridling of Desire*, pp. 77, 79.
6 See Aquinas, *Summa theologiae* 2–2.141.6 as explained in Payer, *Bridling of Desire*, pp. 151–3.
7 *Jacob's Well. Part I. An English treatise on the cleansing of Man's Conscience*, ed. A. Brandeis, EETS OS 115 (London, 1900), Chapter XXXIV.
8 *Instructions for Parish Priests by John Myrc*, ed. E. Peacock, EETS OS 31 (London, 1868), 1365.
9 *Dan Michel's Ayenbite of Inwyt or Remorse of Conscience in the Kentish Dialect 1340 AD*, ed. Richard Morris, EETS OS 23 (London, 1866), p. 46.
10 See Thomas Laqueur, *Making Sex: Body and Gender from the Greeks to Freud* (Cambridge, MA, and London, 1990), p. 33.
11 For the Middle English translations of Lanfranco of Milan's work (c. 1380 and c. 1420), see *Lanfrank's Science of Cirurgie*, part one, ed. Robert Fleischhacker, EETS OS 102 (London, 1894), section II. ix, p. 175.
12 Joan Cadden, *Meanings of Sex Difference in the Middle Ages: Medicine, Science, and Culture* (Cambridge, 1993), p. 135.

> And þe maris haþ ij brode ballokis in þe necke, & wiþ þe ilke ij ballokis ben maad fast ij vessels of sperme [the womb has two ovaries and two spermatic ducts (fallopian tubes)] . . . And of þese vessels, a wommans sperme goiþ to the botme of þe maris/ And in þe tyme of conseyuynge þe wommans sperme [is] medlid wiþ a mannes[13]

– and that, if the woman did not emit sperm, conception could not take place, as is suggested in the *Canon* or medical compendium of Avicenna:

> There is no shame in the doctor speaking about the increase in the size of the penis, or the narrowing of the receptive organs, or of the woman's pleasure, since these are factors that play a part in reproduction. For the small size of the penis is often a hindrance to climax and emission in the woman. Now, when the woman does not emit any sperm, conception cannot take place.[14]

A woman's pleasure was recognised to aid conception, and debate occurred as to whether men or women experience more pleasure in sex, with many concluding that it was women who did.[15] Joan Cadden observes that the formula for sexual pleasure that was perpetuated recognised that 'man's pleasure came from the emission of his own semen, whereas woman's pleasure derived only partially from her own emission and depended for the rest upon the man'.[16] Danielle Jacquart and Claude Thomasset conclude that the belief that woman's pleasure played a role in conception

> created the possibility of making room for the beginnings of an erotic art: the quest for pleasure as such was to be one of the components of every discourse on the conditions for performing the sexual act, since in the background loomed the necessity of encouraging conception.[17]

Medical works contained advice to encourage a woman's enjoyment of sex. There were things that a woman could do for herself, such as using recipes for vaginal constrictives. The *De Curis Mulierum* [On Treatments for Women], a work ultimately derived from the Latin *Trotula* ensemble, suggested that sexual pleasure could be promoted by artificially constricting the vagina.[18] This might be done by the twice-daily insertion of a tampon, soaked either in egg whites mixed with water in which pennyroyal and pre-cooked, heat-producing herbs had been steeped, or in newly ground holm oak bark mixed with rainwater.[19] Men had to play their part too. In cures for female sterility erotic touching as foreplay was

---

[13] *Science of Cirurgie*, II. ix, p. 175.
[14] Avicenna, *Canon*, bk III, fen. 20, tr.1, ch. 8, as quoted in Danielle Jacquart and Claude Thomasset, *Sexuality and Medicine in the Middle Ages* (Princeton, 1988), p. 130.
[15] Joyce Salisbury, 'Gendered Sexuality', *Handbook of Medieval Sexuality*, ed. Vern Bullough and James Brundage (London and New York, 1996), pp. 81–102 (p. 93).
[16] *Meanings*, p. 161.
[17] *Sexuality and Medicine*, p. 130.
[18] The standardised ensemble comprises these three texts: the *Liber de Sinthomatibus Mulierum* [Book on the Conditions of Women], *De Curis Mulierum* and *De Ornatu Mulierum* [On Women's Cosmetics]. See Monica Green, ed. and trans., *The Trotula: A Medieval Compendium of Women's Medicine* (Philadelphia, 2001).
[19] Green, *The Trotula*, p. 42.

recommended. To encourage simultaneous emission one fourteenth-century medical author recommended that the husband 'smoothly stroke his lady, breasts and belly, and excite [her] for having intercourse'.[20] The *Rosa Anglica* of John of Gaddesden, the fourteenth-century Oxford doctor of physic appointed to Edward II, was much more detailed in its advice, and took into consideration the woman's erogenous zones:

> To excite and arouse a woman to intercourse, a man ought to speak, kiss and embrace [her], to touch her breasts, to caress her breasts and to touch the whole [area] between her perineum and her vulva and to strike her buttocks with the purpose that the woman desires sex... and when the woman begins to speak with a stammer, then they ought to copulate.[21]

The medical text recommended precisely the combination of words, kissing and touching that spiritual advisors such as John Myrc, Dan Michel and the author of *Jacob's Well* warned led to sexual sin.

The Wife of Bath's prologue reveals the influence wielded over men's and women's lives by patriarchal discourses purporting to know women's sexuality. In her admission that she cannot deny any good man her 'chambre of Venus' (618), the Wife of Bath lacks the measured and thoughtful response to sex required by canon law. In her discussion of her sex life we hear her living up to every man's worst nightmare of women's sexuality. But at the same time that she confirms male fear of uncontrollable female sexuality, the Wife of Bath resists this formulation by presenting knowledge different from this dominant tradition, exposing 'the fraud of male knowledge'.[22] Alisoun knows only too well that whoever paints the lion governs the perspective given. If women had written the stories of their sexuality, the tales would be very different from those told by clerks: Alisoun understands her genitals are more than simply 'maked for purgaciuon/ Of uryne, and, ... to knowe a femele from a male' (120–2), and 'ese/ Of engendrure' (127–8). Experience has taught her that her *bele chose* is an organ of pleasure, and the 'diverse practyk' (44d), with five husbands, that erotic sensuality is not a given within the marriage bed. In her comparison of her first three marriages with her fifth, Alisoun reveals that women have an attitude towards sex and that a husband's sexual prowess and skill do not always satisfy his wife's expectations.

Alisoun describes how from her first three marriages she gains much in terms of power (in economic terms), but remains unsatisfied sexually and emotionally. She admits that she 'suffre hym do his nycetee' (412), suggesting that any desire and satisfaction experienced was on the part of her husbands only, as she lay back and thought of the 'raunson' or penalty that she would exact in return for what

---

[20] '*De impedimentis conceptionis*. maritus... debet dominam suaviter palpare mamillas et ventrem et excitare ad coytum' (Cadden, *Meanings*, p. 252, n. 86).

[21] 'Mas excitare foeminam debet ac sollicitare ad coitum, loquendo, osculando, amplectendo, mamillas contractando, tangendo pectinem et perinaeum totamque vulvam accipiendo in manus et nates percutiendo hoc fine atque proposito ut mulier appetat venerem... et cum mulier incipit loqui balbutiendo, tunc debent se commiscere' (John of Gaddesden, *Rosa Anglica* (Augsburg, 1595), p. 555, as quoted in Jacquart and Thomasset, *Sexuality and Medicine*, p. 222, n. 99; translation mine).

[22] E. Jane Burns, *Bodytalk: When Women Speak in Old French Literature* (Philadelphia, 1993), p. 39.

amounted to servicing her husbands' lust. Alisoun's confession of enduring sex and faking desire,

> For wynnyng wolde I al his lust endure,
> And make me a feyned appetit;
> And yet in bacon hadde I nevere delit (416–18),

indicates that she did not enjoy a mutually affectionate and sensual relationship with any of her first three husbands. Even though they 'pitously a-nyght . . . swynke!' (202), her husbands are physically unarousing, as is suggested by the Wife's ironic reference to the competition held annually in Dunmow in Essex for the Flitch or side of bacon. This was awarded to any married couple who could live a year and a day without arguing.[23] In none of her first three marriages has Alisoun enjoyed bacon – metonymic of each husband's sexual member. Alisoun's sexual experiences with her three, old husbands recall those of May in *The Merchant's Tale*, whose sixty-year-old spouse, Januarie, 'laboureth . . . til that the day gan dawe' (1842). Although she says nothing, Helen Phillips and Anne Laskaya concur that 'preyseth nat his pleyyng worth a bene' (1854) is, indeed, May's evaluation of Januarie's wedding night performance.[24] Alisoun's and May's sex lives with their much older husbands indicate that, even if the man is fortified by the aphrodisiacs (1807–8) recommended by Constantine the African in his *De Coitu* [On Intercourse],[25] frequent sex is not enough to arouse a woman: technique is crucial. From the Wife's perspective, her first three husbands indulge in laboured, mechanical, decidedly unerotic copulation.

In her hunt for a fourth and fifth husband, Alisoun prioritises the erotic so conspicuously absent from her first three marriages, even though this means that her spouse brings rather less financially to the union than that to which she has become accustomed. In her relationship with husband number four Alisoun discovers that, in the same way that she failed to find her first three husbands a turn-on, her fourth husband is immune to her sex appeal. She is forced to acknowledge that the erotic is in the eye of the beholder.

Although Alisoun considers herself still 'yong and ful of ragerye,/ Stibourne and strong, and joly as a pye' (455–6), her fourth husband does not, and she is denied her sexual right by a man for whom she represents nothing erotic and who satisfies his sexual needs with a mistress. Faced with a sexual stalemate, the Wife of Bath moves swiftly to her marriage to Jankyn, sex with whom she reveals is a mutually pleasurable, tactile, satisfying but all too infrequent experience:

---

[23] The couple was required to swear their oaths on the 'Kneeling Stones', which may still be seen in Little Dunmow Priory today. It is likely that the bacon was given by the ecclesiastical authorities of the Augustinian Priory of St Mary the Virgin at Little Dunmow, as a kind of edible bonus if people took marriage vows with the Church's blessing (details from the anonymous *Little Dunmow Priory. A Brief History and Guide to the Parish Church Today* ([n.p.], [n.d.], no pagination).
[24] Helen Phillips, *An Introduction to the Canterbury Tales: Reading, Fiction, Context* (Basingstoke, 2000), p. 129. Anne Laskaya, *Chaucer's Approach to Gender in the Canterbury Tales* (Cambridge, 1995), p. 94.
[25] Paul Delaney, 'Constantinus Africanus' *De Coitu*: A Translation', *Chaucer Review* 4:1 (1969), pp. 55–65 (p. 55).

> But in oure bed he was so fressh and gay,
> And therwithal so wel koude he me glose,
> When that he wolde han my *bele chose* ...
> I trowe I loved hym best, for that he
> Was of his love daungerous to me. (508–10; 513–14)

It is not merely a matter of Jankyn's youth, fine legs and curly hair. Nor is it that Jankyn, in a spirit of 'treat them mean, keep them keen', gives his wife a taste of her own medicine and, on occasion, denies her his love and body. Rather, when Jankyn does make love to Alisoun he is able and willing to engage in prolonged and pleasurable foreplay, recommended in medical works, that satisfies his wife's erotic desires and encourages her to experience pleasure in intercourse.

In examining the Wife of Bath's appreciation of her fifth husband, comparison between Jankyn's sexual technique and that of Damyan, May's lover, is illuminating. May's encouragement of Damyan indicates that she has 'han no plesaunce' (1434) with Januarie, and that what she desires from the much younger man is sexual pleasure, pure and simple. Elaine Tuttle Hansen's view is compelling that May's behaviour with her squire is illustrative of her 'awakening' as she comes into a subjectivity and sexuality of her own.[26] The actual sex scene, however, is an anticlimax. It is *coitus interruptus* and not just from Damyan's point of view. Missing is any statement that May enjoyed the sex, as did Alison in another fabliau, *The Miller's Tale*, about whose night of passion with the 'hende Nicholas' we are told that the couple both 'lith . . ./ In bisynesse of myrthe and of solas,/ Til that the belle of laudes gan to rynge' (3653–5). We are given instead a very blunt description, from the Merchant's perspective, of how Damyan 'Gan pullen up the smok, and in he throng' (2352) and then Januarie's outcry ' "Ye, algate in it wente!/ . . . / He swyved thee" ' (2376, 2379). May says nothing (even though Proserpina has granted to her and all women the ability to talk themselves out of tricky situations), at the very moment in which she might be expected to voice her opinion about men's sexual performance, for having had two lovers she is now in a position to judge. The Merchant's description of May's coupling with Damyan disappoints because of May's emotional absence from the moment: she is the smock to be lifted and the hole to be filled, reduced to the stereotypically voracious vagina that characterises many a wicked wife. There is no access to May's thoughts at this point; how May might feel about this young man's sexual ability, if she has enjoyed the experience, or if she might want more sensuality and erotic satisfaction than that provided by Damyan's hasty thrusting in. The focus of the encounter is the reaction of the Merchant and Januarie to Damyan's actions. It is the bare-faced cheek that they criticise, not the sexual performance that, most tellingly, neither perceives as lacking in any way nor as anything other than is desired by May. The Merchant-narrator refuses his female lead space to create a sexual-textual discourse of her own. In solidarity with a patriarchy that had much to lose should men acknowledge that women assess men's sexual performance as much as men do women's, and that men too can be found wanting, the Merchant balks at giving May opportunity to admit that women prefer young, virile men or, even

---

[26] *Chaucer and the Fictions of Gender* (Berkeley, Los Angeles and Oxford, 1992), p. 258.

worse, that men, old and wealthy, young and attractive alike, simply do not know how to sexually satisfy their women.

Although the Wife of Bath accuses her first three husbands of precisely the sexual ineptitude that the Merchant fears that May will voice, Alisoun gives praise where praise is due. She recalls fondly Jankyn's performance, which she describes in a very different fashion from that of her first three husbands whose efforts are akin to the Merchant's portrayal of the 'swyving' up the pear tree experienced by May. Alisoun reminisces that Jankyn was 'fresshe and gay' in bed, a description that conveys a variety of meanings; fresh, new, vigorous, lusty, joyous, wanton and amorous, any number of which indicate that he brought virility, pleasure and invention to his lovemaking. She reveals also that Jankyn could 'glose' her so well when he wished to sleep with her. To 'glose' can mean to pursue favour through cajoling and flattery, suggesting that Jankyn began his lovemaking with erotic speech, seducing his wife mentally before attempting the physical.[27] The verb also means to gloss a body of writing, that is, the insertion of an explanatory or interpretive comment between the lines or in the margins of a text after its careful scrutiny. The Wife of Bath is familiar with this second meaning and also that some 'glose' or interpret more accurately than others, for she uses the term to dismiss both the Gospels' interpreters' stance on digamy, 'Men may devyne and glosen, up and doun' (Prologue, 26), and clerical interpretation of the purpose of the genitalia, 'Glose whoso wole, and seye bothe up and doun/ That they were maked for purgacioun/ Of urine . . .' (119–21). As a clerk, Jankyn would be familiar with the concept of 'glosing' texts. Glossing implies a slow and careful study of a text, fingering the lines on the manuscript as it is read, taking the time to explore and understand its minutiae. The Wife of Bath is appreciative that, during their lovemaking, Jankyn applies the same close reading techniques of studying one membrane to another skin that also bears similar lines, hairs, scar marks and discolorations. Jankyn 'gloses' his wife's body, suggesting the slow, careful touching of its lines, lacunae or orifices, scars and birthmarks, such as the one of Mars that she bears upon her 'privee place' (620), that is indubitably erotic. Alisoun recalls that he does this 'so wel', intimating that Jankyn learned to understand her body and Alisoun finally achieved sexual arousal. Like Pygmalion, at whose kisses and touch the woman of ivory 'temptatum mollescit ebur positoque reigore subsidit digitis ceditque' ('lost its hardness, and grew soft: his fingers made an imprint on the yielding surface'),[28] so the Wife of Bath softened under Jankyn's touch, the memory of which still retains its power to move her. Chaucer's audience might have expected Jankyn to succeed where her other husbands had failed. Andreas Capellanus' *De Amore* (1184–86) placed clerks at the summit of the hierarchy of lovers because of their attention to detail that extended to making love:

---

[27] See 'glosen', 3b, in *MED*, ed. Sherman M. Kuhn with John Reidy (Ann Arbor, 1963), vol. 4 (G–H), p. 173.

[28] Latin text of Ovid's *Metamorphoses* from P. Ovidius Naso, *Metamorphoses*, ed. Rudolf Ehwald, *Metamorphoseon* (2 vols, Leipzig, c. 1904), 10.283–4, *Electronic Text Center*, University of Virginia Library, stable URL: <http://etext.lib.virginia.edu/latin/ovid/>), trans. Mary M. Innes, *The Metamorphoses of Ovid* (Harmondsworth, 1955), Book X, 283–4, p. 232.

Clerkus enim in cunctis cautior et prudentior quam laicus invenitur, et maiori moderamine se suaque disponit et competentiori mensura solitus est omnia moderari, et quia clerkus omnium rerum scientiam habet scriptura referente peritiam. Unde potior ipsius quam laici amor est iudicandus, quia nil in mundo tam necessarium invenitur quam omnium industria rerum amorosum esse peritum.

(The clerk is seen to be more careful and wise in all things than the layman. He orders himself and his affairs with greater control, and is accustomed to governing everything with more fitting measure; because he is a clerk he has knowledge of all things, since scripture gives him this expertise. So his love is to be accounted better than the layman's, because nothing on earth is established to be so vital as that the lover should have experience in diligent application of all things.)[29]

Here clerks are praised as far better lovers than any layman because of their ability to apply to their love-making the knowledge gained from study of scripture and the control that they practised in all other areas of their lives. Jacquart and Thomasset have gone so far as to claim that what Capellanus has encoded here is clerical ability to practise *coitus interruptus*.[30] John Metham's *Physiognomy*, or study of the meaning of certain physical attributes, makes a direct link between the soft hands, possessed by one such as a clerk, and a quick mind and sexuality: 'Handys the qwyche be passyng soft sygnyfye that a body hath an abyl wytt to lerne, and thei sygnyffye leccherusnes.'[31] Alisoun intimates that Jankyn practised measured love-making and even the possibility that he tried to avoid making her pregnant. It is of little wonder that Alisoun loved him best of all. Alisoun delights in Jankyn's exploration of her, expressing sentiments similar to the unnamed female narrator of the lyric, *Our Sir John*, who readily admits that when

> Ser Iohn ys taken In my mouse-trappe:
> ffayne wold I haue hem [Sir John/his penis] bothe nyght and day.
> he gropith so nyslye a-bought my lape,
> I haue no pore to sa[y hym nay].[32]

Alisoun is 'glosed wel' and the lyric narrator is 'nyslye gropith', much to their enjoyment.

Alisoun argues throughout her prologue that male-produced texts sought to constrain sexual pleasure, women's in particular, and failed to address that women had erotic needs that their husbands simply did not meet. Men need not worry, however. The Wife of Bath's appreciation of Jankyn's 'glosing' reinforces, as does the lyric quoted above, that what women really desire is to be the recipient of the rigid, male member of a husband who has taken the time to study his wife's body, and erotically touch and arouse her when they make love. The Wife of Bath's

---

29 De Amore, VI. Loquitur nobilior nobiliori, Sections 487–8, quoted from the online version at *The Latin Library* (stable URL: http://www.thelatinlibrary. com/capellanus1.html>), trans. from Jacquart and Thomasset, *Sexuality and Medicine*, p. 104.
30 *Sexuality and Medicine*, p. 104.
31 *John Metham's* Physiognomy, ed. Hardin Craig, EETS OS 132 (London, 1916), p. 137.
32 *Secular Lyrics of the XIVth and XVth Centuries*, ed. Rossell Hope Robbins (Oxford, 1952, repr. 1961), number 26, p. 20.

praise of Jankyn's sexual technique acknowledges that a man can perfect the art of sex, if, with her tutoring, he diligently reads and responds to his wife's body. Not all men take the time or have the ability to learn. The Merchant admits when he comes to describe May's and Damyan's coupling up the pear tree, that he cannot 'glose': 'Ladyes, I prey yow that ye be nat wrooth;/ I kan nat glose, I am a rude man' (*The Merchant's Tale*, 2350–1). This admission, perhaps, explains the lack-lustre description of sex that he provides in his tale and the sorry state of his marriage after only two months' duration. Good sex may not solve all ills, and the Wife of Bath and Jankyn had issues around sovereignty to resolve, but it helps.

The Lady's Man:
Gawain as Lover in Middle English Literature

CORY J. RUSHTON

EROTICISM and the heroic go hand in hand for today's audiences: the male hero is often only as good as his ability to bed attractive women, a trait that allows the male reader or viewer to identify with the hero's serial love affairs. An integral part of the James Bond myth is that Bond can have any woman he wants, despite (or perhaps because of) his misogynistic attitudes:

> With most women his manner was a mixture of taciturnity and passion. The lengthy approaches to a seduction bored him almost as much as the subsequent mess of disentanglement. He found something grisly in the inevitability of the pattern of each affair. The conventional parabola – sentiment, the touch of the hand, the kiss, the passionate kiss, the feel of the body, the climax in the bed, then more bed, then less bed, then the boredom, the tears and the final bitterness – was to him shameful and hypocritical. Even more he shunned the *mise en scène* for each of these acts in the play – the meeting at a party, the restaurant, the taxi, his flat, her flat, the week-end by the sea, then the flats again, then the furtive alibis and the final angry farewell on some doorstep in the rain.[1]

Bond often sleeps with women who are his enemies as well as allies; either way, his lovers often end up dead, leaving him free to pursue further sexual encounters. Byron's Don Juan and the historical Casanova are renowned for little else beyond their romantic escapades, becoming heroes of the boudoir rather than the battlefield. The trend has been brought to its logical conclusion in George MacDonald Fraser's Harry Flashman, a coward whose only real skills lie in the bedroom:

> Let me say that while there have been hundreds of women in my life, I have never been one of those who are forever boasting about their conquests. I've raked and ridden harder than most, no doubt... That's by the way; unless you are the kind who falls in love – which I've never been – you take your tumbles when you've the chance, and the more the better.[2]

---

[1] Ian Fleming, *Casino Royale* (1953), repr. in *Casino Royale, Live and Let Die, Moonraker* (Harmondsworth, 2003), p. 112.
[2] George MacDonald Fraser, *Flashman* (1969; London, 1999), p. 22.

The presence of male wish-fulfilment is readily apparent in these love-them-and-leave-them characters; do the English Middle Ages have an equivalent figure, a character whose serial adventures involve sex and violence in equal measure?

The medieval era has famous lovers (Lancelot, Tristram), but their stories concern a single intense dedication on the part of a hero for a particular woman, not a series of sexual conquests; their stories are also largely written in French rather than English, at least until late in the period. There is, however, one prominent medieval philanderer whose reputation for numerous love affairs has become well-known in modern criticism of romance literature: Sir Gawain.[3] Thomas Hahn notes that Gawain fits the archetype of 'the Young Man, available for both adventure and love' as well as 'the paragon against which manhood is measured' who nevertheless came to be seen as 'the natural target for attacks on the volatility and solipsism of knighthood' in the *Queste del Saint Graal*;[4] subsequent French texts develop this attack even where they did not entirely share the ethos and concerns of the original *Queste*. Yet the *Queste* is, for all its continuing popularity with readers, not a typical medieval text and certainly not a typical romance, and Gawain is there portrayed atypically: older, more vengeful, doomed. A more representative comment may be found in Chaucer's vast canon, albeit as the only reference to Gawain therein: it is, perhaps not coincidentally, the Squire (certainly a 'Young Man') who mentions Gawain as a paragon of the 'olde curteisye'.[5]

In the late Middle English ballad *King Arthur and King Cornwall* (found only in the sixteenth-century Percy Folio), King Cornwall's insulting behaviour towards Arthur and the Round Table (he claims to have a better table at home, and Guenevere agrees) leads to a series of oaths, the fulfilment of which will avenge the dishonour. Arthur vows to be ' "the bane of Cornwall Kinge" ' (135), but Gawain, traditionally Arthur's most loyal and capable knight in English texts, promises only to kidnap Cornwall's daughter and bring her back to 'Little Brittaine' for his personal pleasure: ' "Ile hose her homly to my hurt,/ And with her Ile worke my will" ' (155–6). The poem's most recent editor writes that Gawain's 'vow, unfulfilled in the surviving text . . . recalls his rakish character in the later French romances'.[6] The tacit assumption that Gawain's best defence of

---

[3] Larry D. Benson, *Art and Tradition in* Sir Gawain and the Green Knight (Brunswick, NJ, 1965), pp. 104–5.

[4] 'Gawain and popular chivalric romance in Britain', *The Cambridge Companion to Medieval Romance*, ed. Roberta L. Krueger (Cambridge, 2000), pp. 218–34 (p. 220). The best introduction to the French Gawain remains Keith Busby, *Gauvain in Old French Literature* (Amsterdam, 1980), and a follow-up article, which provides a corrective to his own general argument, 'Diverging Traditions of Gauvain in Some of the Later Old French Romances', *The Legacy of Chrétien de Troyes*, ed. Norris Lacy, Douglas Kelly and Keith Busby, 2 vols (Amsterdam, 1988), II, pp. 93–109. Other valuable articles include Fanni Bogdanow, 'The Character of Gauvain in the Thirteenth-century Prose Romances', *Medium Ævum* 27 (1958), pp. 154–61; and Per Nykrog, 'Trajectory of the Hero: Gauvain, Paragon of Chivalry 1130–1230', *Medieval Narrative: A Symposium*, ed. Hans Bekker-Neilson et al. (Odense, 1979), pp. 82–93.

[5] Geoffrey Chaucer, *The Squire's Tale*, ed. Larry D. Benson, *The Riverside Chaucer*, 3rd edn (Boston, 1987), line 95. See B. J. Whiting, 'Gawain: His Reputation, His Courtesy and His Appearance in Chaucer's Squire's Tale', *Medieval Studies* 9 (1947), pp. 189–234.

[6] Thomas Hahn, ed., *Sir Gawain: Eleven Romances and Tales*, TEAMS (Kalamazoo, 1995), p. 420. For ease of reference, all citations of *The Wedding of Sir Gawain and Dame Ragnelle*, *Sir Gawain and the Carle of Carlisle*, *The Avowyng of Arthur*, *The Greene Knight*, *The Carle of Carlisle*, *The Marriage of Sir Gawain* and *The Jeaste of Sir Gawain* come from this edition.

the Round Table is abduction or seduction (or both) hints at a combination of eroticism and violence that might seem familiar to fans of the Flashman series and other masculine fantasies of sexual adventure.

Gawain's reputation as a philanderer precedes him; the best-known example is the comment of Bertilak's wife in *Sir Gawain and the Green Knight*, whose disbelief that the famous and courteous Gawain could be alone with her and not crave a kiss is notorious (1292–1301).[7] Gawain's reputation concerns courteous seduction, the kind that Bond finds distasteful, and critics have pointed out time and again that the Lady seems to have every reason to believe that Gawain can provide both 'luf-talkyng' and its physical fulfilment. As early as Chrétien's *Yvain*, the French Gawain (or Gauvain) was considered, at the very least, light in love.[8] His promise to be at Lunette's service (313), unfulfilled when she is in danger of execution and Gawain does not appear to champion her (339–42), seems to herald a French tradition of a Gawain untouched by the excesses of courtly love and unencumbered by any lasting *amour*.

The French Gawain does indeed have his fair share of erotic adventures, more so than his English counterpart (*plus ça change*, some might say). In *Le Chevalier à l'épée*, Gawain risks his life to preserve his reputation as a lover.[9] Sent to bed with his host's not entirely unwilling daughter, Gawain is warned that to 'bring to a conclusion' the sexual act will result in his death by magic sword (pp. 93–5). Faced with death, Gawain nevertheless worries about his reputation back home: 'But on the other hand he considered that it could not be concealed or be kept from being known everywhere that he had lain beside her in her bed, with both of them being naked ... and he had failed to take his pleasure' (p. 97). He concludes that he would never recover from the shame, and tells her that she ' "really can't avoid it!" '; although the sword does, in fact, protect her just as she had predicted (pp. 97–8).[10] This Gawain is unable to resist temptation until sorely wounded, but other depictions show a far more circumspect figure often enough that we might at least provisionally question the dominant interpretation of his character.

In *Perlesvaus*, an odd Grail romance apparently produced in Glastonbury Abbey, the questing Gawain is propositioned by not one but two ladies, who are camped along his path; aware of the sacred nature of the Grail quest, he declines. This *ménage à trois* is only offered because Gawain's reputation inferred that he would make good use of the opportunity: the ladies, agreeing that this cannot be the great lover and suspecting 'an imposter', argue that if they had 'wished to keep vigil for three nights, then he would do so for four'.[11] In *Sir Gawain and the Green*

---

7   *Sir Gawain and the Green Knight*, ed. J. R. R. Tolkien and E. V. Gordon, rev. by Norman Davis, 2nd edn (Oxford, 1967).
8   Chrétien de Troyes, *Arthurian Romances*, ed. and trans. D. D. R. Owen (London, 1993). All subsequent references to Chrétien's poems are to this edition.
9   Trans. and ed. Ross G. Arthur, *Three Arthurian Romances: Poems from Medieval France* (London, 1996).
10 The poem then descends into fabliau territory when the lady, having been given to Gawain, chooses to ride away with another man: she has already tested Gawain in bed, and is curious about the abilities of other men – as the poet puts it, 'you know the kind of prowess I mean' (pp. 100–2).
11 *The High Book of the Grail*, trans. Nigel Bryant (Cambridge, 1996), p. 64. The blasphemous use of religious terminology, sexual escapades as a vigil, is entirely appropriate for *Perlesvaus*, a strange

Knight, Bertilak's wife makes the same accusation: ' "Sir, ȝif ȝe be Wawen, wonder me þynkkez" ' (1481). In the Pucelle de Lis episode from the *First Continuation* of *Perceval*, Gawain meets a girl who has always loved him from afar; she carries an embroidered image of him, created by a Saracen woman who once saw him at court. That this image is itself either an erotic or a romantic image (or both) is made clear from the outcome: nature takes its course and Gawain sleeps with her, promising to return once his current quest is complete. Her father, meanwhile, discovers the affair and challenges Gawain over the dishonour; the fact that Gawain had earlier killed the Pucelle's brother adds to the bitter dispute. Gawain kills the father, as well, and is subsequently challenged by yet another sibling, Bran de Lis, this last battle ending in a draw.[12]

In Gerbert de Montreuil's *Fourth Continuation*, Gawain rapes a woman who has seduced him in order to kill him (shades of James Bond again). Hoping to avenge the death of one of her brothers, the lady has hidden a knife in her bed; Gawain finds it, hides it and rapes her: 'Weille ou non, sosfir li estuet/ Le ju de mon seignor Gavain' (12638–9): 'Like it or not, she has to submit to Sir Gawain's game' is Ad Putter's translation.[13] Gerbert's crowing exaltation in Gawain's victory is unmistakable; when the lady falls in love with her rapist, the male fantasy of total sexual conquest is fulfilled. In fact, Gawain is able to go back to bed with her between killing her cousins and fleeing from her brothers. We might see a dark hint of the fate of King Cornwall's daughter in that of the raped lady, simply another in the long line of lovers collected (in the latter case quite literally) by Gawain.

The English Gawain generally avoids these entanglements in the first place, his inherent courtesy protecting him from making costly social mistakes. Gawain often acts as the special champion of ladies in the Middle English tradition, but in almost all cases these are directly based on French sources. The *Stanzaic Morte Arthur* claims that Gawain will not attend the burning of Guenevere because he 'wolde never be ner beside/ There any woman sholde be brent'.[14] Gawain defeats a troublesome knight and would-be rapist named Menealfe in the Middle English *Avowyng of Arthur*, whom he then recommends for inclusion in the Round Table (561–4). Gawain's foes, especially in Middle English texts, invariably tend to join the Round Table; here, the kidnapped damsel provides an excuse for the battle and the subsequent, all-important homosocial bonding. As one might expect, in this case Gawain's advocacy is enough for the court, and they immediately 'fochet furth a boke' on which Menealfe can swear his allegience to the Round Table (565–72).

Menealfe's story, like that of Gawain's sexual revenge against his would-be female killer, concerns the taming of sexually attractive women (just as Shakespeare's *Taming of the Shrew* does). Theorists of male sexuality acknowledge that

---

and violent work of almost fanatic Christian intensity. Gawain's ability to resist this temptation indicates the importance of chastity on the quest of the Grail, and his resolve in doing so contrasts neatly with his amorous reputation in other French romances.

[12] Busby, *Gauvain*, pp. 161–2. Bran de Lis becomes a regular character in French and Middle English romance, including Malory; a fragment of a Middle English adaptation of this exact story, *The Jeaste of Sir Gawain*, is discussed below.

[13] *Sir Gawain and the Green Knight and French Tradition* (Oxford, 1995), p. 113.

[14] *King Arthur's Death: The Middle English* Stanzaic Morte Arthur *and* Alliterative Morte Arthure, ed. Larry D. Benson, rev. by Edward E. Foster (Kalamazoo, 1974), lines 1938–9.

the masculine impulse to rescue and the impulse to threaten are so closely linked as to be often indistinguishable:

> The heroine in jeopardy ... is trapped, a woman without resources to help herself. Heroes in jeopardy do something about it; heroines don't. And the pleasure we get from seeing these sequences is that of seeing a woman in peril. We're supposed to get off on her vulnerability, her hysteria, her terror. In the way such sequences are put together, we are encouraged to take up a traditional male role in relation to the woman, one that asserts our superiority and at the same time encourages us to feel the desire to rape and conquer.[15]

Modern film, particularly horror film, will allow the viewer to see the female victim just as the villain does, often from the exact same viewpoint through the agency of the camera.[16] The medieval romance, with its emphasis on the ties between men, is overt in its acknowledgement of the male gaze: the reader's view of the damsel in *Avowyng* shifts easily from moment to moment, depending on which knight is looking at her.

Menealfe tells Sir Kay, his first opponent, that he captured her in battle:

> 'And this Lady sum I the telle:
> I fochet hur atte Ledelle,
> Ther hur frindus con I felle
>   As foes in a fighte.
> So I talket hom tille
> That muche blode conne I spille,
> And all agaynus thayre awne wille
>   There wan I thus wighte.' (309–16)

Menealfe's overtly belligerent attitude, designed to provoke a fight with the woman's companions, is found elsewhere in Arthurian romance, where the so-called 'custom of Logres' requires knights to leave an unaccompanied female traveller alone, but allows her to be captured if an attacking knight can defeat any male companions (*Lancelot*, 223–4).[17] Gawain himself participates in a variant of this custom in the *Prose Tristan*, a scene that makes its way into Malory:

> Than wythin two or three dayes sir Lamerok founde a knyght at a welle slepynge, and his lady sate with hym and waked. Ryght so com sir Gawayne and toke the knyghtes lady and sette hir up behynde hys squyer.[18]

The lady has no discernible reaction, and is soon rescued by her knight, Bellyaunce le Orgulus: as in *Avowyng*, the abduction exists only to prompt a combat, on this occasion between Bellyaunce and Gawain's fellow Round Table knight, Lamorak.

---

[15] Richard Dyer, 'Male sexuality in the media', *The Sexuality of Men*, ed. Andy Metcalf and Martin Humphries (London and Sydney, 1985), pp. 28–43 (p. 38).
[16] Dyer, 'Male sexuality', pp. 39–41.
[17] See also Corinne Saunders, *Rape and Ravishment in The Literature of Medieval England* (Cambridge, 2001), pp. 250–1. As she states elsewhere in her book, 'the chivalric custom of winning a lady through battle ensures that rape is never far from the action of romance'; of course, as with hagiography, rape is almost always avoided in romance despite the necessity of its threat (187–8).
[18] Thomas Malory, *The Book of Sir Tristram de Lyones*, ed. Eugène Vinaver, *Malory: Works*, 2nd edn (Oxford, 1971), p. 280, lines 16–19.

Lamorak has an obligation to defend members of Arthur's court even when they are clearly in the wrong; his combat with Bellyaunce ends in mutual reconciliation as 'they were sworne togydyrs that none of hem sholde never fyght ayenste other' (281/39–40). Gawain is entirely excluded from this pact of friendship, his position of scorn one shared by Malory and his source.[19]

In *Avowyng*, the lady's beauty is constantly contrasted with her weeping: 'Gay in hor gere' (324), she 'wepputte wundur sore' and prays for both the protection of her ' "madunhede" ' and the violent defeat of her captor (280–2). The woman's weeping ('her vulnerability, her hysteria, her terror') prompts Kay to attempt a rescue for 'chesun of that Lady free' (362), his language at first respectful towards the victim. When the battle results in Kay's customary defeat, he saves his life by mentioning Gawain's immanent arrival (333–48). When Gawain defeats Menealfe in turn, Kay's language suddenly changes: within a series of taunts directed at the defeated Menealfe, Kay notes that he has 'hade a falle,/ and thi wench lost wythalle' (426–7). The second time the lady changes hands seems to fix her now as a prize, and little else: Kay's interpretation of the woman has shifted as his gaze turns from that of would-be rescuer to one of passive observation. He has become an audience. Following his victory, Gawain commands Menealfe to take ' "this damsel schene" ' to Guenevere, where Menealfe will be judged. Once safely at court, the damsel laughs and praises 'God and Sir Gawan' (510–11), praise echoed by Guenevere, who prays that God will always protect Gawain, who ' "thus for wemen con fighte" ' (557–60). The rescued damsel disappears from the narrative, her status as prize a comfortable one (she will likely not be raped at Arthur's court), but also obviously less important than the relationship between Menealfe and Gawain, 'Now gode frindus' (573). Here, the eroticism of an abducted sexual prize is made acceptable through the reader's identification with the heroic Gawain, whose refusal to enjoy his prize absolves readers of any responsibility for whatever threatening fantasies they may have earlier experienced: the 'camera puts us in the position of the rapist, but the plot puts us reassuringly back in the position of the saviour'.[20]

The ballad retelling of *Sir Gawain and the Green Knight*, the fifteenth-century *The Greene Knight*, drains the earlier poem of its subtlety, but it also gives Sir Bredbeddle (this poem's Bertilak) a new role. Bredbeddle's mother-in-law, called Agostes and here Morgan le Fay's textual replacement, arranges a liaison between Gawain and her daughter:

> To her daughter can shee say,
> 'The man that thou hast wisht many a day,
>   Of him thou maist be sped,
> For Sir Gawaine, that curteous knight,
> Is lodged in this hall all night.'
>   Shee brought her to his bedd. (366–71)

---

[19] Bonnie Wheeler, 'Romance and Parataxis in Malory: The Case of Sir Gawain's Reputation', *Arthurian Literature* 12 (1993), pp. 109–32 (p. 129).
[20] Dyer, 'Male Sexuality', p. 39.

She then encourages Gawain to take her daughter ' "boldly in thine armes" ', promising that ' "noe man shall doe thee harme" ' (372–6); the poet has already informed us that Bredbeddle's wife has long loved Gawain despite having never seen him (46–8).[21] Bredbeddle later asserts that he knew Gawain would ' "doe me no villanye" ' despite his wife's desire (486), and he then asks Gawain to take him to ' "Arthurs court" ' (490): ' "Then were all to my pay" ' or satisfaction (491). Gillian Rogers laments that 'Bredbeddle is reduced to the status of procurer for his own wife, apparently in full knowledge if what he is doing'.[22] Bredbeddle is the head of a dysfunctional family manipulating Gawain's reputation as lover and gate-keeper to the Round Table in order to create for themselves a story in which they are Gawain's antagonists, and the fulfilment of their ambitions is thus assured. As in *Avowyng*, the poet's interest here is primarily in the relationships between men, although there is an increased (and misogynistic) emphasis on the motivations of the female characters.

Malory's Gawain has far more of the lecher than the selfless champion about him, especially in the story of Pelleas and Ettarde. Pelleas, after winning a tournament and presenting the prize to Ettarde, 'seyde opynly she was the fayrest lady that there was, and that wolde he preve uppon ony knyght that wolde sey nay' (100/19–21). Malory's Pelleas is typically courtly in other ways as well: he continually seeks to bring himself to his beloved Ettarde's attention by alternating displays of martial prowess and humiliating surrender for the express purpose of seeing her (100/32–4). Ettarde wants nothing to do with him, and, after witnessing Pelleas' humiliation and promising to help him win his lady's affections (101/41), Gawain meets with her, pretending to have slain the suffering lover and hoping to provoke some feeling of sympathy in her (102/6). Any good intentions Gawain has are quickly lost when Ettarde promises to ' "do onythynge that may please" ' him as a reward for ridding her of such a pest (102/16–17). Gawain wins a promise from her that she will do what she can to win his lady's love for him, and when she so promises reveals that she is the object of his desire; ' "I may not chese ... but if I sholde be forsworne" ', Ettarde laconically replies (102/23–9), in exactly the kind of give-and-take 'luf-talkying' that Bertilak's wife craves. This is also the roguish behaviour of a confirmed rake: cunning and charming by turn, Gawain has 'all his desyre' (102/30), betraying a fellow knight by taking advantage of an opportunity that has unexpectedly come his way.

Malory's Gawain does not always take his 'tumbles' where he can, as Flashman put it. It is particularly interesting that the Gawain of the *Mort Artu* tries to seduce the Fair Maid of Escalot, thinking that 'the knight would be happy indeed who could take his pleasure and satisfaction with such a maiden'; when she rejects him in favour of Lancelot, he is 'afraid that Lancelot would learn of it' and is thus eager

---

[21] In this she is far more typical than *Sir Gawain and the Green Knight*'s lady, who seems to feign affection as part of Morgan's game; as J. J. Anderson writes, 'the lady's loving manner is a means to an end', one of the poem's many signs that appearances can be deceiving (*Language and Imagination in the* Gawain-*poems* (Manchester, 2005), p. 198). In essence, Bertilak's wife (or, perhaps, Morgan) creates an erotic tableau for Gawain's perusal.

[22] Gillian Rogers, 'The Grene Knight', *A Companion to the Gawain-poet*, ed. Derek Brewer and Jonathan Gibson (Cambridge, 1997), pp. 365–72 (p. 369).

to 'make his peace' with the maiden.[23] The Gawain of the *Stanzaic Morte* is not shown wooing the girl, but talking of Lancelot (576–95), although his reaction upon seeing her dead body is telling:

> Sir Gawain his eyen then on her cast
> And beheld her fast with herte free,
> So that he knew well at the last,
> That the Maid of Ascolot was she,
> Which he some time had wooed fast
> His owne leman for to be,
> But she answerd him ay in haste
> To none but Launcelot wolde she te. (1008–15)

The *Stanzaic*-poet seems to be undecided on Gawain's initial intentions towards the Maid, but Malory has no such problem. Having both the French and English versions to choose from, Malory eliminates any reference to Gawain's wooing altogether. Malory's Gawain seems only too happy for Lancelot and Elaine without any complications (especially at 631/16–17). It appears that for both the *Stanzaic*-poet and Malory, any sexual opportunity that involves rivalry with Lancelot is no opportunity at all.

Normally in Middle English texts Gawain's sexual opportunism is linked with a courtesy test (as it is in *Sir Gawain and the Green Knight*). Benson cites *Sir Gawain and the Carle of Carlisle* as an English example of Gawain's inability to resist temptation, making no distinction between the daring Gawain of *Le Chevalier à l'épée* and the Gawain ordered to kiss the Carle's wife before being gently restrained from taking matters further (449–68).[24] The Carle sets up courtesy tests for Gawain and his companions, Kay and Baldwin, tests that the latter knights fail. Gawain succeeds through strict adherence to the rules of the game, absolute obedience to the Carle's demands. Certainly the poet tells us that Gawain's 'love was on her lyght', and he attempts to 'doun the prevey act' with her under the Carle's gaze (454–68). Yet he stops immediately when ordered to do so by the Carle (467–8), and is given the Carle's daughter as a reward. This typically unnamed female character is never asked if she wishes to sleep with Gawain, but the poet believes that she was happy enough to do so (487–92). The daughter herself notes that of all the knights ' "that her hathe benne" ', none has matched Gawain (494–5); whether she means in courtesy or sexual skill (or both) is uncertain. Whichever is the case, she is clearly impressed on the morning after, praying at Mass for another visit:

> 'Mare, marce,' seyde that Lady bryght,
> 'Wher I schall se eny mor this knyght
> That hathe le my body so ner?' (505–10)

---

[23] Norris Lacy, ed., *Lancelot-Grail: The Old French Arthurian Vulgate and Post-Vulgate in Translation*, 5 vols (New York, 1993–6), IV, p. 97.

[24] Benson, *Art and Tradition*, pp. 104–5. In fact, retrospectively we can see in *Chevalier* a profound difference that may well have partially prompted the English poems: when Gawain's host offers his daughter as a ' "beautiful diversion to entertain and amuse you" ', we are specifically told that the host 'was no churl' (pp. 90–1).

Her prayer is answered positively: Gawain marries her on the day that her father becomes a knight of the Round Table (631–6), another example of homosocial bonding in which marriage once again cements ties between men (Gawain, the Carle, Arthur).[25]

Gawain's common role as a facilitator of social bonding between Arthur and various potentially hostile figures leads to a notorious propensity for getting married. The poet who composed *The Wedding of Sir Gawain and Dame Ragnelle*, surveying the Middle English tradition, could rightly note that 'Gawen was weddyd oft in his days' – but that he never loved another woman as much as he loved Ragnelle (832–4).[26] Yet love was not Gawain's primary motivation here, any more than it seemed to be the primary factor in his marriage to the Carle's daughter; his willingness to marry a foul hag like Ragnelle is based in his loyalty to Arthur, who needs to find an answer to a question which the hag can provide. ' "I shall wed her and wed her agayn" ', Gawain declares, if it means saving Arthur's life (343–52). The Arthur of *Wedding*, at least, asks Gawain if he is willing; in the later ballad version, *The Marriage of Sir Gawain* (again in the Percy Folio), Arthur promises the hag that she will ' "have gentle Gawaine, my cozen,/ And marry him with a ring" ' (79–80). No consultation seems to be necessary, again implying that Gawain's love life, at least for most Middle English authors, was a matter of state policy and not erotic nor domestic love. That the poet subsequently tells us that Gawain never 'lovyd woman always' or constantly (832–3), despite his earlier insistence that Ragnelle's death after 'butt yerys five ... grevid Gawen alle his lyfe' (820–1), seems indicative of the knight's role in the political life of Arthur's realm even as it confirms his philandering nature.

Malory uses the inherited tradition of Gawain's amorous nature to bolster two of his thematic points; the first is that Gawain is untrustworthy, a fact repeated throughout the *Morte*. But secondly, Gawain inadvertently sets up a defence of married love against the courtly tradition that dominated Malory's sources. Pelleas' eye-witness experience of Ettarde's unfaithfulness is not intended as erotic

---

[25] The later *Carle of Carlisle* ballad in the Percy Folio separates the two happy occasions: Gawain is married to the daughter before he returns to Arthur's court (427–8), after which the Carle is knighted (483–4). For more on the homosocial nature of Gawain's adventures, see Hahn, who writes, in the general introduction to his edition, that the scenes set in the 'intimate, domestic space' of the bedroom 'strengthen the bonds of male solidarity', just as the various combats navigate between 'enmity and reconciliation within a politics of national cohesion' (pp. 26–9). Elizabeth Edwards makes a similar argument when she discusses homosociality in Malory (although not exclusively concerning Gawain): 'The way in which love of the lady animates homosocial bonds is seen in exactly those almost ritual combats which occur so frequently in the *Morte Darthur*' ('The Place of Women in the *Morte Darthur*', *A Companion to Malory*, ed. Elizabeth Archibald and A. S. G. Edwards (Cambridge, 1996), pp. 37–54 (pp. 45–7)).

[26] In this poem, Ragnelle is also the mother of Gyngalyn (799–801), a character who appears in Malory, the earlier *Carle of Carlisle*, the Prose *Tristan*, and on the Winchester Round Table in addition to being the hero of another poem, *Lybeaus Desconus* (and its French source *Le Bel Inconnu*). In French texts, Gyngalyn (Guinglain) is either the son of the unnamed sister of Bran de Lys (the *First Continuation*) or of a fairy character named Floree (the *Lancelot-Grail Cycle*) or Blanchemal la Fée (*Le Bel Inconnu*). He is nearly always associated with the supernatural, and is the most consistently named son of Gawain. This may partially explain *Wedding*'s insistence on Gawain's particular love for Ragnelle, a sign of her son's chivalric superiority. For more on Gawain and his sons in *Lybeaus Desconus* and Malory, see my 'Absent Fathers, Unexpected Sons: Paternity in Malory's *Morte Darthur*', *Studies in Philology* 101:2 (2004), pp. 136–52 (pp. 143–7).

for either Pelleas or the viewer, and the attendant despair and anger over their deception make him ripe for the machinations of the Damsel of the Lake Nimue, who proves to be a true lover. Nimue's efforts on Pelleas' behalf are continually reiterated throughout the *Morte* as a picture of domestic bliss akin to that between Gareth and Lyonesse, as Wilfred Guerin rightly points out.[27] In most cases Malory has added mention of Pelleas and Nimue, and their happiness, where his source does not mention them. Sue Ellen Holbrook writes that Nimue 'punishes Ettard [sic] for being merciless to a true lover', and reiterates the essentially courtly nature of the relationship between Pelleas and Ettarde: 'Pelleas is as extreme in his dedicated misery as Ettard is in her haughty hatred'.[28] The fact that Malory turns Nimue into a beloved wife, a role she has nowhere else in medieval literature, bears witness to the story's role as an *exemplum* of the triumph of proper married love over the troublesome and often divisive courtly tradition. Malory's refusal to follow his source completely and allow for a reconciliation between Gawain and Pelleas furthers the decline of the former's reputation, and helped form the post-medieval portrait of Gawain as over-sexed and treacherous in matters of the heart.

This portrait seems to have already been in development, however, as *The Jeaste of Sir Gawain* indicates. This fragmentary, possibly fifteenth-century, text is a Middle English version of the feud between Gawain and the family of the Pucelle de Lis (here not even given that title). Gawain happily indulges in his amorous encounter with the lady, as 'in hys armes he gan her brace,/ With kyssynge of mowthes sweete'; 'he had her countenance/ Withoute any more delaye' (5–10). Gawain is unable to enjoy himself for long: the girl's father, here called Sir Gylbert, and his sons Gyamoure, Terrye and Brandles challenge him. He defeats all but Brandles, their duel ending only because the combatants 'wante lyght of the daye' (459–69); in the *First Continuation* Gawain suffers the opening of an old wound and must request a cessation of hostilities. The English poem also insists that to the intense relief of both Gawain and Brandles 'after that tyme they never mette more' (533–4); by contrast, the French text effects a reconciliation between the two knights through the existence of Gawain and the Pucelle's son Guinglain.

The poem's insistence that Gawain cannot beat Brandles even though he is here untroubled by an old wound (although he does claim to have ' "bene bestad todaye full soore" ' (428); this is a standard romance trope – the knight tested by his equal) hints at the English poet's disapproval. As in Malory, Gawain has allowed a sexual affair to problematise his relationship with a fellow knight. Gawain returns home shamed: 'On foote he went full werylye/ Tyll he to the courte came home' (528–9). Gawain does little to help the girl, asking Brandles to ' "be frende to that gentle woman" '; Brandles makes it clear he will do no such thing:

> 'She hathe caused today, pardye, much shame.
> Yt ys pyttye she hathe her syght.' (489–90)

---

[27] ' "The Tale of the Death of Arthur": Catastrophe and Resolution', *Malory's Originality*, ed. R. M. Lumiansky (Baltimore, 1964), pp. 233–74 (pp. 254–5).
[28] 'Nymue, the Chief Lady of the Lake in Malory's *Le Morte Darthur*', *Arthurian Women: A Casebook*, ed. Thelma S. Fenster (New York, 2000), pp. 171–90 (pp. 181–2).

The girl is beaten 'bothe backe and syde' by Brandles (509), who further assuages his wounded pride by forcing Gawain to promise mortal combat when next they meet (479–84, 516–20). The girl runs away from home, and her family 'sawe her never after that daye;/ She went wandrynge to and fro' (525–6). Her wanderings are atypical of romance, although they might remind the reader of the fate of Criseyde in Henryson's *Testament of Cresseid*;[29] rejected after Diomed 'had all his appetite', 'desolait sho walkit up and down', eventually turning to prostitution (71–7). In *Jeaste*, the sense that both Gawain and the girl have been punished every bit as much as Criseyde is inescapable (the girl certainly more than the knight).

Gawain's sexual opportunism, in both French and English, is thus continually linked with family: in many texts Gawain's willingness to jump into bed is beneficial to the stability of Arthur's realm, in others that same willingness disrupts congenial ties between and within families. Regardless of the consequences, Gawain usually remains the same, eager for and often unable to resist sexual encounters; he rarely gives those consequences much thought. Gawain's lovers and wives die or disappear, as the poet of *Wedding* realised, leaving him (like Bond) free to pursue new partners. In fact, we may now question Chaucer's single reference to Gawain: the Squire may not mean anything by it, but Gawain's inclusion as an exemplar of courtesy in a tale concerned with masculine betrayal of women may not be entirely innocent.[30] Gawain's sexual adventures often have a wider political or historical resonance: like Flashman, Gawain has 'raked and ridden harder than most', leaving a trail of both broken families and impromptu political alliances behind him. Gawain's role as Arthur's right-hand man is not only saddled with his reputation as a lady's man, it is at least partially predicated upon it – but that is not to say that he cannot also play a role in the fulfilment of male fantasy in the Middle Ages. Hahn called Gawain an exemplar of the 'Young Man', by which we might now mean a 'Lad's Lad'.

---

[29] Robert Henryson, *Selected Poems*, ed. W. R. J. Barron (Manchester, 1981), pp. 27–45. Criseyde's wandering is directly linked with sexual experience:
When Diomed had all his appetite,
And mair, fulfillit of this fair lady,
Upon ane uther he set his haill delite,
And send to hir ane libel of repudy,
And hir excludit fra his company.
Than desolait sho walkit up and down,
And, sum men, sayis, into the court, commoun. (71–7)
[30] A. E. Christa Canitz, 'Courtly Hagiography and Chaucer's Tripartite Genre Critique in the "Legend of Good Women"', *From Arabye to Engelond*, ed. A. E. Christa Canitz and Gernot Wieland (Ottawa, 1999), pp. 131–53 (pp. 135–6).

Erotic Magic:
The Enchantress in Middle English Romance

CORINNE SAUNDERS

> I met a lady in the meads,
> Full beautiful – a faery's child.
> Her hair was long, her foot was light,
> And her eyes were wild.
> (John Keats, 'La Belle Dame Sans Merci', 13–16)

THE POWER of romantic desire is one of the great leitmotifs of literature, and it is in romance writing most of all that this motif is played out. We need only think of the haunting narratives of Tristan and Isolde or Lancelot and Guinevere to be reminded of the compelling quality of desire both within the fictions of romance and for readers and listeners. One aspect of such desire is, of course, the erotic – or more exactly, the pursuit of the erotic. The erotic gestures towards, but is not synonymous with, the sexual, and romance does not treat all sexual encounters as erotic. As with Palomides' hunt for the Questing Beast, pleasure may be situated in impossibility, in the constant re-enactment or narrative of pursuit. The object of desire is desirable precisely in his or her otherness, even unattainability, while the force of love is both transfiguring and alienating. It is not coincidental that there is in romance a powerful link between desire and enchantment. Somewhere behind the clichés of the magic of love, from 'You put a spell on me' to 'There's magic in the air' to 'Some enchanted evening', is a recognition of the fear and fascination of violent and inexplicable desire, so vividly expressed in the ancient notions of the wound or illness or madness of love, in the image of the heart pierced by the arrows of the God of Love, and in the idea of love as hunt or siege. Desire seems to stem from elsewhere, to respond to some external and mysterious force, and the beloved is coloured with that otherness. Thus in romance writing the motif of enchantment is often interwoven with the narrative of desire.[1] Keats's 'La Belle Dame Sans Merci', with its eerie evocation of the faery lady, the pale and loitering knight, and the fearful fascination of desire and death, presents the nexus of enchantment and the erotic in vivid miniature.

---

[1] Derek Brewer's essay, 'The Interpretation of Fairy Tales' (*The Companion to the Fairy Tale*, ed. Hilda Ellis Davidson and Anna Chaudhri (Cambridge, 2003), pp. 15–37), probes the way that romance, like fairy tale, engages with the deepest human instincts, rituals and desires.

In medieval writing, the idea of enchantment takes on a special force in its realism. Enchantment was not simply a convenient metaphor for desire, but an actual possibility, and invested with some anxiety. The medieval thought world included a complex blend of ideas of the supernatural: a strong notion of the planetary gods with their shaping of both character and destiny; a sense of the possibility of miracle and of God's providential intervention in the human world, but also a fear of demonic threat and temptation; a familiarity with folk traditions of faery, with their origins in pagan, especially Celtic, belief; and an awareness of magic as 'science', an area of knowledge that might actively be pursued. Belief in the practice of magic and in the supernatural or otherworld are in a sense interdependent, since magic tends to involve the summoning of demons or spirits, and offers a kind of access to the otherworld.[2] It is not surprising that, in a social context where faith in god and devil, and a spirit world between, was ready and natural, the possibility of magic should also have seemed ready and natural. Its practitioners might be human or supernatural – demonic, divine or simply 'other' – belonging to the world of faery that is a conventional feature of romance, a parallel sphere of marvellous adventure and the provenance of the enchanters and enchantresses and the marvellous or magical objects of romance narratives.[3]

While otherworldly figures and those with access to the otherworld may be male or female, women, it seems, enjoy a special relation with the supernatural, as the range of medieval terms for female practitioners of magic suggests: fées, enchantresses, sorceresses, witches, charmeresses, Phitonesses. In romance, their magic is most of all concerned with the feminine domain of love and desire, and the power over women gained by men through prowess is balanced by the power of the supernatural. Female agency may also, however, be threatening, and practitioners of magic may be represented as powerful and menacing representatives of the otherworld. The figure of the enchantress thus becomes a focus for the fears as well as the desires associated with ideas of love and sexuality. As Keats's 'La Belle Dame Sans Merci' suggests, she may be the faery mistress, image of wish-

---

[2] Important studies of the history of magic include Richard Kieckhefer, *Magic in the Middle Ages* (Cambridge, 1989, Canto edn, 2000); Valerie I. J. Flint, *The Rise of Magic in Early Medieval Europe* (Oxford, 1991); Karen Jolly, Catharina Raudvere and Edward Peters, *Witchcraft and Magic in Europe: The Middle Ages* (2001; Philadelphia, 2002); and Keith Thomas, *Religion and the Decline of Magic: Studies in Popular Beliefs in Sixteenth and Seventeenth Century England*, 2nd edn (London, 1977). For a study of the origins and cultural resonances of medieval belief in the supernatural, focused on the idea of the double, see Claude Lecouteux, *Fées, sorcières et loups-garous au moyen âge: Histoire du double* (Paris, 1992). See further Kathryn S. Westoby, 'A New Look at the Role of the Fée in Medieval French Arthurian Romance', *The Spirit of the Court: Selected Proceedings of the International Courtly Literature Society*, ed. Glyn S. Burgess and Roberta A. Taylor (Cambridge, 1985), pp. 373–85.

[3] Michelle Sweeney, in *Magic in Medieval Romance from Chrétien de Troyes to Geoffrey Chaucer* (Dublin, 2000), offers a brief study of the social and spiritual resonances of magic in romance. See also two wide-ranging collections of essays on magic in French literature: *Le Merveilleux et la magie dans la littérature*, ed. Gerard Chandès, CERMEIL 2 (Amsterdam and Atlanta, 1992), and *Magie et illusion au moyen âge*, Centre Universitaire d'Etudes et de Recherches Médiévales d'Aix, *Senefiance* 42 (Aix-en-Provence, 1999). For a popular account of the supernatural in literature and folk belief, see Maureen Duffy, *The Erotic World of Faery* (1972; London, 1987), in particular, pp. 1–109. See also my essay, 'Violent Magic in Middle English Romance', *Violence in Medieval Courtly Literature: A Casebook*, ed. Albrecht Classen, Routledge Medieval Casebooks (New York and London, 2004), pp. 225–40.

fulfilment, but she may equally be the witch, wielding the powers of necromancy. The enchantress is often a deceptive or ambiguous figure, who strays across the boundary of the forbidden or the fearful, dangerous in her desirability. Medieval English writers take up the emphasis of French romance, intrigued yet troubled by the notion of the actively desiring woman empowered by magic. In Marie de France's *Lanval* and its retellings, in particular, *Sir Launfal*, we find the positive aspect of the enchantress, the otherworldly lady who pursues her lover from afar, and the otherworld is the locus of an idealised eroticism. Later English romances such as *Partonope of Blois* and *Melusine*, which also translate and adapt French works, play on this pattern, linking it in particular to the motif of the otherworldly hunt, while in *Sir Gawain and the Green Knight* the nexus of enchantment and the hunt is more menacing. Malory's *Morte Darthur* provides an extended treatment of the enchantress as a force of disruption, troubling the male landscape of chivalry with the actions of desire and the threat of the erotic. In all these works, the ideas of heterosexual, romantic desire, magic and the supernatural interweave, sometimes to create a positive notion of the erotic, at others to suggest the disruptive and threatening force of desire and sexuality. The female practitioner of magic arts moves in and out of the human world, empowered yet also subject to the constraints of gender. Works in which the otherworldly figure is male, by contrast, stray less into the realm of the erotic, while Chaucer subverts our expectations of the enchantress in *The Wife of Bath's Tale*.

Marie de France's *Lanval* offers a paradigm for the faery mistress motif in its narrative of Lanval's encounter with the unnamed otherworldly lady who has sought him from afar.[4] Marie's understated, elegant verse skilfully presents the beautiful body and countenance of the lady as the exquisite gems at the heart of the extravagant tent and its coverlet:

> Mut ot le cors bien fait e gent;
> Un cher mantel de blanc hermine,
> Covert de purpre alexandrine,
> Ot pur le chaut sur li geté;
> Tut ot descovert le costé,
> Le vis, le col e la peitrine;
> Plus ert blanche que flur d'espine. (100–6)

(Her body was well formed and handsome, and in order to protect herself from the heat of the sun, she had cast about her a costly mantle of white ermine covered with Alexandrian purple. Her side, though, was uncovered, as well as her face, neck and breast; she was whiter than the hawthorn blossom.)[5]

While the faery quality of the lady is suggested by the mysterious trembling of Lanval's horse and her quest from afar for her beloved, her identity is not made explicit. As is typical of this narrative pattern, however, the lady sets Lanval a test of secrecy, proving a harsh mistress when Lanval reveals her existence to the

---

4 Ed. A. Ewert, *Marie de France: Lais*, Blackwell's French Texts (1944; Oxford, 1978), pp. 58–74.
5 Trans. Glyn S. Burgess and Keith Busby, *The Lais of Marie de France* (Harmondsworth, 1986), p. 74.

queen, but finally orchestrating his release and departure to Avalon. For the lady, Lanval is the desired object, his body finally borne away on her palfrey to Avalon, and her love is expressed both in the wealth she showers upon him and in the open gift of her body. The *lai* upholds the values of chivalry, in particular largesse, through the erotic pursuit of Lanval by his beloved, and honour is rewarded with physical possession of the idealised, beautiful body. All is couched within the dream-like context of the otherworld, so that the narrative also becomes one of desire and wish-fulfilment.

The late fourteenth-century version by Thomas Chestre, probably mediated through the earlier *Sir Laundevale*, and also drawing on the lay of *Graelent*, fills out Marie's version with considerable realistic detail.[6] In the transformative space of the forest, Launfal is summoned by the faery Tryamour's maidens to her pavilion, where he is welcomed with open arms: ' "Launfal, my lemman swete,/ Al my joye for þe y lete,/ Sweting paramour!" '[7] Tryamour's beauty, the luxury of her pavilion, and the extravagance of the feast there respond to Launfal's privation, and the exotic otherworld reverses the harshness of Arthur's court and Kaerleon. The Middle English version adds the concrete explanation that Tryamour is the daughter of the King of Faery, and employs striking realism in the depiction of her eroticised body:

> For hete her clothes down she dede
> Almest to here gerdilstede;
> Than lay she uncovert.
> She was as whit as lilie in May
> Or snow that sneweth in winteris day –
> He seigh nevere non so pert. (289–94)

We hear the detail of her hair shining 'as gold wire' (298), her priceless attire and the costly gifts she gives to Launfal, as well as of the wonderful feast complete with three kinds of wine, and Thomas is realistic too in his depiction of the lovers' pleasure: 'For play litill they slepte that night,/ Till on morn hit was day light' (349–50). Their natural delight in love-making, sustained by night in Launfal's bower, is set against the queen's unnatural lechery (47–8) and her implication later that Launfal is unnatural in his dislike of women (689–90). The experience of erotic, natural love illuminates the contrast between the failed ideals of the court and the perfection of an ideal otherworld. Tryamour's desire allows Launfal to fulfil his destiny and to shape his identity as a great knight, providing him with a space in which to enact his chivalric virtues, and the text works through the opposition of open desire, freely expressed within the otherworldly space of the forest, and secret desire within the court. Ultimately, *trouthe* aligns with licit, mutual desire.

The Middle English *Partonope of Blois* (extant in two fifteenth-century versions, both finding their origins in versions of the late twelfth-century French *Partonopeus*

---

6   For further discussion of *Sir Launfal*, see Corinne Saunders, *The Forest of Medieval Romance: Avernus, Broceliande, Arden* (Cambridge, 1993), pp. 142–8.
7   *Sir Launfal*, ed. Donald B. Sands, *Middle English Verse Romances*, EMETS (Exeter, 1986) pp. 203–32, lines 301–3. All subsequent references to *Sir Launfal* will be cited by line number.

de Blois) employs a similar paradigm – but here the pursuing lady is a human rather than otherworldly figure, an enchantress through her learning of magical arts rather than through faery blood, and correspondingly the treatment of her desire is more complicated and ambiguous. The romance employs a literal and compelling image of the pursuit of the erotic, the motif of the otherworldly hunt, used, for instance, by Marie de France in the *lai* of *Guigemar*.[8] Lost in the forest in pursuit of a great boar, Partonope enters a mysterious ship, which he himself identifies as ' "a Shyppe of ffayre/ Or thyng made be Enchauntemente" ' (743–4) and which carries him to what seems an enchanted country constructed through 'nygromansy' (876), where he finds an opulent castle, feast and bedchamber.[9] When the 'yonge mayde' (1193) Melior joins Partonope in the bed, the narrator is careful to tell us that despite her shame and silence, she has brought him there, 'for alle here delyte/ And alle here plesaunce was hym to haue/ To here husbande' (1221–3).

As pursuit is replaced by actual erotic encounter, however, the motifs of the faery mistress and otherwoldy hunt are replaced by a much more ambivalent portrayal of love, in which the free expression of desire seems to be in opposition to the constraints of gender expectations. Melior's fear of being judged harshly is set against Partonope's anxiety that all is a demonic illusion, and the love of the pair unfolds in a comic but troubling play of unwillingness. If Melior has orchestrated the meeting, the narrator explicitly places Partonope as orchestrating the consummation. She turns away 'and lyethe as stylle as a stonne' (1525), while 'He soghte faste tylle that he fonde/ Thys yonge lady' (1530–40); much is made of his physical pleasure and active desire:

> ... such a-nother creature
> He ffelte neuer of flesche and bonne,
> And nere þys lady he gan to gonne.
> Ouer here hys arme he gan to laye,
> Thys ys soþe as I yowe saye.
> So softe, so clene she was to fele
> Pat where he was he wyste not welle.

---

[8] For a study of the motif of the hunt, see Marcelle Thiébaux, *The Stag of Love: The Chase in Medieval Literature* (Ithaca and London, 1974).

[9] A. Trampe Bödtker, ed., *The Middle-English Versions of 'Partonope of Blois'*, EETS ES 109 (London, 1912 for 1911), 744–5, 876. All subsequent references to *Partonope of Blois* will be from this edition, which takes as its main text the fullest copy of the longer English version, found in British Museum MS Add. 35,288 (late fifteenth century), and will be cited by line number. For a discussion of the emphasis of the English version, see Sandra Ihle, 'The English *Partonope of Blois* as *Exemplum*', *Courtly Literature: Culture and Context. Selected Papers from the 5th Triennial Congress of the International Courtly Literature Society, Dalfsen, The Netherlands, 9–16 August, 1986*, ed. Keith Busby and Erik Kooper, Utrecht Publications in General and Comparative Literature (Amsterdam and Philadelphia, 1990), pp. 301–11. Here as in the following discussions, the detailed relation between French and English texts is too large a subject to be addressed; while all the works considered have French sources and analogues, this essay will focus on the nuances of Middle English writing. On *Partonopeus*, see further *Partonopeus in Europe: An Old French Romance and Its Adaptations*, ed. Catherine Hanley, Mario Longtin and Penny Eley, *Mediaevalia* 25:2, special issue (2004), and the various articles of Penny Eley and Penny Simons, including 'A Romance Revisited: Reopening the Question of the Manuscript Tradition of *Partonopeus de Blois*', *Romania* 115 (1997), pp. 368–405, and 'Male Beauty and Sexual Orientation in *Partonopeus de Blois*', *Romance Studies* 17 (1999), pp. 41–56.

> Plesaunce had hym ouer-come
> Pat all hys wyttes were fro hym nome. (1532–40)

Again she puts him aside, again he lays his hand across her and she 'hyt suffered pasyentlye' (1559). The consummation appears disturbingly close to a rape:

> Than sayde sho to hym full mekely:
> 'For þe loue of Gode, I praye yowe lette be.'
> And wyth þat worde a-none ganne he
> In hys armes her faste to hym brase.
> And fulle softely þen sho sayde: 'Allas!'
> And her legges sho gan to knytte,
> And wyth hys knees he gan hem on-shote.
> And þer-wyth-all she sayde: 'Syr, mercy!'
> He wolde not lefe ne be þer-by;
> For of her wordes toke he no hede;
> But þys a-way her maydenhede
> Haþe he þen rafte, and geffe her hys. (1560–71)

Melior's dismay, suffering and tears seem to place erotic pleasure as illicit and enforced, but the emphasis swiftly shifts when she is revealed to be the Queen of Byzantium, who has sent her envoys in search of the best man in the world; like Tryamour, she has desired the knight from afar, and gone in search of him. On seeing Partonope, she says, ' "myn herte dyd lere/ A-boue alle other to loue yowe beste" ' (1654–5); she has caused ' "þorowe my crafte" ' (1659) the flight of the boar, Partonope's separation from the king on the hunt and the magical ship. Her powers of enchantment are emphatically stated: ' "Alle þys was made by crafte of me./ Thys crafte I dyd, yette more I can./ In alle þys tyme sawe [me] no man" ' (1672–4). The episode is disturbing as well as comic: Melior, rather like the lady who presents Lancelot with a scene of apparent rape in Chrétien's *Le Chevalier de la Charrete*, proves to have been a counterfeit victim, mimicking unwillingness and pain, and representing her desire as force.[10] The mock rape in *Le Chevalier de la Charrete* suggests the eroticism of force: the sight of the near-naked lady apparently about to be raped is intended to incite desire as well as to test military prowess, and Chrétien emphasises Lancelot's lack of desire, as well as his later sense of being a victim of force.[11] In *Partonope* too, there is a sense that Melior's resistance spurs Partonope on, fuelling his desire – but perhaps the scene plays most of all on the unacceptability for the lady of openly expressing sexual desire. Even the lady who has mastered the arts of magic must seem the unwilling, chaste virgin, and only the faery lady may safely pursue her own desire.

At the same time, like the lady in *Lanval*, Melior puts Partonope's devotion to

---

[10] See Chrétien de Troyes, *Le Chevalier de la Charrete, Les Romans de Chrétien de Troyes III*, ed. Mario Roques, Classiques Français du Moyen Age (Paris, 1972), 1062–95.
[11] Chrétien writes of Lancelot, 'si n'en ert mie talentos,/ ne tant ne quant a'an ert jalos' (1085–6: '[it] did not provoke in him any desire or make him jealous in the least' (trans. David Staines, *The Complete Romances of Chrétien de Troyes* (Bloomingdale and Indianapolis, 1990), p. 183)), and later records Lancelot's thoughts, 'Donc est ce force? Autant le vaut;/ par force covient que il s'aut/ couchier avoec la dameisele . . .' (1209–11: 'Was this, then, a forceful prodding? Yes, of course, for he was forced to lie with the young lady' (p. 185)).

the test, decreeing that no man shall see her until she is married: in a sequence that closely resembles the tale of Cupid and Psyche (first told by Apuleius in *The Golden Ass*), Melior insists that she may come to Partonope only at night: ' "Ye shalle not fayle no nyghte to haue me/ Redy to parforme yowre hertes desyre./ In kyssynge, in felynge, and in all þat may be plesyre" ' (1798–1800). On the one hand the test heightens the erotic: Partonope's knowledge of his lady only by touch adds to the sensual quality of their relationship, and the expression of love cannot rely on the recitation of the conventions of beauty. As in *Lanval*, the secrecy of the lovers' intimacy enhances the effect of passion. At the same time Melior's mysterious magical powers are situated in Partonope's ignorance of her appearance. The work contrasts positive and negative magic: Partonope is warned by Melior not to attempt to see her ' "Be crafte of Nygromansy" ' (1872), while his mother fears her potentially monstrous nature and places her as ' "a þynge of ffeyre" ' (5072) who has taken her son through ' "þe deuyllys Enchauntemente" ' (5056). In fact, we are told that Melior's magical crafts are rooted in honest, Christian learning, and by contrast Partonope's mother practises 'fals enchawntemente' (5518), first giving her son an enchanted potion that causes him to become a 'fole naturelle' (5448) and plight his troth to the King of France's niece, and later providing him with an enchanted lantern which cannot go out 'for wynde ne weder' (5804), and which shows him Melior's countenance. It is only at this point that we hear the source of Melior's magic: her father, the Emperor of Constantinople, has had her schooled in the seven arts, medicine, divinity, and finally magic: ' "Then to Nygromancy sette I was,/ Then I lerned Enchawntementes/ To knowe þe crafte of experimentes" ' (5933–5). Her arts of illusion are all effected ' "By þe wytte þat Gode haþe sente" ' (5966). In a strange way, the apparent force of the consummation scene is enacted at this point in the narrative, when Melior is deprived of ' "all þys connynge and all þys crafte" ' (5976), and she bitterly laments the falseness of men and her own shame and weakness.

The message of *Partonope* is complex. The marvellous pursuit of the knight, achieved through Melior's enchantments, places her as powerful agent of her own destiny, shaping her own erotic fulfilment in love. Yet the consummation with its accompanying test of secrecy leads to Melior's loss of power: it is as if once she has succumbed to desire, she succumbs too to the traditional gender balance in which she approaches the status of the victim she has pretended to be. Along with this shift, the erotic fades out of the narrative: the narrative resists exploring the erotic potential of scenes of romantic fulfilment. Melior's independent selfhood is not lost, and the poet emphasises her supernatural beauty when, after a long series of tests, Partonope is brought before her: 'Men seide she was an hevenly þing./ It were Impossible, thei seide, þrugh nature/ Might be brought forþe suche a creature' (11461–63). The convention, used for instance by Chaucer in his depiction of Emilye in the *Knight's Tale*, takes on a new force in the context of Melior's supernatural powers: she seems indeed analogous to a creature of Faery. Yet we hear no more of her magical abilities, and similarly, the narrator draws a veil over the wedding night of Partonope and Melior: 'in what Ioy then they be/ But þis may not be declared for me,/ Ne what her Ioy was, ne her delite' (12186–8). The elaborated expression of the erotic belongs to the otherworldly narrative of the start, to the 'crafte' of enchantment rather than the traditional order of marriage.

Partonope finds a striking parallel in the fourteenth-century English romance of *Melusine*, which also employs the devices of the otherworldly hunt and the testing of the hero, but depends upon the concealment of otherworldliness.[12] Melusine is placed at the start as a creature of faery, and the tale is set in the context of the supernatural beings who in ancient times inhabited Poitou – goblins, 'bonnes dames' who play pranks on children, 'fauntasyes' who appear in the likeness of old women, and faeries who 'toke somtyme the fourme & the fygure of fayre & yonge wymen', binding their husbands to covenants which when kept brought prosperity and happiness (i, 4). Melusine is in fact half human: her mother is the faery Pressyne, her father the King of Albany, who is ravished by Pressyne's marvellous beauty and song when he encounters her by a spring in the forest (the motif so memorably used in Debussy's opera, *Pelleas et Melisande*). Pressyne, like Melusine later, binds her husband to the condition that she must not be seen in childbed, and flees with her three daughters when he forgets his promise; Melusine, the oldest, conspires with her sisters to punish her father by imprisoning him in a mountain in Northumberland – but is condemned by Pressyne to be transformed each Saturday into a serpent. Harmony of her divided being, which her part-serpent body emblematises, may only be achieved through the loving faith of a husband who obeys the condition not to see her on Saturdays, nor to speak of her deeds to others: if he does not transgress, she will live her ' "cours naturell" ' and ' "dey as a naturel & humayn woman" ', begetting a fair line; otherwise, she will revert to her part-serpent form until the Day of Judgement, appearing to the inhabitants of Lusignan for three days to signify either a new lord or the death of a descendant (i, 15). As in *Partonope*, marriage is the condition that denies the supernatural, but here such denial is portrayed as desirable, the condition for happiness and mutuality in love.

The first part of the work, however, narrates Melusine's careful orchestration of her love and marriage through her supernatural powers, and as in *Partonope*, the love pursuit is enacted through the device of the otherworldly boar hunt. The mysterious powers of destiny are emphasised, as Raimondin's uncle, the Earl of Poitiers, reads in the stars his accidental death at the hands of his nephew. At midnight, Raimondin's horse leads him while he sleeps to a 'fontayne of fayerye', the 'fontayne of soyf' (v, 27), where three ladies play, and he wakes to see the marvellous beauty of Melusine and to hear that she knows all his adventure. Like Melior, she defends her knowledge, which is not ' "be fauntesye or dyuels werk" ' but ' "of god" ': her belief is ' "as a Catholique byleue oughte for to be" ' (vi, 31). Her magic arts are employed to assist Raimondin in gaining lands, create an opulent wedding feast and oversee the construction of the castle of Lusignan. This narrator, however, offers little detail regarding the love relationship: once the Bishop has drawn the curtains round the bed, 'of this matere recounteth no ferther thystorye' (xviii, 57). The focus is not erotic but on the shaping of a dynasty, and

---

[12] The story of Melusine is told in the fourteenth century by Jean d'Arras in verse (c. 1382–94) and La Coudrette in prose; Jean d'Arras' work is translated into English prose c. 1500 as *Melusine*, and La Coudrette's perhaps slightly earlier as *The Romans of Partenay*. This essay will use the English translation of Jean d'Arras' verse romance, ed. A. K. Donald, *Melusine*, EETS ES 68 (London, 1895). All quotations will be cited by chapter and page number. For a recent study of Jean d'Arras' *Melusine*, see Stacey L. Hahn, 'Constructive and Destructive Violence in Jean d'Arras' *Roman de Melusine*', *Violence*, ed. Classen, pp. 187–206.

on the maternal love of Melusine for her children, although her marvellous beauty and active pursuit of desire has orchestrated the union. The narrative shifts to the detailed evocation of grief once Raimondin, urged on by his brother, has seen Melusine's serpent form. His long lament, ' "Farwel beaute, bounte, swetenes, amyablete . . ." ' (xxxvii, 298), seems to recognise his own role in disallowing Melusine her human form and wifely role, while she swoons at his reproaches to her as ' "fals serpente" ' (xlii, 314), and laments not only the loss of their love, but also that she will now not live the ' "cours natural as another woman" ', buried and honoured in the chapel at Lusignan (xliii, 316). Despite her powers, Melusine cannot escape her fate: the unthinking actions and words of Raimondin condemn her to her supernatural existence, caught within which she must forfeit human joy – even while her supernatural powers have shaped that joy for her in the first place. Ultimately, her shape-shifting identity is a curse. Yet Melusine's words also make clear the dangers of active female desire: ' "Ha/ a Raymondyn/ the day that first tyme I sawe the was for me ryght doulourous and vnhappy/ in an euyl heure sawe I euer thy coynted body, thy facion, & thy fayre fygure/ euyl I dyde to desire and coueyte thy beaute . . ." ' (xliii, 315). In Melusine, otherworldly pursuit of the eroticised male body promises freedom and transcendence of the monstrous, but ultimately, she is betrayed, caught once again within her supernatural identity. Thus female practitioners of magic, human and faery, seem to move in and out of empowerment in their relations with men: magic allows them to pursue desire, yet desire also proves threatening to them. They become sympathetic figures partly through their loss of power as a result of male betrayal, and the human and the supernatural appear to be in conflict within their characters, even while their destinies depend on this interweaving of magic and vulnerability. Melusine cannot escape her serpent self; Melior, wholly human from the start, regains her knight and her status once she has suffered the loss of her powers.

Enchantresses who do not lose their powers play altogether more threatening roles. *Sir Gawain and the Green Knight* offers a memorable example of the interweaving of the erotic and the menacing in its portrayal of the Lady, whose other face is that of loathly old woman, Morgan le Fay. Throughout the poem, we are reminded of the potential violence of the otherworld, most disturbingly in the uncanny beheading of the Green Knight, whose powers seem to extend far beyond the natural, to overcome death itself. The world of Hautdesert appears to be a refuge for Gawain, setting against the hostile outside world rich feasting, sumptuous clothing and an opulent bedchamber. It is a world of material delight approaching that of *Partonope*, and it is not coincidental that Bertilak's lady is characterised by surpassing beauty: 'Ho watz þe fayrest in felle, of flesche and of lyre/ And of compas and colour and costes, of alle oþer,/ And wener þen Wenore, as the wyʒe þoʒt.'[13] Gawain is cocooned in a feminised world, sleeping on in his luxurious bed while Bertilak rises early to hunt; the conversation and 'dere dalyaunce' (1012) with the lady sustains this sense of the feminine. The poet is careful to

---

[13] *Sir Gawain and the Green Knight*, ed. Malcolm Andrew and Ronald Waldron, *The Poems of the Pearl Manuscript: 'Pearl', 'Cleanness', 'Patience', 'Sir Gawain and the Green Knight'*, EMETS (Exeter, 1978), 943–5. All subsequent references to *Sir Gawain and the Green Knight* will be from this edition and will be cited by line number.

suggest the eroticism of the bedroom scenes, from the moment of the lady's secret entrance to sit by the sleeping Gawain's bed so that he is caught, unclad and alone. Her offer of sexual delight is explicit and almost immediate, ' "3e ar welcum to my cors/ Yowre awen won to wale" ' (1237–8), and she seems to suggest the kind of force that Melior leads Partonope to enact, ' "Me behouez of fyne force/ Your seruaunt be, and schale" ' (1239–40); ' "3e ar stif innoghe to constrayne wyth strenkþe, 3if yow lykez" ' (1496). While the comedy arises from Gawain's desire elegantly to escape her wiles, there is no doubt of his pleasure in the dalliance, or of the physicality of their 'comlyly' kissing (1505). The third encounter seems particularly to emphasise Gawain's pleasure and desire in its evocation of the lady's loving approach, 'Þe lady luflych com, la3ande swete,/ Felle ouer his fayre face and fetly hym kyssed' (1757–8). He welcomes her warmly, and his vivid appreciation of her physical beauty is clearly placed by the poet as dangerous:

> He se3 hir so glorious and gayly atyred,
> So fautles of hir fetures and of so fyne hewes,
> Wi3t wallande joye warmed his hert.
> With smoþe smylyng and smolt þay smeten into merþe,
> Þat al watz blis and bonchef þat breke hem bitwene,
>   And wynne,
> Þay lauced wordes gode,
> Much wele þen watz þerinne.
> Gret perile bitwene hem stod,
> Nif Maré of hir kny3t mynne. (1760–9)

It is crucial for the 'earnest' of Gawain's testing that the erotic game should be real, characterised by genuine delight and desire, for his strength in resisting too must be real. The peculiar menace of the test is heightened by the interwoven narrative of Bertilak's hunt, which echoes the violence of the beheading scene, most memorably in the graphic description of the dismemberment of the deer, but also in the detailed images of chase, capture and death of the prey in the successive hunts of deer, boar and fox. Within the rarefied courtly world of Hautdesert, the repeated images of imprisonment, capture and binding used by the Lady parallel the vocabulary of the hunt, so that the bedchamber scenes seem, like *Partonope* and *Melusine*, to depict an otherworldly chase of the enchantress for her prey. Gawain is ultimately revealed to have been playing a potentially fatal erotic game, the stakes of which are death. The mores of Arthur's court and of chivalry are tested by the enchantress, in this strange otherworldly castle of Hautdesert with its rival court presided over by Morgan le Fay.

The menacing castle of the enchantress was a powerful literary convention. The fourteenth-century *Lybeaus Desconus*, attributed, like *Sir Launfal*, to Thomas Chestre, balances out the positive portrayal of the faery mistress in *Sir Launfal* with the image of the Dame d'Amour, the powerful enchantress who 'Kowþe moch of sorcery,/ More þen oþer wycches fyfe', and keeps Lybeaus from his lady, persuading him through her arts that he is 'In paradys alyue': 'Wyth fantasme and fayrye/ Þus sche blerede hys y3e.'[14] A century later, Malory's *Morte Darthur* offers

---

[14] *Lybeaus Desconus*, ed. M. Mills, EETS OS 261 (London, 1969), Cotton MS, 1424–5, 1431–3. This

us a more extensive treatment of enchantment, which repeatedly links magic, sexual desire and force in negative ways. In the *Morte*, writes Geraldine Heng, 'magic is a direct mode of feminine play'.[15] Through the female enchantresses of the *Morte* – Morgan, Nenyve, Hallewes, Brisen – desire and magic interweave, often threateningly, around the bodies of the knights of the Round Table. Morgan le Fay is the central practitioner of magic in the *Morte*, perhaps indeed the archetypal enchantress of all romance. In Malory's narrative, as is conventional, she takes on the face of the younger, beautiful lady while retaining the power of the ancient duenna of *Sir Gawain*: she is 'the false sorseres and wycche moste that is now lyvyng'.[16] She is firmly associated with the Arthurian court: as well as being Arthur's half sister, she has her own rival court, and is set up as the great opponent of Arthur. Whereas a male rival would use deeds of arms and military force, however, Morgan's means are those of magic. Rather than emphasising Morgan's intrinsic supernatural quality as 'le Fay', Malory tells us that she 'was put to scole in a nonnery, and ther she lerned so moche that she was a grete clerke of nygromancye' (I.2, 5). These, like Melior's, are human arts, but are connected explicitly with the dark, demonic side of magic, 'nygromancye'. Morgan possesses the arts of illusion and shape-shifting typical of the magician, changing herself into the shape of great stones when pursued, and creating the false sword and scabbard and the destructive gifts that she sends to the court. Her enchantments are frequently extreme in their potential violence, and are most often aimed at orchestrating the downfall of Arthur, although her jealousy can take other forms, as in her imprisonment of a lady 'naked as a nedyll' in boiling water 'many wyntyrs and dayes' because she is 'the fayryst lady of that contrey' (XI.1, 478). But Morgan is also characterised by sexual desire: much is made of her love for Accolon and, as well, of her desire either to gain Launcelot for her own lover or destroy him. Accolon's fear, when he finds himself on a magical ship, that he is the victim of demonic enchantment is mistaken, for the enchantment has been effected by Morgan, his own lover, but his statement also contains truth: ' "thes damysels in this shippe hath betrayed us. They were fendis and no women",' he says; they are ' "false damysels that faryth thus with theire inchauntementes" ' (IV.8, 84). Ultimately, Morgan will cause Accolon's death when she causes him to fight Arthur with Excalibur, and her arts of enchantment are indeed treacherous ones.

Enchantment in the *Morte* is repeatedly and explicitly linked to the possession of male bodies and to predatory sexual desire: the threat of enchantment complements the physical challenges encountered by Arthur's knights, in particular Launcelot, who figures both as protector and victim of women. Thus Morgan le Fay

---

romance has many cognates, the closest of which appears to be the first half of Renaut de Beaujeu's *Li Biaus Desconeus*, but Thomas Chestre's source is not known: see Mills, 42–64.

[15] 'Enchanted Ground: The Feminine Subtext in Malory', *Courtly Literature*, ed. Busby and Kooper, pp. 283–300, p. 289. Heng's consideration of the ways love and magic interweave in feminine play and authority is an important one.

[16] Ed. Eugène Vinaver, *Malory: Works*, 2nd edn (Oxford, 1971; pbk edn, 1977), VIII.34, 270. All subsequent references to Malory's *Morte Darthur* will be from this edition and will be cited by book, section and page number. I use this edition as the most accessible to readers, since the third edition, revised by P. J. C. Field (Oxford, 1990), is now out of print. See also my discussion in 'Violent Magic', pp. 232–6.

and three queens, having abducted the sleeping Launcelot to a 'chambir colde', require his love: ' "Now chose one of us, whyche that thou wolte have to thy peramour, other ellys to dye in this preson" ' (VI.3, 151–2). The scene provides a neat counterpart to the many abductions of damsels by villainous knights in the *Morte*: the power of enchantment allows women to employ force, to abduct even the best of knights. Nenyve's entrapment of Merlin, the benign practitioner of magic, similarly replaces force with enchantment, turning his powers back on him when she imprisons him within the wondrous cave that he himself shows to her:

> So by hir subtyle worchyng she made Merlyon to go undir that stone to latte hir wete of the mervayles there, but she wrought so there for hym that he come never oute for al the craufte he coude do, and so she departed and leffte Merlyon. (IV.1, 77)

Merlin, with all his arts and foreknowledge, cannot resist the disruptive forces of sexuality, embodied in the dangerously desirable enchantress, that conspire to shape his destiny. Yet Malory offers Nenyve a rationale too: she fears Merlin's pursuit of her maidenhood, 'for cause he was a devyls son, and she cowde not be skyfte of hym by no meane' (IV.1, 77). Merlin's desire for her unleashes the negative enchantment and, unlike Tennyson's Vivien, Nenyve remains a morally ambiguous figure, motivated by human and comprehensible fears.

The desiring enchantress, half-human, half-otherworldly, is perhaps most strikingly depicted in the *Morte* in the lady Hellawes, who may find her origins in *Perlesvaus*, but is very much Malory's invention.[17] Malory explicitly links her, like Morgan le Fay, to necromancy: she is 'Hallewes the Sorseres, lady of the castell Nygurmous' (VI.15, 168). The strange otherworldly adventure of the Chapel Perilous turns out to be a complicated snare for Lancelot, who, if he had not refused Hellawes' request for 'one kiss,' would have lost his life, his corpse surrendered to the enchantress:

> 'Than wolde I have bawmed hit and sered hit, and so to have kepte hit my lyve dayes; and dayly I sholde have clypped the and kyssed the, dispyte of quene Gwenyvere.' (VI.15, 168)

Sex and death are equated in a highly threatening way, and the predatory woman is written as the enchantress who desires the body at all costs, even the cost of life itself. Enchantment again replaces physical force, and traditional gender roles are reversed, although, unlike female victims, Launcelot is ultimately able to save himself – and in fact Malory, as so often, effects a rapid reversal. We learn that after all it is Hellawes who dies of unrequited love for Launcelot: despite all her powers of enchantment, the woman becomes the victim.

Throughout the *Morte*, magic is ambivalent, a potentially negative force, but in Malory's tale of the Sankgreall, marvellous enchantment is rewritten as the illusory art of the devil himself: here sexual desire, evil and death are equated, and the lure of the erotic is fatal. This is especially striking in the narrative of the adventures of Perceval, who on his barren rocky mountain is tempted by 'a jantillwoman

---

[17] See also my discussion in *Rape and Ravishment in the Literature of Medieval England* (Cambridge, 2001), pp. 247–8.

of grete beauté' (XIV.8, 548). The parallels with the *Lanval* pattern and with *Partonope* are clear: the lady, 'the fayryst creature that ever he saw', kindles Perceval's desire by providing a marvellous feast and 'the strengyst wyne that ever he dranke', and urging him on through her apparent resistance, 'she refused hym in a maner whan he requyred her, for cause he sholde be the more ardente on hir' (XIV.9, 549). Having sworn to be her servant, he lies down naked beside her, only to see her disappear into the winds and burning sea when he crosses himself: she was a manifestation of the devil himself. Bors undergoes a similar attempted seduction by a lady who disappears with 'a grete noyse and a grete cry as all the fyndys of helle had bene aboute hym' (XVI.12, 571). Literal and symbolic interweave as what appear to have been physical realities prove demonic illusions: Perceval is told that ' "that jantillwoman was the mayster fyende of helle, which hath pousté over all other devyllis" ' (XIV.10, 551). The enchantress here becomes the demonic temptress, illusory yet capable of the most extreme act of force, of sending knights to eternal damnation. As in *Sir Gawain and the Green Knight*, it is crucial for the testing of virtue that the Grail knights should experience real desire, the lure of the erotic.

The enchantress, then, is repeatedly identified both with pursuing and inciting erotic desire. Such feminine and sexual power brings with it unease, and thus the practice of magic is unstable, the experience of it shifting from marvellous to demonic. The romances in which the supernatural protagonists are male provide a thought-provoking contrast. In *Sir Orfeo*, Orfeo's wife Heurodis wakes to reveal that she has been bidden to accompany the King of Faery to his world: ' "thou shalt with us go/ And live with ous ever-mo" '.[18] Despite the guard of Orfeo and a thousand armed knights, the King of Faery's words are fulfilled: Heurodis is spirited away. The violence of the act is explicit in Heurodis' madness and self-mutilation:

> 'Thy body, that was so white y-core,
> With thine nailes is all to-tore!
> Alas, thy rode, that was so red,
> Is all wan as thou were ded!
> And also thine fingers smale
> Beth al blody and all pale!' (81–6)

Its purpose, however, is left enigmatic: the King of Faery seems to want to possess – but not in sexual terms – bodies, and the Kingdom of Faery is eerily adorned with bodies all caught in the throes of violent death. The King of Faery's company is defined by the action of hunting – though they catch 'no best' (263). Yet erotic desire does not characterise the King of Faery's actions, and his taking of Heurodis, indeed, is set against Orfeo's loving desire for his wife and acute sense of loss, enacted in his exile.

Sir Degarré similarly depicts an act of faery-taking, this time one that is explicitly sexual but again not presented as erotic: the rape of the unnamed princess by a

---

[18] Ed. Sands, *Middle English Verse Romances*, pp. 187–200, lines 143–4. All subsequent references to *Sir Orfeo* will be from this edition and will be cited by line number. See further my discussion in *Rape*, pp. 228–33. See also 'Violent Magic', pp. 237–9, for a discussion of *Sir Orfeo* and *Sir Degarré*.

faery knight at the start of the romance.[19] While the eponymous hero is conceived through this act, it is startling in its violence:

> Þo no þing ne coude do ȝhe
> But wep and criede and wolde fle;
> And he anon gan hire atholde
> And dide his wille, what he wolde.
> He binam hire here maidenhod ... (109–13)[20]

By contrast with *Partonope*, here the distress and rape of the damsel are bizarrely at odds with the physical attractiveness of the fairy knight and the setting, and the courtly language of the knight heightens the shock of force:

> 'Iich have i-loved þe mani a ȝer,
> And now we beþ us selve her;
> Þou best mi lemman ar þou go
> Weþer þe likeþ wel or wo.' (105–8)

Desire intersects with violence but the scene is not depicted in terms of erotic pleasure: rather, what is articulated as love by the faery knight is enacted as the violent theft of property, 'He binam hire here maidenhod', and 'what he wolde' is not elaborated. The viewpoint is that of the lady. The faery knight is portrayed as beyond the norms of the human world, his otherworldly nature affirmed in his statement that he is to beget a child on the woman. It seems only a small step to the demonic rapist of *Sir Gowther*. Yet in fact the faery rapist of *Sir Degarré* becomes an ambiguous figure, ultimately reclaimed as Degarré's father and rewritten as the lady's beloved, sending her a pair of magical gloves from fairyland. The erotic, however, is left for Degarré's own pursuit of love.

There seems to be, then, a special link between the female arts of enchantment and the erotic. The enchantress may contravene gender expectations by actively pursuing desire, and is intriguing for this. If she is not to be portrayed as the evil necromancer or as demonic, however, she is likely to combine power and potential vulnerability. The experience of enchantment brings with it the desire to undo, to possess and demystify the female body. Chaucer plays both comically and more seriously on the dramatic possibilities of the motif of the otherworldly lady. In *The Knight's Tale*, when Arcite perceives Emilye as a goddess, part of the power of attraction lies in the apparent otherness, the beauty beyond the ordinary, of the beloved; in the same way, it might be argued that Troilus fails to perceive Criseyde as an earthly, inevitably flawed woman, and that his sublimation of her underpins the profundity of his betrayal. In these works, the tension lies in the difference between perception and actuality: Emilye and Criseyde are precisely not supernatural. Thopas' elf-queen, by contrast, provides us with a parodic representative of 'Fayerye', while *The Wife of Bath's Tale* offers a more sustained instance, which

---

[19] Ed. A. V. C. Schmidt and Nicolas Jacobs, *Medieval English Romances*, London Medieval and Renaissance Series, 2 vols (London, 1980), vol. 2. All subsequent references to *Sir Degarré* will be taken from this edition and cited by line number.
[20] See further my discussion in *Rape*, pp. 213–18.

blends game with earnest.[21] Here the otherworldly lady or enchantress functions to correct the violence of rape, committed by an Arthurian knight. The knight's vision 'under a forest syde' of a dance of 'ladyes foure and twenty, and yet mo' who suddenly disappear 'he nyste wher' cannot but suggest the marvellous and otherworldly, yet the marvellous is undercut when the ladies' place is taken not by a beautiful enchantress but by an old hag, 'A fouler wight ther may no man devyse'.[22] As so often in Chaucer's writing, convention is rewritten, and we are presented with a 'loathly old hag', who combines transformative, conspicuously faery powers with her highly philosophical, moral teaching on *gentillesse*, a didactic role that might seem more appropriate to a wholly different kind of otherworldly figure, such as Boethius' Lady Philosophy. Yet at the same time, the hag's actions neatly align with those of the enchantress in her pursuit of the male body. The loathly old hag effectively gains the knight's body for herself, and Chaucer plays humorously on the lack of eroticism in the description of their first night in bed:

> Greet was the wo the knyght hadde in his thoght,
> Whan he was with his wyf abedde ybroght;
> He walweth and he turneth to and fro.
> His olde wyf lay smylynge everemo ... (1083–6)

The tale indeed resists the association of female desire with sexual pleasure, 'lust abedde' (927), replacing it with a much more serious notion of desire for 'sovereynttee' (1038). Yet Chaucer does not completely abandon the convention of the desiring enchantress, for once the knight has yielded his lady 'maistrie' (1236), she becomes the beautiful, desirable young lady, her body his to love, and their delight mutual. With the final act of enchantment, paradoxically, she is brought back within the realms of the human.

Chaucer's play on the convention of the otherworldly lady and her pursuit of love affirms its familiarity and its potential for romance writers. The figure of the enchantress was versatile, allowing for a multi-faceted presentation of love, desire and gender within individual works as well as across romance writing. The enchantress may be a fantasy creature, her appearance and pursuit responding to desires and dreams of ideal love, but she may also be, or may become, a monster, wish-fulfilment quickly changing to nightmare. There is always the fear that the apparently divine figure may turn out to be a demon, and the possibility that her arts may be tamed, or that she may not be supernatural at all. Around her weave fears as well as fantasies of sexuality, transformation, death and desire, and ultimately the wish to know and to possess, as well as the fascination of the other, the unknown.

---

[21] See further my discussion in *Rape*, pp. 301–9, and in 'Woman Displaced: Rape and Ravishment in Chaucer's Wife of Bath's Tale', *Arthurian Literature XIII*, ed. James P. Carley and Felicity Riddy (Cambridge, 1995), pp. 115–31. For a general discussion of Chaucer's use of the supernatural, see my essay, 'Magic, Science and Romance: Chaucer and the Supernatural', *Medieval English Literary and Cultural Studies. SELIM XV*, ed. Juan Camilo Conde Silvestre and Mª Nila Vásquez González (SELIM, 2004), pp. 121–43.

[22] Geoffrey Chaucer, *The Wife of Bath's Tale*, ed. Larry D. Benson, *The Riverside Chaucer* (1987; Oxford, 1988), pp. 116–22, lines 990, 992, 996, 999. All subsequent references to *The Wife of Bath's Tale* will be from this edition and will be cited by line number.

'wordy vnthur wede':
Clothing, Nakedness and the Erotic in some Romances of Medieval Britain

AMANDA HOPKINS

CLOTHING plays a vital role in many Middle English romances. Dress can identify the social rank of the wearer, as it does in various ways in the Middle English redactions of Marie de France's *Lanval*, or be a public demonstration of social condition, like Criseyde's widow's weeds.[1] It can even aid personal recognition, as when Orfeo discovers his queen in the Otherworld: 'Be hyr clothys he hyr knew'.[2] As recent scholarship has demonstrated, it is clothing rather than anatomy that is the 'prime indicator of gender identity' in medieval texts.[3] It can be a valuable gift, like the cloth studded with gems presented to the emperor in *Emaré*, later

---

[1] 'All people use material culture to express their social identities, in terms of a personal sense of self and membership of wider groups defined according to structural divisions in society, such as family, household, gender, social class, occupation, ethnicity, and so on' (Roberta Gilchrist, 'Medieval Bodies in the Material World: Gender, Stigma and the Body', *Framing Medieval Bodies*, ed. Sarah Kay and Miri Rubin (Manchester, 1994), pp. 43–61 (p. 44)). In Geoffrey Chaucer's *Troilus and Criseyde* (ed. Larry D. Benson, *The Riverside Chaucer*, 3rd edn (Oxford, 1987); all citations of Chaucer's works refer to this edition), there are several references to Criseyde's widow's dress (e.g. I, 109, 177, 309; II, 534), and the narrator makes it clear that the black (or 'broun' at I, 109) garb of a widow was considered (deliberately?) unattractive in the Middle Ages: he alludes to Criseyde's obvious beauty *despite* her weeds ('Criseyda,/ In widewes habit blak; *but natheles*,/ . . ./ In beaute first so stood she, makeles' (I, 169–72, my emphasis)); elsewhere, Pandarus insists she should discard the weeds to enhance her appearance, telling her to ' "cast youre widewes habit to mischaunce!/ What list yow thus yourself to disfigure/ . . .?" ' (II, 222–4).

[2] *Sir Orfeo*, ed. A. J. Bliss, 2nd edn (Oxford, 1966), Ashmole 61 text, 395. Bliss edits all extant versions of the text in this volume; the reference to Orfeo's recognition of Heurodis specifically (and solely) by her clothing appears in all three MSS (cf. Harley 3810, line 378; Auchinleck, line 408).

[3] E. Jane Burns, 'Refashioning Courtly Love: Lancelot as Ladies' Man or Lady/ Man?', *Constructing Medieval Sexuality*, ed. Karma Lochrie, Peggy McCracken and James A. Schultz, Medieval Cultures 11 (Minneapolis, 1997), pp. 111–34 (p. 113); cf. Burns's monograph, *Courtly Love Undressed: Reading Through Clothes in Medieval French Culture* (Philadelphia, 2002), p. 24 et passim; Ad Putter, 'Transvestite Knights in Medieval Life and Literature', *Becoming Male in the Middle Ages*, ed. Jeffrey Jerome Cohen and Bonnie Wheeler (New York, 1997), pp. 279–302. Timothy Taylor observes that the invention of clothing 'gave rise to the idea of gender – the extension of aspects of sex beyond obvious biological attributes. Clothing was from the outset "male" or "female" ' (*The Prehistory of Sex: Four Million Years of Human Sexual Culture* (London, 1996), p. 7, cf. p. 224).

made into a robe for the eponymous heroine,[4] and descriptions of costly clothing and rich materials serve to add an exotic quality to many texts. Allusion to nakedness in romance may refer to poor clothing rather than complete nudity, as at the beginning of *Havelock* when the author writes: 'Þe tale is of Havelock imaked;/ Wil he was litel, he yede ful naked'.[5] The editor glosses *naked* as 'poorly dressed';[6] in medieval texts, then, nakedness is not necessarily an absolute concept, but can indicate that the social status of the wearer is compromised by garments that do not echo his true social rank. Similarly, references to nudity sometimes evoke the context of *largesse*, intimately connected with gifts of clothing, for example in the criticism of the late merchant's overspending in *Sir Amadace*:

> 'He cladde mo men agaynus a yole
> Thenne did a nobull knyghte...
> Burdes in the halle were nevyr bare,
> With clothes richeli dighte.'[7]

Clothing is a major feature, sometimes the only feature, of descriptions of feminine beauty, as demonstrated in *Lybeaus Desconus*, attributed to Thomas Chestre.[8] In one episode, the hero encounters a knight, Gyffroun, who has announced that he will give a gerfalcon to any man who has a lady more beautiful than his own, but he will fight any contender whose lady proves less beautiful. Chestre goes on to supply descriptions of Lybeaus' companion Elene (on the left in the quotations below)[9] and of Gyffroun's lady (on the right):

Mayde Elene, also tyte,	After hym [Gyffroun] com ryde
Jn a robe of samyte	A lady proud yn pryde,
Anoon sche gan her tyre	Was clodeþ yn purpel pall.
To þo Lybeaus profyte,	Þat folk com fer and wyde
Jn keue[r]chers whyt	To se her bak and syde:
Arayde wyth gold wyre.	How gentyll sche was and small.
A veluwet mantyll gay	Her mantyll was rosyne,
Pelured with grys and gray	Pelured with ermyne,
Sche caste abowte her swyre;	Well ryche and reall.

---

[4] Ed. W. H. French and C. B. Hale, *Middle English Metrical Romance* (2 vols, New York, 1930; reiss. as a single volume, 1964), vol. 1, pp. 423–55. The origins and appearance of the 'cloth of golde' (243), woven, by an Emir's daughter, of 'ryche golde' (113, cf. 129) and set with precious stones, are described at length (85–168).

[5] Ed. Diane Speed, *Medieval English Romances*, Durham Medieval Texts 8, 3rd edn, 2 vols (Durham, 1993), vol. 1, pp. 25–121, lines 5–6.

[6] Speed, *Medieval English Romances*, vol. 2 (Glossary, p. 413).

[7] Ed. Edward E. Foster, *Amis and Amiloun, Robert of Cisyle and Sir Amadace*, TEAMS METS (Kalamazoo, 1997), 158–9, 161–2. On the distribution of luxury clothing as part of the construct of *largesse*, see Burns, *Courtly Love Undressed*, pp. 25–9 et passim.

[8] Ed. M. Mills, *Lybeaus Desconus*, EETS OS 162 (Oxford, 1969). This volume comprises facing-page editions of MSS Cotton Caligula A. II and Lambeth Palace 306; quotations included here are taken from the Cotton text, but Lambeth ms citations are also supplied where appropriate for comparison.

[9] Elene has already been conventionally and briefly described in the text, in a passage that focuses primarily on her clothing and seemly bearing (Cotton 110–17, cf. Lambeth 119–26). At this point the narrator seems more enthusiastic about his portrayal of the lady's dwarf companion, who is supplied with a full twenty lines of description (Cotton 121–41, cf. Lambeth 130–50).

> A sercle vp-on her molde A sercle vp-on her molde.
> Of stones and of golde: Of stones and of golde,
> Þe best yn þat enpyre. (832–43) Wyth many amall. (868–79)

The public display depicted is less a beauty contest than a demonstration of male wealth and power communicated in terms of rich female clothing, whose perfunctory conventionality is indicated by the similarity of the ladies' garments and the exact repetition of the detail of the circlet (841–2, 877–8, cf. Lambeth 870–1, 906–7). As so often in medieval romance, female sexual attractiveness is expressed by means of valuable and exotic clothing, and here the ladies' beauty is expressed primarily by means of the garments they wear.

Chestre's description of Gyffroun's lady, however, extends further:

> As þe rose her rode was red;
> Þe her schon on hyr heed
> As gold wyre schyneþ bry3t.
> Ayder browe as selken þrede
> Abowte yn lengþe and yn brede;
> Hyr nose was strath and ry3t.
> Her eyen gray as glas,
> Melk whyt was her[r] face:
> So seyde þat her sygh with sy3t.
> Her swere long and smal;
> Her bewte telle all
> Ne man with mouþe ne my3t. (880–91)

This description evokes the female physical attributes with which the reader of medieval romance is familiar. It is essentially a list of perfect features: colour of complexion and eyes, shape of nose, brow and neck, added to the overall body shape of *bak and syde* mentioned earlier (872). The skin is white, emphasising the lady's aristocracy: she need not labour under the skin-darkening sun and she has access to washing facilities. Here the lady's skin is compared to milk; medieval authors also favoured snow as a model for female skin, as in Criseyde's 'snowissh throte' (III, 1250) or the throat of Bertilak's wife, which 'Schon schyrer þen snawe þat schedez on hillez'.[10] Equally conventional, the colouring in the lady's face is rose-like. The hair colouring most admired in medieval romance is blonde, and Chestre's comparison with *gold wyre*, such as that which decorates Elene's kerchief (837), evokes the prized materials of the period.[11] His closing remark about the impossibility of describing the lady's beauty is a frequent statement in romance, a

---

[10] *Sir Gawain and the Green Knight*, ed. J. R. R. Tolkein and E. V. Gordon, 2nd edn, rev. by Norman Davis (Oxford, 1967), 956.

[11] As well as illustrating physical beauty and social status in medieval texts, gold is one of various valuable materials often used to exemplify the moral value of characters explicitly associated with it. There are numerous examples, such as the story of Emaré, who is taught 'Golde and sylke for to sewe' (59) as a child; later in the text, her working of costly materials is used as an index of her appropriate noble feminine accomplishments. The robe made from the gold cloth given to her father, which he intends her to wear in his incestuous wedding to her, becomes a key symbol of the text, an expression both of Emaré's moral purity in defying wickedness, and of her true aristocratic status when she travels incognito. On the symbolism of the cloth and its employment as a device to detract from moral problems in the text, see Amanda Hopkins,

reference to the difficulty of expressing differentiation between one lady and another when perfect beauty and perfect clothing adhere to a conventional template.

In *Sir Gawain and the Green Knight*, the reader is presented with the depiction of a lady deliberately dressing in such a way as to enhance her sexuality, as Bertilak's wife carefully prepares for her final attempt to seduce the hero. In describing the first two days of temptation, the author has focused on the lady's behaviour and speech; but having failed to tempt Gawain, and having only one more opportunity, for the third bedroom scene the host's wife is seen to prepare herself with absolute purpose:

> Bot þe lady for luf let not to slepe,
> Ne þe purpose to payre þat pyȝt in hir hert,
> Bot ros hir vp radly, raked hir þeder
> In a mery mantyle, mete to þe erþe,
> Þat watz furred ful fyne with fellez wel pured,
> No hwez goud on hir hede bot þe haȝer stones
> Trased aboute hir tressour be twenty in clusteres;
> Hir þryven face and hir þrote þrowen al naked,
> Hir brest bar bifore, and bihinde eke. (1733–41)

The lady's deliberate preparations make her intentions plain, and the luxurious clothing and jewellery contrast with her naked face, throat, décolletage and back. The areas of skin left uncovered are those which Gawain has already admired from a distance in the chapel, when the lady 'Hir brest and hir bryȝt þrote bare displayed' (955). Like the presentation of Elene and Gyffroun's lady in *Lybeaus Desconus*, the depiction of the lady's appearance in the chapel scene is an example of the comparison method used by medieval authors; again dress is a prominent basis of comparison, but here it involves comparing the areas of skin displayed by the younger woman with the layers of clothing worn by the elder (950–65), of whom 'noȝt was bare . . . bot þe blake broȝes,/ Þe tweyne yȝen and þe nase, þe naked lyppez' (961–2). The comparisons are multiplied, for Gawain's admiration has already been implied by the narrator's reference to another beautiful woman: the lady at Hautdesert is 'wener þen Wenore' (945), 'Þe comlokest to discrye' in Arthur's court (81).[12] Yet the erotic qualities of the later description, in which the host's wife arrays herself for her third private interview with Gawain, are not permitted to fulfil their potential, for the audience sees the lady not though the gaze of the hero whom the elaborate dress is intended to move, but through the objective eyes of the narrator, and when the lady is in her own apartment; when

---

'Veiling the Text: the True Role of the Cloth in *Emaré*', *Medieval Insular Romance: Translation and Innovation*, ed. Judith Weiss, Jennifer Fellows and Morgan Dickson (Cambridge, 2000), pp. 71–82.

[12] Arthur's queen makes a single, brief appearance in the text, in Fitt I; while she is presented as surrounded by luxurious curtains and canopies (74–80), her clothing is not described and a single curt reference comprises the detail of her personal appearance ('yȝen gray' (82)). Yet the audience is clearly intended to note the fact of her beauty for future reference, since the narrator insistently tops the superlative of line 81 almost immediately: 'A semloker þat euer he syȝe/ Soth moȝt no mon say' (83–4).

Gawain himself sees the lady, in his bedchamber, the intensity of the moment is reduced by the generality of the depiction:

> He seȝ hir so glorious and gayly atyred,
> So fautles of hir fetures and of so fyne hewes,
> Wiȝt wallande joye warmed his hert. (1760–2)

The focus is carefully placed on a generalised 'joye', rather than any specifically defined erotic response, but the nature of the effect of the lady's preparations is made more explicit in the narrator's subsequent warning that 'Gret perile bitwene hem stod/ Nif Maré of hir knyȝt mynne' (1768–9), its reference to the Virgin Mary, whose likeness is painted on the inside of Gawain's shield as a reminder of his own moral aspirations (640–50), standing in stark contrast to the erotically clothed lady and the sexually charged situation.

For Middle English authors at least, it seems to have been easier to describe female repulsiveness than beauty, as the loathly lady narratives demonstrate.[13] John Gower's description in 'The Tale of Florent' takes the form of a list of familiar physical features now seen as gross and ugly in the hag's form, exactly reversing the conventional depictions of female beauty:

> Florent his wofull heved uplefte
> And syh this vecke wher sche sat,
> Which was the lothlieste what
> That evere man caste on his yhe:
> Hire nase bass, hire browes hyhe,
> Hire yhen smale and depe set,
> Hire chekes ben with teres wet,
> And rivelen as an emty skyn
> Hangende doun unto the chin,
> Hire lippes schrunken ben for age,
> Ther was no grace in the visage.
> Hir front was nargh, hir lockes hore,
> Sche loketh forth as doth a More,
> Hire necke is schort, hir schuldres courbe –
> That myhte a mannes lust destourbe!
> Hire body gret and nothing smal,
> And schortly to descrive hire al,
> Sche hath no lith withoute a lak;
> Bot lich unto the wollesak
> Sche proferth hire unto this knyht... (I, 1675–93)

---

13 *The Weddyng of Syr Gawen and Dame Ragnell for Helpyng of King Arthoure*, ed. Stephen H. A. Shepherd, *Middle English Romances* (New York, 1995); John Gower, 'The Tale of Florent' in *Confessio Amantis*, ed. Russell A. Peck, Medieval Academy Reprints for Teaching 9 (Toronto, 1980), Book I, 1407–1882; Geoffrey Chaucer, *The Wife of Bath's Tale* in *The Canterbury Tales*. Susan Crane notes that the Wife of Bath alone fails to describe the loathly lady, but rather 'masquerades in the split body of her tale's heroine', the lack supplied by the narrator in *The General Prologue* and Alisoun's allusions to her form in her own prologue (*Gender and Romance in Chaucer's Canterbury Tales* (Princeton, 1993), p. 129).

Clothing and nakedness also feature in the loathly lady narratives, as each author demonstrates that the hag's appearance cannot be improved by expensive clothing, and each depicts the wedding night, with its nude participants. In *The Weddyng of Syr Gawen*, when the hag arrives to marry her chosen knight, the text contrasts the hag's anatomical appearance with her newly acquired, incredibly expensive garments:

> She was arayd in the richest maner
> (More fressher than Dame Gaynour);
>
> Her arayment was worth .iij. .m. mark
> Of good red nobles styff and stark,
> So rychely she was begon.
> For all her rayment she bare the bell
> Of fowlness that ever I hard tell –
> So fowll a sowe saw never man! (590–7)

The juxtaposition of female body and rich dress in this passage mimics its use in many texts as an enhancement of feminine beauty and worth,[14] emphasising the author's deliberate failure to attain the usual result: the exaggeratedly costly garments cannot make the hag any easier on the eye. Gower, too, remarks that the replacement of the lady's rags with valuable clothing results in no improvement in her appearance, precisely the opposite, in fact: 'Bot when sche was fulliche arraied/ And hire atyr was al assaied,/ Tho was sche foulere on to se' (1757–9). The usual romance chemistry is evoked and reversed: instead of the costly clothing enhancing the lady's appearance, in Gower's text it increases her ugliness by its contrast to her physical features.

It is telling that none of the texts describes the lady's transformed appearance in any detail, which begs the question Susan Crane poses: 'If both bodies are female, what are the defining characteristics of femaleness? In every case the transformed body recalls its other form by the perfect opposition of its qualities: Chaucer's hag "so loathly, and so oold also" now "so fair was, and so yong therto" (III 1100, 1251).'[15]

Only in *The Weddyng of Syr Gawen* is there no wedding-night negotiation. Gawain's unfailing courtesy makes him turn to Dame Ragnell in bed to fulfil his promise to marry her gladly, and embrace his full obligations in marriage. 'Shewe me your cortesy in bed', says the hag, 'kiss me att the leste' (630, 635), but Gawain staunchly replies, 'I woll do more/ Then for to kysse, and God before!' (638–9). At once, she becomes 'the fayrest creature/ That ever he saw, without mesure!' (641–2), with, as the narrator later comments, 'her [hair] . . . to her knees, as red as gold wyre' (743).

Elsewhere, the knights are reluctant to pay their marital debts. In 'The Tale of Florent', when the newlyweds are 'abedde naked' (1781), framed by bedcurtains of 'cendal thinne' (1787) in a room 'full of lyght' (1786), the graceless, unwilling

---

[14] Burns notes that courtly literature often details clothing in terms of value (*Courtly Love Undressed*, p. 35).
[15] *Gender and Romance*, p. 88.

and ungrateful bridegroom turns away from the sight of the wife to whom he owes his life (1783-5). At the lady's demand for the fulfilment of the marital debt, he turns back and 'syh a lady lay him by/ Of eyhtetiene wynter age,/ Which was the faireste of visage/ That evere in al this world he syh' (1801-5), so attractive that now 'he wolde have take hire nyh' (1806), had the lady not prevented him by opening her variation on the discussion about *maistrie* in marriage. The Wife of Bath's equally unwilling knight, having acceded to his ugly bride's request for *maistrie*, is told to ' "Cast up the curtyn, look how that it is" ' (III (D) 1249) and his ardour, too, is enflamed by the lady's new appearance:

> And whan the knyght saugh verraily al this,
> That she so fair was, and so yong therto,
> For joye he hente hire in hise armes two.
> His herte bathed in a bath of blisse,
> A thousand tyme a-rewe he gan hir kisse,
> And she obeyed hym in every thyng
> That myghte doon hym plesance or likyng. (III (D) 1250-6)

Sexual disgust has been transformed into lust, at least on the part of the knight, suggesting that, for the medieval male, female obedience is itself erotic.[16] The hag's own lust, described in all the texts,[17] is transmuted into a tacit acquiescence fitting to a virgin bride; and although the narrators specify the visual effect on, and immediate ardent response by, the bridegrooms, none describes the elements of the naked wife's new appearance that have inflamed the husband's sexual passion; but, in nearly every case, eroticism is fulfilled in the dissolving of the aggressive expression of female desire into what is clearly a more seemly, and erotic, passive acceptance of appropriate (male) ardour.[18] As Judith Weiss states, 'The courtly lady, though admired and adored, tends to be a passive object of desire. The uncourtly lady, who woos, usurps the male role by trying to constrain or force, by becoming the active partner.'[19] If the knight of the loathly lady tales (other than the gentlemanly Gawain) is forced to learn humility and the correct treatment of

---

[16] A point that recurs throughout the Marriage Group of *The Canterbury Tales*, where male characters frequently emphasise the desirability of obedience in their wives or potential wives, and the narrators often denigrate its absence in their own spouses, in contrast to the Wife of Bath, who explicitly prefers the reversal of the customary gender roles both in her biography and (at least until its ending) in the story she tells. It is notable that Chaucer stresses obedience – in the opposite sex – as appealing to both genders. How far the reader is to understand the obedience as reaching into the bedroom, and what form it might take there, is beyond the scope of the present essay.

[17] The relevant page is missing from the manuscript of *The Weddyng of Syr Gawen*, but the description of the lady's enthusiastic and vigorously physical approach to her food at the feast (604-15) suggests an analogy for other physical appetites, which may also have been described by the author. Compare Thomas H. Crofts' analysis of the paralleling of descriptions of voracious appetites for food and for sex, again notably in a 'monstrous' figure, elsewhere in this volume.

[18] The exception is 'The Tale of Florent', where the narrative ends with Florent's acquiescence and the lady's promise that she will remain beautiful for the rest of her life (1822-52); since the tale is recounted by Genius to Amans in order to demonstrate the benefits of obedience to his lady's commands (1856-641, 227-1406), as one of a series of lessons in the practice of courtly love, the lady retains *sovereinete*.

[19] 'The Wooing Woman in Anglo-Norman Romance', *Romance in Medieval England*, ed. Maldwyn Mills, Jennifer Fellows and Carol Meale (Cambridge, 1991), pp. 149-61 (p. 160).

women by marrying against his inclinations, once she has won her chosen husband the lady (other than Florent's wife) must also embrace an unaccustomed role, passivity, in order to fulfil her erotic desires with the object of her choice; the final negotiations and the achievement of compromise are carried out in private with the participants' physical nudity suggesting a symbolic psychological nakedness.

James A. Schultz reiterates Caroline Walker Bynum's 'caution against assuming that medieval people eroticised the body in the same ways as we do';[20] and he notes that, where specific bodily parts are described as desirable, they are usually those common to both sexes: hair, head, arms.[21] While the bare areas displayed by Bertilak's wife are clearly intended to provoke an erotic *frisson*, complete nakedness seems to be of minimal erotic interest to romance authors. In the wider context, nudity 'was accepted and represented in the Middle Ages without either false shame or exhibitionism';[22] and, although texts sometimes refer to nakedness in bed, Jean Verdon's observation that in the Middle Ages 'It was customary to sleep in the nude'[23] suggests that romance authors may often fail to specify an unclothed state that must be obvious to them. Of course, a focus on nakedness is not always appropriate. In *Lybeaus Desconus*, for example, the kiss of the hero transforms a woman-faced serpent into a naked lady, who is clearly discomforted by her lack of clothing: 'sche stod be-fore hym naked/ And all her body quaked:/ Per-fore was Lybeauus wo' (2014–16). In alluding to Lybeaus' sympathetic reaction to the lady's discomfiture, the narrator deliberately circumvents the erotic potential of the passage, and neither the narrator nor the hero allows his gaze to linger on the lady's form; rather they hasten to find clothing for her so she might appear in her public identity as a suitable prize for the knight's achievements in rescuing her from peril (2071–94). Similarly, the author of *The Erle of Tolous* carefully removes any hint of titillation from the bedroom scene.[24] Here, two corrupt guards selected by the Emperor to look after his wife, Dame Beulybon, importune her in turn; she rejects them firmly, but they are unconvinced by her promise that she will not expose their attempts, and instead enact a plan to have her executed for adultery. To this end, they hide a naked squire in her bedchamber, planning to rush into the room later to catch the 'adulterers' apparently *in flagrante delicto*. When they burst in, they kill the young man before he can protest his innocence; but, while his nakedness is crucial to the plot and is mentioned several times (726, 733–4, 776–7),[25] the author concentrates on Dame Beulybon's innocence and the guards'

---

[20] 'Bodies that Don't Matter: Heterosexuality before Heterosexuality in Gottfried's *Tristan*', *Constructing Medieval Sexuality*, ed. Lochrie et al., pp. 91–110 (p. 92), citing Bynum, 'The Body of Christ in the Later Middle Ages: A Reply to Leo Steinberg', in her collection *Fragmentation and Redemption: Essays on Gender and the Human Body in Medieval Religion* (New York, 1991), pp. 79–117 (p. 85).
[21] 'Bodies', pp. 92–3.
[22] Françoise Piponnier and Perrine Mane, *Dress in the Middle Ages*, trans. Caroline Beamish (New Haven, 1997), p. 9.
[23] *Night in the Middle Ages*, trans. George Holoch (Notre Dame, 2002), p. 159, cf. p. 155, and Piponnier and Mane, *Dress*, pp. 99–100.
[24] Ed. French and Hale, *Middle English Metrical Romances*, vol. 1, pp. 383–419.
[25] In the plan, the squire is to be 'nakyd saue þe breke' (727), but the breeches are not mentioned

treachery, ignoring her vulnerable nudity: yet, since she is 'in bedde on slepe' (745) when the traitors rush in, her nakedness must be assumed.

Male nudity, conversely, can be presented with humour. The overall sense of evil in the passage in *The Erle of Tolous* when the guards convince the squire to follow their plan, for example, is countered by a comic edge: it is difficult to take completely seriously the young man's naïve acceptance of their plan as 'a yoly play' (730) when he has been described as 'Twenty wyntur . . . oolde' (713).[26] Again, the bedroom scenes in *Sir Gawain and the Green Knight* are overtly comic, with the hero, 'a man lying (naked) in bed',[27] trapped in his unclothed state by the determined lady sitting on the bedside. John Burrow describes the first bedchamber scene as 'pure comedy, the comedy of embarrassment', similar to that found in *Troilus and Criseyde*.[28] In the first *Gawain* bedroom scene, the author employs comedy to intensify the eroticism by emphasising the hero's discomfiture and his reasons for it; conversely, in *The Erle of Tolous* the humour in the squire's ridiculous naïvety defuses any eroticism from the episode.

In *Troilus and Criseyde*, the erotic potential of the lovers' consummation is suggested in the moment when Troilus kneels by Criseyde's bed:

> This Troilus ful soone on knees hym sette
> Ful sobrely, right be hyre beddes hed,
> And in his beste wyse his lady grette.
> But Lord, so she wex sodeynlich red!
> Ne though men sholde smyten of hire hed,
> She kouthe nought a word aright out brynge
> So sodeynly, for his sodeyn comynge. (III, 953–9)

Yet here the erotic potential is compromised both by Troilus' uncertainty and swooning, whose comedy switches the focus to the emotional rather than the erotic plane, and by the sinister nature of Pandarus' plotting. His close kinship to Criseyde has been revealed in Book I (975) and the impropriety of his involvement articulated by Troilus: ' "Al this drede I, and ek for the manere/ Of the, hire Em, she nyl no swich thyng here" ' (I, 101–2). Pandarus' declaration to Criseyde, ' "For me were levere thow and I and he [Troilus]/ Were hanged, than I sholde ben his baude" ' (II, 532–3), not only places his actions within a context the audience might not otherwise contemplate – Pandarus the Pimp – and thus invites consideration of his motivations, but provides in its rider an unequivocal reminder of their kinship: ' "I am thyn em; the shame were to me/ As wel as the, if that I sholde assente,/ Thorugh myn abet that he thyn honour shente" ' (II, 355–7). His presence in the bedchamber in Book III, reading romances at the fireside (978–80), thus presents an unsettlingly inappropriate voyeurism, echoing his earlier behav-

---

when he is discovered in the lady's bedchamber: 'The younge knyght, verrament,/ Nakyd founde they thore' (776–7).

[26] The author attempts to emphasise the young man's naïvety by repeatedly referring to him as 'chylde' (712, 721, 733, 748).

[27] J. A. Burrow, *Gestures and Looks in Medieval Narrative*, Cambridge Studies in Medieval Literature 48 (Cambridge, 2002), pp. 150–1.

[28] *A Reading of Sir Gawain and the Green Knight* (London, 1965), p. 78.

iour when he forces Criseyde to accept Troilus' love letter: 'in hire bosom the letter down he thraste' (II, 1155).[29]

Later, however, Chaucer does move towards a lyrical eroticism, focused on Criseyde's naked form. Towards dawn, when Troilus finally overcomes his fears, Chaucer removes external distractions to focus on the love-making:

> Hire armes smal, hire streghte back and softe,
> Hire sydes longe, flesshly, smothe, and white
> He gan to stroke, and good thrift bad ful ofte
> Hire snowissh throte, hire brestes rounde and lite.
> Thus in this hevene he gan hym to delite,
> And therwithal a thousand tyme hire kiste,
> That what to don, for joie unnethe he wiste. (III, 1247-53)

Troilus' explorations of his lady's body are ardent, if conventionally concentrated on the pallor of her skin, and the body parts of arms, back, sides and throat, now augmented by the reference to Criseyde's breasts. Troilus' enthusiasm and pleasure are evoked through the physicality of the description and the hyperbole that follows it. Like the loathly lady narratives, the passage demonstrates the fact that 'romance depicts male ideals of chivalric prowess and male fantasies';[30] the response of Criseyde, who, as a widow, is presumably sexually experienced, to the inexperienced Troilus' attentions has little place: where earlier she was voluble and reassuring, now she neither speaks nor stirs, but merely lies naked beneath his moving hands, her desires, if any, subsumed by his, her pleasure defined only in relation to mutual pleasure, 'hire delit or joies' (III, 1310).[31] With Criseyde, Chaucer negates the active female erotic response he embraces so fully in the character of the Wife of Bath, and abnegates his responsibility to feminine sexuality in favour of the convention of female passivity.[32] In romance, the focus is on male pleasure and satisfaction, and the eroticism of romance's idealistic female passivity

---

[29] Medieval concern about incest, and its reflection in the literature of the period, has been documented and explored by numerous commentators; see, e.g. Elizabeth Archibald's article, 'Incest in Medieval Literature and Society', *Forum for Modern Language Studies* 25:1 (1989), pp. 1-14, and her book, *Incest and the Medieval Imagination* (Oxford, 2001); James A. Brundage, *Law, Sex, and Christian Society in Medieval Europe* (Chicago and London, 1987), passim; Ruth Mazo Karras, *Sexuality in Medieval Europe: Doing unto Others* (New York and London, 2005), passim.

[30] Elizabeth Archibald, 'Women and Romance', *Companion to Middle English Romance*, ed. Henk Aertsen and Alasdair A. MacDonald (Amsterdam, 1990), pp. 155-69 (p. 166).

[31] Elsewhere in this volume, Corinne Saunders examines an episode from *Partonope of Blois*, which depicts Melior, having created the opportunity to fulfil her desire for the eponymous hero, accepting his erotic ministrations with complete passivity.

[32] The depiction of extreme passivity by Chaucer and other authors seems to conflict with Karras's view that the passivity expected of females in the Middle Ages means that they were the sexually receptive participants, not that women 'were expected to lie still on their backs' (*Sexuality*, p. 4); the concept of such passivity is supported by Simone de Beauvoir's observations of patriarchal ideals: men, she states, require that the beautiful female body display 'les qualités inertes et passives d'un objet' (the inert and passive qualities of an object: *Le Deuxième Sexe 2: Les faits et les mythes*, Folio Essais 37 (Paris, 1949), pp. 263-4; translation mine). Sue Niebrzydowski's essay in this volume explores the implications of the presence or absence of female commentary on male sexual techniques in *The Canterbury Tales*, based on a comparison of Dame Alisoun's detailed and explicit descriptions of sexual satisfaction (or lack of it) in her marriages with May's silence about the quality of Januarie's and Damyan's sexual performances in *The Merchant's Tale*.

provides a parallel to the eroticism of obedient wives, such as Dame Alisoun's transformed hag.

Partial nudity can be more erotic than complete nakedness, as Roger Middleton observes in his examination of Enide's torn clothing in Chrétien de Troyes' *Erec et Enide*: 'a dress with holes in the sides is quite as good as one that is completely tattered; in fact, it is rather better because it focuses on the area of most interest. This point is not lost upon fashion designers of our own day, and it was not lost upon Marie de France who is responsible for the dress of this type in the lay of *Lanval*.'[33]

Lanval provides a rare opportunity to compare the medieval approach to the erotic by male and female authors, since several Middle English redactions of Marie's lay survive; it is likely that all were male-authored, and one is by an identified male writer, Thomas Chestre. In Marie's version, Lanval, a knight unjustly neglected by Arthur, is taken as lover by an unidentified lady, who gives him the means to display extraordinary *largesse*, on condition that he conceal their relationship. His new wealth attracts the queen's attention, but the hero spurns her advances and insults her by comparing her appearance unfavourably with his lady's poorest servant girl. The queen makes a carefully edited complaint against Lanval, and King Arthur has him imprisoned pending a trial for treason in which Lanval must prove his boast. However, the lady, as threatened, has vanished. After making him suffer a year's separation, the lady arrives at court to vindicate her lover, who leaves the court with her for Avalon.[34]

The revealing dress features in the second of two scenes in which the author consciously juxtaposes clothing and nakedness to achieve an erotic effect. In Marie's text, the despondent and ignored Lanval rides away from the court, and is met by two richly dressed maidens who lead him to their mistress, who has already selected Lanval to be her lover. The lady is, of course, a *fée*, a woman of the fairy world, to whom human rules of sexual behaviour do not apply: 'The *fée* of the early romances . . . had close ties with the supernatural and these gave her the relative sexual and moral freedom to seduce knights without comment and to carry them away from society to an ill-defined otherworld';[35] and it is her autonomy that contributes to the eroticism of her appearances in the text. Further, as William MacBain observes, it is her very autonomy that serves to keep her outside the

---

33 Roger Middleton, 'Enide's See-through Dress', *Arthurian Studies in Honour of P. J. C. Field*, ed. Bonnie Wheeler (Cambridge, 2004), pp. 143–63 (p. 154). I should like to express my thanks to the author for supplying me with a copy of this article.
34 Quotations from *Lanval* are taken from *Marie de France: Lais*, ed. Alfred Ewert (Oxford, 1944, reiss. with a new introduction by Glyn S. Burgess, London, 1995). Translations are my own. Marie is herself a representative of the literature of medieval Britain since she is generally believed to have been writing in the Plantagenet court of Henry II (see, for example, the introduction to *The Lais of Marie de France*, trans. Glyn S. Burgess and Keith Busby, 2nd edn (Harmondsworth, 1999), passim).
35 Kathryn S. Westoby, 'A New Look at the Role of the *Fée* in Medieval French Arthurian Romance', *The Spirit of the Court. Selected Proceedings of the Fourth Congress of the International Courtly Literature Society (Toronto 1983)*, ed. Glyn S. Burgess and Robert A. Taylor (Cambridge, 1985), pp. 373–85 (p. 385); cf. Weiss, 'Wooing Woman', p. 149 and n. 2.

society of the human world,[36] a society which, in *Lanval*, includes women distributed as spoils by King Arthur to his knights, 'Femmes e tere departi' (17, he distributed wives and land), an implicit critique of the powerlessness of women omitted by all the Middle English redactors.

The lady herself is gradually, but almost completely, revealed: first Marie describes, in loving detail, the *fée*'s expensive pavilion, then the bed on which the lady lies, and finally the lady herself, 'an eroticised damsel stretched out on lavish bedclothes inside her ornate tent, a paragon of seductive beauty undressed':[37]

> Ele jut sur un lit mut bel. . .
> En sa chemise senglement.
> Mut ot le cors bien fait e gent;
> Un cher mantel de blanc hermine,
> Covert de purpre alexandrine,
> Ot pur le chaut sur li geté;
> Tut ot descovert le costé,
> Le vis, le col e la peitrine;
> Plus ert blanche que flur d'espine. (97, 99–106)

(She lay on a very fine bed, in her shift alone. Her body was well-made and handsome; for warmth, she had thrown over herself a costly white ermine cloak, covered with Alexandrine purple. Her sides, her face, her neck and her breast were all uncovered. She was whiter than hawthorn blossom.)

The eroticism is carefully stated: the lady's status and power are emphasised through the materials described, but these are not allowed to overwhelm the sensuality of the scene. Marie's technique here is to supply a long, leisurely movement, representing the view through Lanval's eyes, from the meeting of the *fée*'s attractive and richly dressed maidens (53–79), via the exterior view of the costly tent, topped with its gold eagle, and the interior, dominated by the bed whose covers 'valeient un chastel' (98: were worth as much as a castle), and then the description of the lady's luxurious fur mantle, to conclude in sharp focus on the heady combination of valuable fur and cloth with the clean, healthy, aristocratic form of the lady, whose beauty 'resides in her sumptuously white skin, seductively bared among the *riches dras* and costly mantle that both clothe and reveal her body'.[38]

A. C. Spearing identifies the first view of the lady as corresponding to male erotic fantasy,[39] although, as he rather grudgingly admits elsewhere, the erotic fantasy of *Lanval* may appeal to both sexes: 'Doubtless there are also elements of female fantasy involved in the lady's self-display and more generally in her role as wealthy, self-pleasing, and successful seductress.'[40] Yet, as Kathryn S. Westoby

---

36 'The Outsider at Court, or What is so Strange about the Stranger?', *The Court and Cultural Diversity. Selected Papers from the Eighth Triennial Congress of the International Courtly Literature Society*, ed. Evelyn Mullally and John Thompson (Cambridge, 1997), pp. 357–65 (p. 361).
37 Burns, *Courtly Love Undressed*, p. 171.
38 Burns, *Courtly Love Undressed*, p. 172.
39 *Medieval Love-Narratives* (Cambridge, 1993), pp. 97–119 (p. 100).
40 'Marie de France and Her Middle English Adapters', *Studies in the Age of Chaucer* 12 (1990), pp. 117–56 (p. 135, n. 25).

explains, *fées* 'were creatures with whom the courtly lady of the audience would be eager to associate. They had the autonomy which the courtly lady lacked and exercised the power over men which the courtly lady perhaps tried, less successfully, to exert herself.'[41] In the context of the Middle Ages, however, it is not only the *fée*'s sexual autonomy that ladies of the audience might admire, but the freedom to dress as she wishes, to use clothing both to please herself and to attract male admiration.[42] The *fée*, as Lanval's mistress clearly demonstrates, is outside the limitations imposed by medieval sumptuary laws, which dictated that female dress should be cheaper and less varied than male clothing.[43] She can select, and publicly display, her clothing and accoutrements without fear of any man's reproof or any society's reprisal, displaying an autonomous power that is, in itself, erotic.[44]

Middle English redactions, such as *Landavale*, Thomas Chestre's *Sir Launfal*, and *Sir Lambewell*,[45] adopt a different approach to the erotic qualities of the pavilion scene. The maidens, pavilion and bed are still present, but the sense of exotic mystery has been removed by the texts' provision of an identity for the lady: in *Landavale*, the author tells the audience that the hero 'founde yn that pavilion/ The kyngys doughter of Amylion' (92),[46] while Chestre gives the lady a name: 'He fond in þe pauyloun/ Þe kynges douȝter of Olyroun,/ Dame Tryamour þat hyȝte' (277–9).[47] The figure of the lady herself is described with less subtlety than in Marie's version:

> There was a bede of makyll price,
> Couerid with purpill bise;
> Thereon lay that maydyn bright,

---

41 'A New Look', p. 385.
42 'One source of sensual delight [in medieval England], which involved colour and display, was clothing. For those who could afford them, the latest styles in fashionable dress were an expression of position, pleasure, and wealth. The enjoyment of nice clothing became so pronounced, in fact, that the social establishment attempted to restrict certain types of clothing to designated strata of society' (Compton Reeves, *Pleasures and Pastimes in Medieval England* (Stroud, 1997), p. 49).
43 'When the given data make comparison possible, it is confirmed that a garment or an outfit made for a princess almost always cost less than the equivalent made for a man of equal rank' (Piponnier and Mane, *Dress*, p. 77; cf. Burns, *Courtly Love Undressed*, pp. 31–5).
44 The eroticism of her autonomy seems antithetical to the obedient, passive lady idealised in romance, but in fact her erotic domain corresponds to another in which the male is submissive to the female: courtly love. As suggested in the context of the loathly lady tales (discussed above), the erotics of the Middle Ages, no less than the modern western world, allows for the coexistence of both dominant and submissive females, and, by extension, dominant and submissive males. On the dynamics of courtly love, see, for example, Georges Duby, 'The Courtly Model', trans. Arthur Goldhammer, *A History of Women in the West. II: Silences of the Middle Ages*, ed. Christiane Klapisch-Zuber (Cambridge, MA, and London, 1992), pp. 250–69.
45 *Landavale* and *Sir Launfal*, ed. A. J. Bliss, *Thomas Chestre: Sir Launfal* (London, 1960); *Sir Lambewell*, ed. John W. Hales and Frederick J. Furnivall, *Bishop Percy's Folio Manuscript, Vol. 1: Ballads and Romances* (London, 1867).
46 In Marie's text, the lady's home is not revealed until the end of the narrative, when *fée* and knight set out for Avalon (641).
47 Elizabeth Williams notes that in *Sir Lambewell* the lady remains a king's daughter, but the fairy quality is removed; the suppression means the author 'is in danger of exchanging the houri for an exceptionally well-to-do courtesan: removing the magic also removes the "excuse" for sexual freedom' (' "A damsell by herselfe alone": Images of Magic and Femininity from Lanval to Sir Lambewell', *Romance Reading on the Book: Essays on Medieval Narrative Presented to Maldwyn Mills*, ed. Jennifer Fellows, Rosalind Field, Gillian Rogers and Judith Weiss (Cardiff, 1996), pp. 155–70 (p. 161)).

> Almost nakyd, and vpright.
> Al her clothes byside her lay:
> Syngly was she wrappyd, parfay,
> With a mauntell of hermyn,
> Coverid with alexanderyn.
> The mantell for hete down she dede
> Right to hir gyrdillstede. (*Landavale*, 95–104)
>
> Jn þe pauyloun he fond a bed of prys
> Jheled wyth purpur bus,
> Þat semylé was of sy3te:
> Perjnne lay þat lady gent
> (Þat after Syr Launfal hedde ysent),
>   Þat efsom lemede bry3t.
>
> For hete her cloþes down sche dede
> Almest to her gerdylstede:
> Þan lay sche vncouert. (*Sir Launfal*, 283–91)

The author of *Sir Lambewell* is less subtle still:

> therin sate a lady bright,
> from the Middle shee was naked vpright,
> and all her cloathing by her lay;
> fful seemlie shee sate, I say,
> all in a mantle of white Ermines
> was fringed about with gold fine.
> her mantle down for heat shee did
> full right to her girdle steed... (117–24)

As Elizabeth Williams, comparing the Middle English redactions of *Lanval* with their source, suggests,

> the total effect is remarkably different because the translator lays a far greater emphasis on the lady's state of undress. Marie works this in tastefully with the other details, but where she begins by mentioning the one garment which the lady wore under her cloak, the translator instead draws attention to those she has discarded ... Besides this emphatic opening, he makes the point again where Marie does, in the description of the cloak, and the lady's nakedness is far more complete, for he denies her even the *chemise* ... and allows her only the cloak ... Finally, where Marie says that the lady had drawn the cloak round her for warmth..., the translator states that she had discarded it for the heat.[48]

Pace Mortimer J. Donovan, who, without further explanation, states that in the Middle English redactions, the hero's 'love for the *fée*, in the pavilion scene, is

---

[48] '*Lanval* and *Sir Landevale*: A Medieval Translator and His Methods', *Leeds Studies in English*, NS 3 (1969), pp. 85–99 (p. 89). For a different interpretation of the relationship between external temperature and sexuality in this text, see Robert Rouse's essay, ' "Some Like it Hot": The Medieval Eroticism of Heat', elsewhere in this volume.

more sensual than Marie de France would allow',[49] the greater nakedness in the Middle English texts seems to alter Marie's sensuality to a coarser titillation, although it is not easy to conclude whether this can be attributed purely to the effect of male authorship or whether it is designed to accommodate the changing tastes, sex or class of the intended audience.[50] The Middle English redactors also excise Marie's sensual references to the lady's uncovered anatomy, *le costé,/ Le vis, le col e la peitrine*, which in *Lanval* reflect the knight's gaze, heighten the lady's own awareness of her sensuality and augment the lingering eroticism of the scene.

The erotic register of the later passage, in which the lady arrives to justify her lover, is also changed by the Middle English authors. In Marie's text, the *fée* has dressed deliberately to invite the public's gaze and admiration: 'Ele iert vestue en itel guise:/ De chainsil blanc e de chemise,/ Que tuz les costez li pareient,/ Que de deus parz laciez esteient' (559–62: she was dressed in this way: in a white tunic and a shift which revealed her flanks, being laced on both sides). The editor, Alfred Ewert, refers to contemporary evidence, which shows that this manner of lacing was fashionable in the period,[51] but the detail is omitted by the Middle English authors, who emphasise instead the costliness of the lady's clothing, and thus her social status, rather than its erotic scantiness:

> A crown was vpon her hede,
> Al of precious stones and gold rede;
> Clothis she was yn purpyll pall,
> Her body gentill and medill smale;
> The pane of hir mantell jnwarde
> On hir harmes she foldid owtewarde,
> Which wel became that lady. (*Landavale*, 439–45)[52]

Perhaps this is a reflection of changing fashions; but, like the comparison of the ladies in *Lybeaus Desconus*, this description is less about beauty and the contrasting appeal of *fée* and queen than about the display of wealth and power; indeed, Chestre has the lady carry a *gerfawcon* (961), a bird usually carried by a king,[53] thus

---

49 *The Breton Lay: A Guide to Varieties* (Notre Dame, 1969), p. 146. The basis for this assertion is not obvious, for none of the authors seems to articulate the consummation in terms that might be described as particularly sensual. The narrator of *Landavale* expresses the couple's satisfaction plainly – 'To bedde they went both anon;/ All that nyght they ley yn fere/ And did what thir will were –/ For pley they slepyd litill þat nyght' (148–51, cf. *Sir Launfal* 347–50) – yet Marie's depiction of events is just as clear: 'S'amur e sun cors li otreie./ Ore est Lanval en droite veie!' (133–4: she grants him her love and her body. Now Lanval is on the right road!). One detail differs: in the Middle English redactions, the knight and lady are served a meal before they retire to bed, and the knight stays overnight; in Marie's text they retire at once, suggesting a more urgent desire, and take their meal later; and Lanval returns to the court later the same day.
50 Bliss states in the introduction to his edition that Chestre's narrative was written for 'simpler, less sensitive listeners in market-square or inn-yard', noting that his version is characterised by 'less elegance and less psychological subtlety' (*Sir Launfal*, p. 1).
51 *Lais*, p. 178, n.
52 Cf. *Sir Launfal*, 940–60.
53 *The Middle English Breton Lays*, ed. Anne Laskaya and Eve Salisbury, TEAMS METS (Kalamazoo, 1995), p. 260, n. In Marie's text the lady carries a sparrowhawk (*espervier*, 573) and is escorted by a greyhound (*levrer*, 574); in *Landavale* the bird remains a sparrowhawk, but the number of greyhounds has been increased to three (446–7).

focusing on the challenge to Arthur's social status. The dignity and authority of the *fée* in court in *Lanval* are reduced to visual effects and the barbarism of her revenge on the queen: she 'keeps her magical power yet makes of herself a mere surface, a body whose only gestures are to reveal itself (riding into court and removing her mantle) or conceal itself (blinding Guinevere and departing)'.[54] In Marie's text, once in the court, the lady 'Sun mantel ad laissié chaeir,/ Que meuz la puïssent veer' (605–6: let her mantle fall so that they could see her better), a deliberately sensual gesture that attracts the gaze of the whole court, yet paradoxically emphasises her separateness from it. In *Sir Launfal*, Dame Tryamour also drops her cloak, but in such a way that it evokes, for Elizabeth Williams, not the beauty of a noble lady choosing to display herself for a specific, and valid, reason, but rather 'the image of the stripper'.[55] Yet this interpretation is problematic, since Dame Tryamour is, in fact, more fully dressed beneath her mantle than Marie's *fée*.[56] The removal of the cloak,

> Sche ded of her mantyll on þe flet
> (Þat men schuld her beholde þe bet)
> Wythoute a more soiour, (979–81)

seems in fact a perfunctory gesture: not striptease, but stripping off for action in preparation for her malicious expression of victory in her blinding of the queen.[57] The male authors of fourteenth-century England have expurgated the erotic from Marie's climactic scene.

Some Middle English texts display eroticism through smaller gestures, with their lovers demonstrating a *frisson* of desire while fully dressed and in a public location. Where the author of *The Erle of Tolous* is sensitive to the dangers of inappropriate eroticism in the scene in which Dame Beulybon is arrested, he allows himself a subtle sensuality in his earlier depiction of the meeting of the Empress and the Earl. The Earl has heard of the lady's beauty and offers his prisoner, Trylabas, remission of his ransom and generous payment if he can arrange for the Earl to be able to see the lady for himself. Trylabas tells Dame Beulybon of the Earl's admiration, and attempts to convince her that this is an opportunity to have the hero, her husband's enemy, apprehended; but the lady, whose appreciation of the Earl's noble nature has been attested several times in the narrative, insists that Trylabas keep his word and agrees to appear in the chapel in order that the Earl, disguised as a hermit, can gaze on her.[58] In the chapel, it is clear that she has dressed carefully, 'Wondur rychely sche was cladde,/ In golde and ryche perrée' (329–30), although the public location and her escorts (228) confirm a complete propriety

---

[54] Crane, *Gender and Romance*, p. 158.
[55] ' "A damsell by herselfe alone" ', p. 155.
[56] The lady in *Landavale* does not remove her cloak at all.
[57] Bliss observes that there are no analogues for the queen's blinding in Arthurian literature (*Sir Launfal*, p. 38).
[58] Notwithstanding the medieval Church's continued attempts to regulate sexual expression, religious buildings paradoxically frequently provide the setting for erotic, albeit remote, encounters in medieval texts; the erotics of place, however, is beyond the scope of the present essay.

that adds to, rather than detracts from, the erotic display. The hero is struck by her beauty, and here the author underlines the erotic potential of the naked face: 'Sche stode stylle in that place/ And schewed opynly hur face' (337–8). Dame Beulybon presents herself leisurely to the Earl's gaze:

> Hur eyen were gray as any glas;
> Mowthe and nose schapen was
>   At all maner ryght;
> From the forhedde to the too,
> Bettur schapen myght non goo,
>   Nor none semelyer yn syght.
>
> Twyes sche turnyd hur abowte
> Betwene the erlys þat were stowte,
>   For the Erle schulde hur see.
> When sche spake wyth mylde steuyn,
> Sche semed an aungell of heuyn,
>   So feyre sche was of blee!
> Hur syde longe, hur myddyll small;
> Schouldurs, armes therwythall,
>   Fayrer myght non beel
> Hur hondys whyte as whallys bonne,
> Wyth fyngurs lone and ryngys vpon;
>   Hur nayles bryght of blee. (343–60)

The movements she makes to allow her admirer to view her fully are highly erotic, not least because, like *Lanval*'s *fée*, Dame Beulybon performs them of her own volition and is in complete control of the situation; they share the moment secretly, although in public, and she does not exit to her private chapel until the Earl 'had beholden hur welle' (361). In describing the Empress' appearance, the author, of necessity, focuses on conventional aspects of the lady's anatomy; but, unlike Troilus' view of the oblivious Criseyde in the temple (I, 267–315), here the participation of both parties creates a sensual intimacy, allowing an original articulation of erotics to overcome convention. There is, as well, a certain emphasis on the unclad parts, Dame Beulybon's eyes, hands, fingers, as there was before on her uncovered face. Later, the author returns to the lady's hands, recapturing the sense of the couple's remote intimacy: Dame Beulybon slips a ring from her finger and places into the Earl's hand with alms; when he discovers it, he kisses it many times (401) because of its earlier proximity to the lady's person: 'My dere derlynge,/ On thy fyngyr thys was!' (402–3).

Clothing and nakedness can be seen to have an ambivalent relationship with the erotic in medieval romance, and an author must handle the material skilfully and sensitively to achieve an original sensuality within conventional narrative techniques. While the ideal eroticism of romance is primarily concerned with the articulation of male desire, it would seem that the transmission of the erotic may also express the responses of the object of male desire, an expression of lovers' mutual participation in a sensual moment. It is apparent that medieval authors, while hampered by the conventions of romance, and sometimes their own ineptness, were aware of the potential eroticism of their descriptions and the interplay of the erotic, clothing and nakedness. This is perhaps nowhere more clearly demonstrated than in Josian's plea to the demurring hero in *Sir Beues of Hamtoun*:[59]

> 'Ichauede þe leuer to me lemman,
> Þe bodi in þe scherte naked,
> Þan al þe gold, þat Crist haþ maked,
> And þow wost wiþ me do þe wille!' (1105–9)

---

[59] *The Romance of Sir Beues of Hamtoun*, ed. Eugen Kölbing, EETS ES 46 (1885), 48 (1886), 65 (1894), repr. in one volume (Cambridge, 2000).

'Some Like it Hot':
The Medieval Eroticism of Heat

ROBERT ALLEN ROUSE

THE LATE fourteenth-century romance *Sir Launfal* narrates the financial, martial and erotic adventures of one of the lesser-known knights of the Arthurian court. In Thomas Chestre's popularised version of Marie de France's Breton Lai (*Lanval*), our hero's woes begin when he is excluded from the Arthurian court's *largesse* after he refuses the predatory Guinevere's sexual advances.[1] Shamed by his resulting poverty, which is only amplified by the financial demands of his role as Arthur's royal steward, Launfal takes his leave of the court and departs for Caerleon, where he vainly seeks succour at the hands of the city's mayor, who has benefited in the past from Launfal's own generosity. However, a knight out of favour in the royal court is of no current use to the mayor, who begrudgingly offers only meagre lodgings, and this is only forthcoming after Launfal sarcastically rebukes him regarding the value of past loyalties. Denied not only the company of men owing to his poverty, but also access to the Church, as he lacks clean clothing in which to visit it, Launfal is approaching the depths of despair. After a final humiliation of being excluded from the invitations to a Trinity feast hosted by the mayor, Launfal rides out into the forest to seek refuge both from the ridicule of the townsfolk and from his own sense of shame.

It is in this moment of extreme financial deprivation and social exclusion, the pathos of which is further intensified by his fall into a fen while riding to the forest, that Launfal encounters what turns out to be the unsought answer to his social and pecuniary predicament. Having stopped to rest and to contemplate his woes under a tree in a forest clearing, he is visited by two beautifully arrayed maidens, who greet him nobly before leading him to the pavilion of their mistress, Dame Triamoure. Once there, Launfal comes across a most magnificent scene of exotic opulence:

> He fond in the pavyloun
> The kinges doughter of Olyroun,

[1] The line of textual transmission from Marie's Lanval to Chestre's *Sir Launfal* is by way of the fourteenth-century Middle English *Landevale*. For a discussion of the relationship of the three texts, see Myra Stokes, '*Lanval* to *Sir Launfal*: A Story Becomes Popular', *The Spirit of Medieval English Popular Romance*, ed. Ad Putter and Jane Gilbert (Harlow, 2000), pp. 56–77.

> Dame Triamoure that highte.
> Here fadir was King of Fairie
> Of Occient, fere and nyie,
> A man of mochel mighte.
>
> In the paviloun he fond a bed of pris
> Y-heled with purpur bis,
> That semilé was of sighte.
> Therinne lay that lady gent
> That aftere Sir Launfal hedde y-sent,
> That lefson lemede bright.
>
> For hete her clothes down she dede
> Almest to here gerdilstede;
> Than lay she uncovert.
> She was as whit as lilie in May
> Or snow that sneweth in wintris day –
> He seigh nevere non so pert.[2]

The exotic trappings of the scene, with its obvious connotations of wealth and sumptuousness, and above all Triamoure's half-undressed appearance, combine to present Launfal, and the reader, with an irresistible opening gambit in her offer of romantic love and financial patronage. This scene of apparent erotic tension seems readily accessible to the modern reader, who cannot help but find something familiar in Triamoure's slow titillating uncovering of her naked breasts, glistening, as it appears to Launfal, as white as the snow on a winter's day.[3] The erotic currency of the exposure of female breasts is a dominant one in today's exhibitionist world, to the extent that the commercial success of certain popular newspapers, chains of bars and the careers of media starlets have built upon the exploitation of this mammarian economy. To the modern reader then, the immediate erotic foci of the scene are Triamoure's naked breasts.

However, in the medieval world, the message was somewhat less brazen. Marilyn Yalom has discussed the nature of the symbolism of the female breast, and points towards the primacy of a sacred understanding of the breast in the medieval period.[4] The sacred symbolism of the breast is best encapsulated by the tradition of the Madonna del Latte paintings, demonstrating Mary's privileged position as the maternal provider of Christ. Mary's breast, and the milk that flows from it, are polysemously symbolic: literally and metaphorically they embody divine sustenance, representing in the conception of Saint John Cassian firstly Mary's role as the mother of Christ; secondly, analogously representing the flowing of blood from Christ's wounds; and finally, in an anagogical sense, the flow of divine Grace

---

[2] *Sir Launfal*, ed. Donald B. Sands, *Middle English Verse Romances* (New York, 1966), lines 276–94. All quotations from *Sir Launfal* are from this edition.
[3] Whiteness of skin holds a place of great importance in the rhetoric of female beauty found in the medieval *effictio*, following patterns articulated by Matthew of Vendôme's *Ars versificatorio* and Geoffrey of Vinsauf's *Poetria nova*. It might also be noted, in passing, that for a modern reader, the erotic image of Triamoure's unveiling of her breasts is somewhat reinforced by the suggestive, and often collocative, presence of *pert* in line 294.
[4] Marilyn Yalom, *A History of the Breast* (New York, 1997).

from God to mankind.[5] The other dominant western medieval understanding of the female breast is in terms of its role in the physiology of the body and in the nurturing of infants, and in these medical writings we find little emphasis upon any erotic significance. Danielle Jacquart and Claude Thomasset, commenting on the *Etymologiae* of Isidore of Seville, observe that 'Nothing in the work of later encyclopaedists could enable one to consider the female breasts as being endowed with any particular erogenous sensitivity: only their function as a source of food was indicated.'[6]

Given such a cultural context, an erotic interpretation of Triamoure's display of excessive bodily exposure is problematic, and becomes especially so when examined against the norms of Middle English literature. Firstly, we have the possible reading that Triamoure offers up her naked body not in an erotic manner, but rather as a romance simulacrum of divine grace. Given the widespread appropriation of the rhetoric of religious worship and divine love that we find within the romance genre, with the role of Mary being paralleled by that of the female lover, it would perhaps be within the bounds of interpretative licence to read, on one level, Triamoure's offering of her naked upper body to Launfal as fulfilling a similar sustaining function as Mary does to Christ. Triamoure does, after all, provide Launfal with access to a form of grace, in a monetary sense, through which he manages rise from his fallen state to reclaim his former spotless chivalric reputation. However, while this reading can of course be made, it is perhaps more a reflection of the intrinsic structural parallels that exist between the modes of chivalric 'courtly love' and that of Christian theology. It would also seem unlikely that this reading would be the first to occur to the popular audience of *Sir Launfal*, which leaves us to consider further the nature of Triamoure's seduction.

In addressing the possible erotic import of Triamoure's undressing, we also have to take into account the general lack of representations of nudity and sex in medieval romance. As Donald Sands has observed, 'Tryamour's seduction of Launfal via semi-nudity is an uncommon thing in Middle English romance'.[7] Nakedness in itself seems to rarely take on explicit erotic meaning in romance, perhaps unsurprisingly so given the ubiquity of the naked body in scenes of sleeping and bathing in medieval texts.[8] It must also be noted that sex too seems to occupy a less than prominent place in these romances. Lee C. Ramsey notes that 'Sex occurs in medieval romances because marriage does, but it is understood as a secondary benefit of marriage . . .'.[9] However, in texts that are more deeply influ-

---

5   The anagogical understanding of the milk from Mary's breast as the blood of Christ is one that is both theologically and medically rational (from the point of view of medieval medicine). The Galenic theory of dealbation held that the milk from a lactating breast was transformed from the blood of the mother. Mary's milk was sacred owing to the uncontaminated nature of her virginal body (Danielle Jacquart and Claude Thomasset, *Sexuality and Medicine in the Middle Ages*, trans. Matthew Adamson (Princeton, 1988), p. 12).
6   *Sexuality*, p. 11.
7   Sands, *Middle English Verse Romances*, p. 203.
8   Elizabeth Archibald discusses the wider medieval attitudes towards nakedness, and the notable absence of such scenes in Middle English romance, in her article 'Did Knights have Baths? The Absence of Bathing in Middle English Romance' (*Cultural Encounters in the Romance of Medieval England*, ed. Corinne Saunders (Cambridge, 2005), pp. 101–16).
9   Lee C. Ramsey, *Chivalric Romances: Popular Literature in Medieval England* (Bloomington, 1983), p. 107.

enced by continental models of erotic love, we do find scenes of naked eroticism. Geoffrey Chaucer, in Book III of *Troilus and Criseyde*, presents the following scene of Troilus' ecstasy as he discovers for the first time the body of his lover:

> Hire armes smale, hire streyghte bak and softe,
> Hire side longe, fleshly, smothe, and whit
> He gan to stroke, and good thrift bad ful ofte
> Hire snoissh throte, hire brestes rounde and lite;
> Thus in hevene he gan him to delite . . .[10]

Here Troilus' tentative foreplay, presented, as Helen Phillips has observed, 'predominantly through the male experience', quite clearly articulates an erotic view of the naked body.[11] However, Chaucer, as is often the case, operates in a more sophisticated literary mode than does *Sir Launfal*, and Launfal's experience of seeing Triamoure's naked body seems to hold little in the way of such obvious erotic *frisson*.

So where might we turn next in our search for the significance of Triamoure's striptease? If there is not an immediate erotic purpose behind her actions, then where else may the significance of her actions lie? This scene of the initial meeting of Triamoure and Launfal, and in particular Triamoure's letting slip of her upper garments, are explained within the text as being owing to the heat of the day: *for hete her clothes down she dede*. Of course, how seriously we take this as a reason for her actions depends very much on our reading of Triamoure herself. It is clearly evident from the narrative that she has summoned Launfal to her pavilion for the express purpose of seducing him to be her lover, thus Chestre's causal phrase *for hete* seems very much a convenient excuse for her exhibitionism. From the point of view of such a reading, Triamoure's actions seem very much along the lines of the coquettish 'Oh my, isn't it hot in here . . .' school of seduction techniques.

However, if we widen our focus beyond just this one passage for a moment, and consider how this connection between heat and the erotic operates with the narrative as a whole, we can see a more intriguing and influential theme emerge. The connection between the heat of the weather and the actions of our two lovers can also be witnessed in the events that lead up to their first encounter. After riding away from Caerleon, and exhausted after extricating himself from the mire in a fen, Launfal takes refuge from the heat of the late morning (*undertide*) by resting under a tree:[12]

> Poverly the knight to horse gan spring.
> For to drive away lokinge,
> He rood toward the west.
> The wether was hot the undertide;
> He lighte adoun and gan abide
> Under a fair forest.

---

[10] *Troilus and Criseyde*, ed. Larry D. Benson, *The Riverside Chaucer*, 3rd edn (Oxford, 1988), lines 1247–51.
[11] Helen Phillips, 'Love', *A Companion to Chaucer*, ed. Peter Brown (London: Blackwell, 2004), pp. 281–95 (p. 286).
[12] *Undertide* is a time of day that is also associated with an encounter with the faery in *Sir Orfeo* (line 41), where Herodis falls asleep under the *ympe-tree* and encounters the faery-hunt.

> And for hete of the wedere
> His mantel he felde togidere
> And sette hoim doun to reste.
> Thus sat the knight in symplité
> In the shadwe under a tre,
> Ther that him likede best.
>
> As he sat in sorrow and sore
> He sawe come out of holtes hore
> Gentil maidens two. (*Sir Launfal*, 217–31)

We might expect, if we were reading another genre of medieval literature, that Launfal might fall asleep and encounter a dream-vision that would involve some kind of gloss upon, or even a solution to, his present worldly cares and worries. Instead, he encounters what in many ways appears to be a waking vision of exotic beauty, and an adventure that certainly would not seem at all out of place if it were to be found within a dream. Triamoure's two maidens, themselves dreamy visions of exotic beauty, greet Launfal and lead him off towards his fateful rendezvous with their mistress. In this scene, which acts very much to set the dream-like mood of the following seduction scene, the heat of the weather again plays an important narrative role. It is the fact that the *wether was hot the undertide* that leads Launfal to rest under the tree, and this is re-emphasised when we are told that *for hete of the wedere/ His mantel he felde togidere/ And sette hoim doun to reste*.

From my reading of the scenes of both the seduction and its arboreal prelude within *Sir Launfal*, there seems to emerge an intriguing correlation between the temperature of the day and the behaviour of both Launfal and Triamoure. Launfal's encounter with Triamoure is as dependent upon the heat of the day as Triamoure's actions are, suggesting some kind of important role that this motif of ambient heat plays in their amorous encounter. This potential connection between heat and love, or more particularly, sexual desire, is what I would like to explore further in the remainder of this essay.

A possible correlation between heat and sexual desire also seems to be at play in another, decidedly more sexually repressed, Middle English narrative: that of Margery Kempe. At the beginning of the eleventh chapter of her *Book*, Margery finds herself entangled in a rather heated situation with her long-suffering husband:

> It befel upon a Fryday on Mydsomyr Evyn in rygth hot wedyr, as this creatur was komyng fro Yorkeward beryng a botel wyth bere in hir hand and hir husbond a cake in hys bosom, he askyd hys wyfe this qwestyon, 'Margery, if her come a man wyth a swerd and wold smyte of myn hed les than I schulde comown kendly wyth yow as I have do befor, seyth me trewth of yowr consciens – for ye sey ye wyl not lye – whether wold ye suffyr myn hed to be smet of er ellys suffyr me to medele wyth yow agen as I dede sumtyme?' [Margery replies that she would rather see him dead than see them both return to their uncleanness. She asks him to swear a vow of chastity, but he refuses] ... Than went thei forth to Brydlyngtonward in rygth hoot wedyr, the fornseyd creatur havyng gret sorwe and gret dred for hyr chastité. And, as thei cam be a cros, hyr husbond sett hym down undyr the cros, clepyng hys wyfe

unto hym and seyng this wordys onto hir, 'Margery, grawnt me my desyr, and I schal grawnt yow yowr desyr. My fyrst desyr is that we schal lyn stylle togedyr in o bed as we han do befor; the secunde that ye schal pay my dettys er ye go to Jherusalem; and the thrydde that ye schal etyn and drynkyn wyth me on the Fryday as ye wer wont to don.' 'Nay ser,' sche seyd, 'to breke the Fryday I wyl nevyr grawnt yow whyl I leve.' 'Wel,' he seyd, 'than schal I medyl yow ageyn.' [Margery prays to God for advice; she then offers to pay her husband's debts in return for his agreeing to the vow of chastity – an offer with which he is satisfied – one debt can be seen to pay another here].[13]

In this episode we can see once again a connection between the heat of summer and erotic desire. Margery's husband's repeated threats to *medele wyth* her, and his demands that she *grawnt me my desyr*, make explicit his sexual intentions. In a similar manner to *Sir Launfal*, it seems that there is again an environmental component contributing to his reasons for raising the issue. The emphasis that Margery places upon the *rygth hot wedyr* as the couple leave from York suggests that she views this hot weather as being at least a contributing factor to her husband's behaviour. And after their first exchange, the connection is stressed once again when she tells us that they made towards Bridlington *in rygth hoot wedyr, the fornseyd creatur havyng gret sorwe and gret dred for hyr chastité*. The link here between the temperature and her fears for her chastity suggests that there exists some connection between the heat of the day and her husband's continual demands for her to resume her marital duties. This connection with the heat of summer is perhaps foregrounded in the passage by the setting of the events upon *Mydsomyr Evyn* (traditionally 23 June), the night before the longest day of the year.[14] Summer, and the hot weather that the season brings, seem to occupy a particular place in the rhetoric of love and desire.

Both *Sir Launfal* and *The Book of Margery Kempe* draw upon a conceptual association linking the heat of summer with sexual desire. That these two texts are making use of a similar understanding of this connection suggests that this may be indicative of a literary trope connecting heat, summer and lust. Just such a relationship is expressed at the beginning of Sir Thomas Malory's 'Knight of the Cart' episode, where he digresses on the connections between summer, true love, heat and sexual desire:

> But nowadayes men can nat love sevennyght but they muste have all their desyres. That love may nat endure by reson, and where they bethe sone accorded and hasty, heete sone keelyth. And ryght so faryth the love nowadayes, sone hote sone colde. Thys is no stabylté. But the olde love was nat so. For men and women coude love togydirs seven yerys, and no lycoures lustis was betwyxte them, and than was love trouthe and faythefulnes. And so in lyke wyse was used such love in kynge Arthurs dayes.
>
> Wherefore I lykken love nowadayes unto sommer and wynter: for, lyke as the

---

[13] *The Book of Margery Kempe*, ed. Lynn Staley, TEAMS METS (Kalamazoo, 1996), chapter 11, pp. 37–9.

[14] There exists perhaps another example of a connection between the heat of summer and sexual desire in Margery's account of her sexual temptation with a fellow worshipper on St Margaret's Eve (20 July), related in chapter 4 of her narrative, pp. 28–30.

tone ys colde and the othir ys hote, so faryth love nowadayes. And therefore all ye
that be lovers, calle unto youre remembraunce the monethe of May, lyke as ded
quene Gwenyver, for whom I make here a lytyll mencion, that whyle she lyved she
was a trew lover, and therefor she had a good ende.[15]

Here Malory constructs May, and thus late spring, as the ideal season of love. May
is neither *colde* nor *hote*, but rather consists of a happy medium of the two, and it is
the month's moderate temperature that lies at the core of Malory's seasonal metaphor of love. Malory is, of course, making use of the endemic medieval tradition
positing May as the month of love, a tradition that influenced all genres of literature from the courtly romance to the popular lyric. Malory, however, goes further
than simply perpetuating this association, and provides a comparative gloss on the
merits of May, comparing it with the seasons of winter and summer on the basis of
the effects that temperature has on human desire. Malory views the influence of
heat, or at least the excessive unrelenting heat of summer, as being the cause of
what he terms *lycoures lustis* in men (and women), echoing the concerns that
Kempe holds regarding the behaviour of her husband. As is often his wont, Malory
chooses to interpret the connection between heat and lust in a nostalgic and moralising context, but he also articulates a clear view of the connection between seasons
and types of love: while spring (May) appears to be the season of true or virtuous
love, summer seems to be viewed as the season of immoderate and lecherous love.

Underlying this connection between heat and disproportionate love, or lust, is
of course the theory of the four humours:

> The physiology of the human body, and the medical treatment of it, were fitted
> into the traditional way the world was represented. The four elements, and the
> dual quality that each of them possessed, were correlated with the four humours
> taken from the Hippocratic school, and it was this system, developed in the greatest detail by Galen, which was to constitute the foundation of medieval science.[16]

The associations of behaviour and bodily attributes that were associated with the
humours and their corresponding seasons are revealing: summer is linked to fire,
yellow bile, and the choleric temperament, while spring is allied with the air,
blood and sanguinity. Both seasons are marked out by their association with heat,
differing in that while spring is hot and moist, summer is construed as excessively
hot and thus also overly dry. These seasonal characteristics also impinge upon the
understanding of human sexuality. Joan Cadden comments on the essential
humoural differences between men and women under the Galenic system.[17] Men
were considered to be warm in nature while women tended towards the cooler
humoural temperament. The act of copulation was viewed by many medical
writers as an essential part of the bodily system, regulating both moisture and heat
in both participants: 'just as sneezing keeps the body's level of phlegm in balance,
sexual release regulates the level of generative superfluities. Conversely, the reten-

---

[15] Thomas Malory, *Morte Darthur*, ed. Eugène Vinaver, *Malory: Works* (Oxford, 1977), XVIII, 25.
[16] Jacquart and Thomasset, *Sexuality*, p. 48.
[17] Joan Cadden, 'Western Medicine and Natural Philosophy', *The Handbook of Medieval Sexuality*, ed. Vera L. Bullough and James A. Brundage (New York, 1996), pp. 51–80.

tion of such substances causes imbalance and thus ill health.'[18] In appreciating the perils of excessive heat, we can see that Malory's distinction between spring and summer love is based in the Galenic conception of how heat affects the human body and sexual behaviour. Such a concern for the regulation of bodily moisture can also be seen to underlie the advice found in the popular *Secreta Secretorum*, in which men are encouraged to partake of baths, blood-letting and women during the moist seasons (winter and spring), while being warned to avoid such dangerously dehydrating activities as much as possible during the summer months.[19] Summer, then, was not viewed as a time for love, but rather a time of immoderate lust. Jacquart and Thomasset note the advice of medieval medical texts such as the *Pantegni* and the *Canon* of Avicenna, which advise that, in 'accordance with the rule *similia similibus*, the best season for the pleasures of Venus is the spring, since it is hot and moist in nature, and is thus the time when the sanguine humour predominates. Summer and autumn, during which the bile and melancholy abound respectively, are hardly propitious times'.[20]

It was not only sexual behaviour that was affected by an excess of heat: it was also thought to lead to madness and irrational behaviour. In Thomas Hoccleve's semi-autobiographical *Compleinte and a Dialogue*, we witness how Hoccleve's narrator is plagued by the hazardous reputation of the heat of summer. Although he has recovered from his earlier debilitating mental illness, the narrator is beset by the rumour and gossip of his neighbours, who fear that his madness will return:

> Thus spake manie oone and seide by me:
> 'Althouȝ from him his siknesse sauage
> Withdrawen and passed as for a time be,
> Resorte it wole, namely in suche age
> As he is of,' and thanne my visage
> Began to glowe for the woo and fere.
> Tho wordis, hem unwar, cam to myn eere.
>
> 'Whanne passinge hete is,' quod þei, 'trustiþ this,
> Assaile him wole aȝein that maladie.'
> And ȝit, parde, thei token hem amis.
> Noon effecte at al took her prophecie.
> Manie someris bene past sithen remedie
> Of that God of his grace me purueide.
> Thankid be God, it shoop not as þei seide.[21]

In Hoccleve's poem we again see the connection between *passinge hete*, *someris* and mental *siknesse sauage*. Although, as Hoccleve complains, while the heat of the summer has not in fact triggered a relapse of his madness, his neighbours' belief that the summer heat will eventually do just that is indicative of a widely held

---

[18] Cadden, 'Western Medicine', p. 58.
[19] *Secreta Secretorum: Nine English Versions*, ed. M. Manzalaoui, vol. 1, EETS OS 276 (London, 1977), cited in Archibald, 'Did Knights have Baths?', p. 110.
[20] Jacquart and Thomasset, *Sexuality*, pp. 145–6.
[21] Thomas Hoccleve, 'My Compleinte', ed. Roger Ellis, *'My Compleinte' and Other Poems* (Exeter, 2001), pp. 117–18, lines 85–98.

belief in the connection between heat and irrational behaviour. Lust, glossed by Malory as that *love may nat endure by reson*, is excessive and unreasonable desire, fuelled by an excessive degree of heat within the body of the amatory miscreants.

Summer is constructed in these texts as a component part of a wider rhetoric of the seasons of love, predicated upon the physiological theory of the four humours. In comparison to the way that medieval literature can be seen to make use of spring, and May in particular, for its reputation as the ideal erotic season, summer seems to hold a baser, yet equally important, place within the rhetoric of love. As a season of irrational or immoderate sexual desire, when pious women such as Margery must fend off the unwelcome advances of their husbands, and during which, as Malory admonishes, *men can nat love sevennyght but they muste have all their desyres*, summer stands as a cautionary foil to its more moist and tame predecessor, spring. In this context, then, we can return to our tableau of Triamoure's seductive ungirdling before the entranced Launfal, and question again what exactly is the focus of his gaze. If, as I have argued above, it is not Triamoure's breasts themselves that are the erotic foci of the scene, then perhaps we need to dramatically reconceptualise our understanding of the erotic nature of the scene. If not Triamoure's rapidly descending décolletage, what then, if anything, is erotic about the scene?

The nature of the erotic is, as has been discussed earlier in this volume, continually evasive and in many cases highly particular to the individual reader or audience. However, what seems to be common to many definitions of what is erotic is an element of transgression. Often that which is viewed as erotic is somewhat transgressive of the norms of conventional sexuality, positioning the erotic at the margins of accepted behaviour, perhaps encapsulated best in the modern notion of that which is considered to be risqué. With this in mind, if we re-examine Launfal's first encounter with Triamoure, from his resting in the forest to his meeting her in her pavilion, the element most transgressive of medieval norms is in fact the *hete of the wedere*. Is it perhaps possible that it is in this trope of the excessive heat of summer, with the transgressive sexual behaviour that this foregrounds, that the medieval reader would have found the erotic thrust of the passage? The emphasis upon the heat of summer in the text certainly suggests such a reading, and leads us to a medieval understanding of the Launfal episode as erotic in terms of its transgression of the usual norms of the literary seasonal rhetoric of love. Where one might in romance expect a knight to encounter his lady in the springtime, in an atmosphere of virtuous love, when, as Malory tells us, *was love trouthe and faythefulnes*, instead we witness their meeting in the season of *lycoures lustis*, signalling a very different kind of relationship between the two lovers than one might expect to find in a romance.

However, by returning once more to the underlying connection between the weather and the bodily humours, I feel that we can take this reading of the erotic nature of the scene yet one step further. While the rhetorical trope of summer, as envisaged above, seems to colour a medieval reading of the events with erotic overtones, there is also Triamoure's own nature to be considered. Why, we ask again, does she remove her clothes? Is it in fact due to the hot weather, thereby positing the causal factor of her behaviour as an external force, or can we envisage, perhaps alongside a medieval audience, that she acts thus due to her own internal humoural heat, thus making explicit her own excessively 'hot' nature? As a faery-mistress, is Triamoure by her very nature 'hot'? Do her sexually aggressive actions, transgressive in terms of female norms, present her as innately erotic in her own right? Her active wooing of Launfal, and her highly territorial behaviour during their relationship, supports just such a reading. Triamoure's transgressive nature is also, of course, marked out by her accoutrements, origin and lineage: *Here fadir was King of Fairie/ Of Occient,* presenting a conflation of faery-lover and exotic sexuality and opulence.

If we attribute her actions to her own internal heat, rather than to the external heat of summer (although, of course the former is necessarily exacerbated by the later), then we find yet another erotic resonance within the text, for hot women in the Middle Ages, by their very nature, were considered sexually attractive. Michael Scot, in the *Physionomia*, discusses the aspect of heat in relation to the attractiveness and sexual appetite of women. Drawing on the tradition found in Arab medical texts, Scot presents a number of portraits of different female dispositions, commenting that in order to find the ideal female sexual partner, a man must look for the following:

> ... the highest degree of heat must be sought in woman. The best predispositions are found together in the young girl of more than twelve years of age who has lost her virginity. Small and firm breasts, thick hair in the right places and a highly coloured complexion are good signs. Such a woman likes to behave insolently, shows no sign of piety and is capable of getting drunk; she enjoys singing, going for walks and having fun. She is in a permanent state of desire which she can satisfy in the sexual act. Since her menstrual blood is not very copious, her periods are irregular and she rarely becomes pregnant.[22]

Once again we find this conception of female sexual aggression grounded in the physiological thought of the period. Such women, owing to their humoural heat and dryness, were thought to be inclined to seek out the carnal act continually, seeking to obtain the moisture contained within the male sperm, in order to remedy their own innate dryness. Hot-blooded women, then, are intrinsically erotic, for the reason that they transgress many of the established and conventional norms of female sexual behaviour. Triamoure, in her active and aggressive behaviour, both sexual and otherwise, is suggestive of just the kind of hot-blooded attractive behaviour that Scot describes above, an association that would have been much more readily available to Chestre's medieval audience than to a reader today.

One might suggest, in conclusion, that Chestre's depiction of Triamoure partakes of an established medieval rhetoric of the erotic, drawing upon the negative (depending upon one's point of view) sexual stereotypes of both the season of summer and of Triamoure as an excessively choleric woman. Both of these tropes seem to carry a certain erotic force, pointing towards an understanding of the text as erotically charged in a manner that is not immediately apparent to the modern

---

[22] Jacquart and Thomasset, *Sexuality*, pp. 143–4.

reader. Triamoure is indeed presented as being a 'hot' woman – not only in a modern sense, but also in a medieval one. She is depicted in erotic terms not only on the level of appearance – her lily-white skin, rose-like complexion, hair shining as gold-wire, and beautiful attire – but also in her behaviour. Through her striptease on encountering Launfal – aimed at both the knight and at the audience – Triamoure reveals her hot-blooded choleric nature. Highly fitting for a fairy-lover, this hot-blooded temperament manifests in her initial sexual advances, in the highly territorial constraints that she places upon her human lover, and in her jealous punishment of Gwenere at the end of the tale.

How's Your Father?
Sex and the Adolescent Girl in Sir Degarré

MARGARET ROBSON

MY FOCUS IN THIS ESSAY is ignorance and its converse, knowledge: most particularly I want to look at adolescent knowledge about sex and the body. In this essay I shall be focussing on the development of women. There is an important distinction to be made, however, between what is privately known and what can be articulated publicly: society dictates not what can be done (sexual practices remain largely the same, the results remain the same), but what may be said to be done. This is particularly problematic for the adolescent; how is the developing awareness of sexual identity, sexual desire, to be understood? How do girls find out about their bodies and their desires in a culture where practices such as masturbation are typically subject to prohibition and remain unvoiced? The unspeakable has to obtrude itself into narratives (consciousness?) in some way other than the verbal. One of the most telling forms of communication is through the use of body language, and body language is most eloquent on the subject of sex.

The story of *Sir Degarré* is as follows.

The widowed king of Brittany, who will not allow his eligible daughter to marry anyone unless the suitor is able to defeat him, is met riding with his daughter to a ceremony held each year to commemorate his dead wife. On the way, the princess declares that she must leave the retinue to answer a call of nature and while subsequently lost in the forest she is violently raped by a fairy knight who declares himself her lover and the father of the son she will bear from this union.

The princess reveals her pregnancy to her maid, afraid that the populace will attribute paternity to her father, and the maid arranges for the baby to be exposed, wrapping with him a talismanic pair of gloves, which the fairy knight has sent to the princess: the gloves (which will fit only the princess) are accompanied by the injunction that the boy should love only the woman whom they will fit. Degarré's upbringing is divided into two parts: until the age of ten he lives with the married sister of the hermit who discovered the foundling, and for the next ten years with the hermit himself.

At the age of twenty, Degarré leaves the hermitage to seek his family, having been given the gloves, money and letter with which he was found. He goes unarmed but for an oaken staff, which he cuts himself, and although he is offered the hand of a maiden after he has killed a local dragon, he declines, as he wishes only to find his parents.

Degarré's mother is still being fought for by her father and suitors; however Degarré defeats the old man and marries his mother. It is not until they are about to go to bed that he remembers the gloves and confides in the old king; his bride is revealed as his mother and the princess tells her father the tale of Degarré's begetting. Degarré vows to find his father and his mother gives him the sword, without a point, which the fairy knight had given her at the time of the rape.

On the quest to find his father, Degarré lodges for a night in a castle of maidens (the only man there is a dwarf), where no one speaks and he sleeps an enchanted sleep after listening to the music of a harp. The lady reveals that she is being besieged by a suitor whom she does not love and who has threatened to ravish her. She declares that she will reward Degarré with her hand and her inheritance if he can kill the knight; this he does, but although he betrothes himself to the lady, he first wants to find his father.

He finds and fights his father, during which recognition is achieved by the pointless sword. Degarré tells his father that they must go and find his mother who is in mourning; the tale ends there.

The princess's ability to speak her own story, to recognise her own desires, begins with a piece of body language that begs attention.

> Here chaumberleyn ȝhe cleped hire to,
> And oþer dammaiseles two,
> And seide þat hii moste aliȝte
> To don here nedes and hire riȝte. (49–52)[1]

These lines provide one of the most extraordinary intrusions in courtly poetry in Middle English. On a solemn occasion, the princess effectively halts the ceremony because she has to answer a call of nature. The idea that a ceremonial occasion may be derailed by such needs is anathema to the idea of ceremony itself: as Mary Douglas notes, 'A natural way of investing a social occasion with dignity is to hide organic processes.'[2] Even when ceremony is celebrating the body, be that in marriage or in death, the physical body remains consistently absent: the feasting, or fasting, the ritual and the clothing all act as signifiers for the changes that the body is undergoing; but seldom, in courtly literature, does the body present itself as a site of physical process.[3] In this tale, however, the girl's body is absolutely central; it is the site that is fought over (by her father and any man who has an interest in her inheritance); it is the site of shame (the hidden pregnancy, the hidden child); and it is also the locus that produces the solution to the gap in the

---

[1] All references are to the edition found in *Medieval English Romances*, Part Two, ed. N. Jacobs and A. V. C. Schmidt (London, 1980).
[2] *Natural Symbols* (Harmondsworth, 1973), p. 12.
[3] Another exception is provided by the lay *Sir Gowther* (ed. Maldwyn Mills, *Six Middle English Romances* (London, 1973)), where the infant is seen being breast-fed by a number of wet nurses as well as his own mother, whose nipple he bites off in the process.

transmission of property, title and goods. At the end of the tale, though, we have a woman speaking her own desire for the man whom she has enchanted.

The princess inserts herself into this tale firstly as a body that cannot be ignored, for she announces her physicality in a way that is inappropriate, both to ceremony and the genre, and which begs the question: what is it she stops to do, and why is she so outspoken on the matter? This is an issue that criticism has not engaged with: it is almost as though her statement of need has never been made. What has tended to happen is that criticism has moved – seamlessly – from the journey to the abbey, to the rape. James Simpson, for example, summarises the story thus:

> The story of *Sir Degarré* runs as follows: on the anniversary of the death of a queen, the widower king of Brittany and his beloved daughter ride through a forest to the abbey where his wife is buried; the daughter's retinue is detached from the king's and the daughter from her retinue.[4]

This passive voice does not reflect the events, but it is a version that is commonly promulgated.[5] Nicholas Jacobs and A. V. C. Schmidt are also very careful in their reading of the princess's announcement of her bodily needs. They note that the chamberlain is, unusually, a woman, but without offering any evidence as to why they have come to this conclusion.[6] The narrative is unclear on this issue, for it simply states that the princess called 'here chaumberleyn/ And oþer dammaiseles two' (49–50). The whole issue of the princess's announcement of her bodily needs is elided, avoided and disguised.[7]

What call of nature is being answered here? The obvious assumption is that the princess needed either to urinate or defecate; while one can hardly blame criticism for its unwillingness to engage with the toilet needs of princesses, surely the point

---

4 'Violence, Narrative and Proper Name: *Sir Degaré*, "The Tale of Sir Gareth of Orkney", and the *Folie Tristan d'Oxford*', *The Spirit of Medieval English Popular Romance*, ed. A. Putter and J. Gilbert (Harlow, 2000), pp. 122–41 (p. 127). See also M. J. Donovan: 'On the anniversary of his wife's death, he [the King of Brittany] sets out to visit her grave and while travelling loses his daughter, who with two attendants wanders in the forest and finally on to a heath' (*The Breton Lay: A Guide To Varieties* (Notre Dame, 1969), p. 159).

5 In fact criticism has tended to read the tale as a typical 'hero myth'; John Finlayson's 1984 appraisal is remarkably similar to James Simpson's conclusions of 2000. Finlayson comments: 'In essence, therefore, *Sir Degarré* is a romance of adventure which conforms to the loss of status-restoration pattern. Through his adventures the hero establishes his prowess and identity and the work ends on an appropriate restoration of harmony. Apart from being short and having the marvellous element of a fairy-birth episode (whose potentials are completely underdeveloped and subsequently ignored) *Sir Degarré* is in no way substantially different from any other *roman d'aventure*' ('The Form of the Middle English Breton Lay', *The Chaucer Review* 19 (1984–5), pp. 352–67 (p. 357)).

6 *Medieval English Romances*, p. 241, n. 49.

7 The insertion of the female body into the text is sometimes recognised by such elision, or even distaste: while the female body is present, references to organic processes imply that the reader does not want to know about such matters. I offer the following comment on *Sir Gowther* from M. J. Donovan: 'Although it opens promisingly as the Duke of Austria marries and amid great splendour holds a tournament, it soon loses the reader in the business of Gowther's nursery' (*The Breton Lay*, p. 228). While it seems unsporting to criticise a text published in 1969 for not demonstrating feminist sympathies, such criticism has informed so much of the way in which we have read that I offer it as a measure of the distance it has been necessary to travel to be able to think of an alternative to male-centred readings.

of this extraordinary intrusion of the body into the ceremonial is that we are forced to consider the matter? In reading fabliaux, one makes frequent visits to the privy; it would seem that it is not the act, but rather the genre-bending that causes the discomfort.[8] The combination of princess and ceremony ought to mean that we are not dealing with organic processes, but we cannot escape the narrative fact that the rape and the whole of the subsequent tale, which Finlayson classifies as a *roman d'aventure*, is predicated on a comfort stop.[9] So what *does* the princess stop to do? We are never told: but we are, emphatically, being told of her possession of a physical body; this is where the erotic begins, with attention drawn to the girl's pubescent body.

At the opening of the tale we are presented with a solemn celebration of the anniversary of the mother's death; but we are told, obliquely, that this day marks another anniversary, for it is also the princess's birthday (22–3). The mother's death in childbirth is an annual reminder to the princess of the potential danger of motherhood, a danger that we know will confront the princess at some point because she is her father's only heir (17–18), and as such, she is a conduit for his lands and money.[10] But we are also assured that this is not a prospect that the princess must face soon, for even though she is of age (24), her father will not allow her to marry anyone unless that person is able to defeat him in battle, and as no one has yet been able to do so, she remains, symbolically, a child.

One of the issues that I want to focus on in the tale is an investigation of ideas about age. There are types of behaviour acceptable in children but not in adults, and vice versa, but adolescence is a time when these expectations collide and are either strengthened or collapsed. When is a girl an adult? When she is of marriageable age? When she is of childbearing age? When she has had sex? When the announcement of organic needs is no longer appropriate? Or is a girl an adult when she is able to articulate her sexual desires?

The princess in Sir Degarré provides an interesting example of the collision between childhood and adulthood, so I want to turn now to the way in which she and her father are presented.

There is a whole range of problems suggested by the varying perspectives we are given of father and daughter: the king is described as though he were a young and powerful knight, a man in his prime whom no-one can defeat (7–16). This is not, necessarily, a contradiction of his role as a father, although it stretches credibility that he is being presented in precisely the same terms twenty years later (289). Although we are introduced to the king as the widowed father of a girl of marriageable age, he is first presented as though he were his daughter's champion:

---

[8] See Geoffrey Chaucer, *The Miller's Tale* and *The Merchant's Tale* (*The Canterbury Tales*, ed. L. D. Benson et al., *The Riverside Chaucer*, 3rd edn (Boston, MA, 1987); all citations refer to this edition); the bed-trick of the former is made possible when the Miller's wife gets up to go to the toilet and May's love-letters are read – and disposed of – there.

[9] Finlayson, 'Breton Lay', p. 357.

[10] Unlike Simpson and Finlayson, Schmidt and Jacobs read the tale as being essentially bourgeois, demonstrating a 'preoccupation with money throughout the tale' (p. 241, n. 28). Their comment that such preoccupations are better disguised in aristocratic texts does not, I think, fit with the aristocratic obsession with lineage, which is an obsession with money and property by another means, an obsession that this text manifestly shares.

> Ac þe king answered ever
> þat no man schal here have never
> But ȝif he mai in turneying
> Him out of his sadel bring
> And maken him lessen hise stiropes bayne. (29–33)

This motif of the father who will not allow his daughter to marry unless the suitor can defeat him in a contest inevitably links the tale to those which are predicated on father–daughter incest.[11] This incest motif is emphasised later in the narrative by another near-miss at incest when Degarré marries his mother but is saved, at the last minute, from consummating the marriage. In *Sir Degarré*, the incest is displaced, rather than averted, and it is to the princess's absence from the company following her announcement of her bodily needs that I must return.

When the princess leaves the retinue with her maidens she is raped in the woods. There is a displacement at work here that is worth commenting on, for the princess's departure from the retinue is deliberate; she gets herself lost, even from her companions, presumably after she has performed her call of nature, and it is they who fall asleep while she wanders further into the forest, picking flowers and listening to the birdsong (53–78).[12] Again, this text begs the question: is this princess a child or an adult? We are told that she is of marriageable age, but also that she behaves like a child, in that she is allowed to articulate her bodily needs. However, this child, picking flowers in the woods, is also represented as thinking like an adult woman, for she is not only afraid of wild animals harming her, but of men doing so (88). Her consciousness of the threat posed to an isolated girl by a man is the first indication we are given of her knowledge of what might happen between men and women; and this implicit recognition is closely followed by the explicit. The arrival of the fairy-knight recalls her father, for he is emphatically a man of arms, in his prime; the narrative further identifies him as her father,

---

[11] For an authoritative discussion of incest in medieval narrative see Elizabeth Archibald's *Incest and The Medieval Imagination* (Oxford, 2001) and 'The Flight From Incest: Two Late Classical Precursors of The Constance Theme', *The Chaucer Review* 20 (1985–6), pp. 259–72. Schmidt and Jacobs link the contest with the father for the daughter's hand with the Greek myth of the marriage of Pelops and Hippodameia, whose father, Oenomaus, may have himself fallen in love with Hippodameia. However, there is another Greek myth that seems to me to bear closer resemblance to *Sir Degarré*, and that is the myth of the birth of Theseus. In this tale Theseus' grandfather, Pittheus, is instrumental in bringing Aegeus to the bed of his daughter, Aethra. Aegeus' family narrative is one blighted with incest and punishment, for he is the brother of Procne and Philomela, while Pittheus is one of the sons of Pelops. The incest motif is carried on to the next generation in the family with the attempted seduction of Theseus' son, Hippolytos, by his second wife, Phaedra. In the birth myth of Theseus, the recognition tokens given to Aethra by Aegeus for their son are sword and sandals (see R. Graves, *Dictionary of Greek Mythology*, 2 vols (Harmondsworth, 1955), vol. 1, pp. 323–5 for Theseus and vol. 2, pp. 31–6 for Oenomaus and Hippodameia).

[12] The 'noon-tide demon' is a feature of many tales, most notably *Sir Orfeo* and *Sir Gowther*. For an examination of this motif, see J. Friedman, 'Eurydice, Herodis and The Noon-Day Demon', *Speculum* 41 (1966), pp. 22–9. The princess's response to the forest is an interesting one, which again suggests her ambiguous state. Forests occupy an important place in myths and stories; children are abandoned in them; women meet their lovers in them; men run mad in them; forests have a status that is always meaningful and mark some kind of transitional state. For a discussion of this, see Yi-fu Tuan, *Landscapes of Fear* (Oxford, 1980). The princess behaves in a cross-over fashion: the child enjoying nature, the woman afraid of isolation, the adolescent confused about the world.

because, as we are told: 'þer nas non in al þe kinges londe/ More apert man þan was he' (96–7).[13] The fairy-knight reveals to her that he has loved her long (105) and that he has seized this opportunity to become her lover. We know that the king has jealously guarded his daughter, refusing men access to her, and while this does not, of course, preclude someone with magical powers from doing so, the knight has had to wait for the opportunity that the maiden has created, in order to become her lover. It is as though he has been waiting for her sign, and that sign was the announcement of her bodily needs, made in the presence of her father. This narrative gap, the lost princess, the lost time in the woods, provides the king with exactly what he needs, both literally and figuratively, in order to keep his bloodline pure and keep lands, money and title in the family. The heiress, as I have remarked, is the conduit for all this, but in order to function as such, she has to have reached puberty, childbearing age. While her father has been fighting off potential suitors for her hand, he has not yet been able to secure the succession; he can only do so by begetting an heir himself, and in the absence of his wife, his daughter must supply him with one.[14] But it is she who tells him that the time is ripe; her body is no longer entirely child-like, she leaves the tribute to her mother as a necessary step in the way to adult sexual life.

The encounter in the forest with the fairy-knight results in a brutal rape. The knight declares:

> 'And now we beþ us selve her;
> þou best mi lemman ar þou go
> Weþer þe likeþ wel or wo.' (106–8)

We are left in no doubts about the princess's unwillingness: the rape is as violent as the fairy-king's abduction of Herodis.[15] Here, in *Sir Degarré*, a daughter cannot consent to incest, for such consent would lead to inevitable tragedy.[16] While it is

---

[13] Finlayson comments that 'the fairy-knight might as easily have been a mortal rapist for all the difference his fairy origins make to the nature and quality of the action and poem' ('The Breton Lay', p. 359). See also Cheryl Colopy, '*Sir Degarré*: A Fairy Tale Oedipus', *Studies in Short Fiction* 17 (1982), pp. 31–9, where she observes: 'The forest setting and the many ambiguous features of the fairy knight can encourage us to see the rape as a fantasy of wish-fulfilment: the daughter "dreams" that her own father appears in the forest and rapes her, a projection of her own intense feelings for him. Some stylistic details would even support this – similar adjectives, not used elsewhere in the poem, describe both the king and the fairy knight' (p. 33).

[14] The conflation of the role of wife and daughter is a commonplace one. Phyllis Chester notes: 'Women are encouraged to commit incest as a way of life. As opposed to marrying our fathers, we marry men like our fathers, ... men who are older than us, are taller than us, are stronger than us... our fathers' (quoted in J. Herman and L. Hirschman, 'Father-Daughter Incest', *Signs* 2 (1977), pp. 735–56 (p. 740). The article also comments on the practice of daughters replacing their dead mothers and becoming wives (see p. 748). Rosalind Coward writes: 'The power which the heroine achieves is the power of the mother, the daughter has taken the mother's place' (*Female Desire: Women's Sexuality Today* (London, 1984), p. 196).

[15] See *Sir Orfeo* in *Sir Orfeo and Sir Launfal*, ed. L. Johnson and E. Williams (Leeds, 1984). For a 'disguised' rape, see the tale of Arthur's begetting by Thomas Malory, ed. E. Vinaver, *Malory: Works* (Oxford, 1970). Arthur's begetting is modelled on Zeus's begetting of Heracles on Alcmene (Graves, *Dictionary of Greek Mythology*, vol. 2, pp. 84–7).

[16] Elizabeth Archibald writes: 'I do not know any romances or extended narratives involving mother–son incest, potential or actual, which focus on the mother, or in which the mother initiates the incest' ('Imagination', p. 134). This is not true of exempla, as Archibald points out, the

not always the case in sexual relations, ignorance can provide a get-out clause, so that the clearer it is that the princess is raped – and here it is absolutely unequivocal – the more 'chaste' the princess remains.[17] The narrative provides us with a way of maintaining the princess's honour and thus that of her child, who is then able to succeed to his (grand)father's lands.[18]

The princess, then, has provided her father with the heir he needs; the fairy-knight reveals her pregnancy to her immediately after the rape (116–17) and the child is, of course, to be a boy, an heir in his own right rather than a make-shift link. The practicalities of maintaining a direct line of inheritance done with, the fairy-knight/king can rejoin the retinue, as do the princess and her maidens who are found by the two squires whom her father has sent to look for the women (141–4). The service for the late queen is conducted and the king and his daughter ride side-by-side back to the castle.

The passage that follows this again seems to me extraordinary, in that it reveals, quite explicitly, the princess's knowledge of her father's incestuous desires and, even more importantly, the extent of her own knowledge about sex and its consequences. The section opens with a description of her swelling womb, which she tries to hide (157–8). Clearly, pregnancy is no mystery to her, for when she is confronted by one of her maidservants about her tears, she reveals to her, and to us, what the matter is:

> 'Ich have ever ȝete ben meke and milde;
> Lo, now ich am wiþ quike childe.
> Ȝif ani man hit underȝete,
> Men wolde sai bi sti and street
> Þat mi fader þe king hit wan;
> And I ne was nevere aqueint wiþ man.' (165–70)

Gregory legends providing a famous example. While mother–son incest is rare, there are relations that are contiguous to it that are punished. The model for these is the Potiphar's wife motif, which provides the pattern for Morgause's relations with Lamorak and Guinevere's with Launfal in Thomas Chestre's version, where the promiscuous Guinevere is blinded by the fairy Triamour (see Malory, *Works*, and Thomas Chestre, *Sir Launfal*, ed. A. J. Bliss (London and Edinburgh, 1960). For Potiphar's Wife, see Genesis 39:1–20).

[17] The same still holds true today. Corinne Saunders writes: 'The work of the lawyer Susan Estrich, for example, highlights the fact that the law has favoured classic cases of "stranger rape", where the woman is violently attacked by an unknown individual, while less clear-cut instances, those she classes as "simple rape", are often not prosecuted – cases where force is less apparent, the woman appears provocative, or the rapist is not a stranger' (*Rape and Ravishment in The Literature of Medieval England* (Cambridge, 2001), p. 7). It is also the case that the fact of her pregnancy, to a medieval audience, would indicate consensual sex, for pregnancy could not be achieved without it (see J. A. Brundage, *Law, Sex and Society in Medieval Europe* (Chicago, 1987), p. 450).

[18] Corinne Saunders has argued that the tale rewrites the princess's rape through its product, Degarré. She writes: 'The romance's ambiguous and shifting perspective on sexuality is to an extent typical of the way that the archetypically male, often misogynistic, structures of the genre function, but also reflects the ambivalence of contemporary attitudes to rape. Because the woman is not in the end devalued through an abduction but valued through her son, the crime loses much of its impact, and as the predestined conception of a hero, the rape can no longer be condemned' (*Rape*, p. 216). In fact the tale tacitly recognises Degarré in a range of ways, but one of the most notable is that he is able to defeat the princess's father, and we know that in twenty years no one else has; only the son can be a match for the father; the son proves himself to be the son by virtue of the fact that he defeats the father. Furthermore the child of a strange *father* would be outcast from position on the grounds of illegitimacy: a son who is not acknowledged as his father's heir cannot be lineally successful, as Degarré is.

Nothing about what this princess says suggests ignorance: her analysis of the situation is entirely accurate; not only does she understand the signs of pregnancy but she is in possession of that most crucial piece of sexual information – how babies get there. Notably, she also displaces her knowledge of the incestuous nature of relations with her father on to others; it is one spoken of openly in the streets (168). She articulates the fact of her pregnancy and provides the explanation of the need for it to remain secret; this 'open secret' is of course the fact that the sexual relations that have produced this child are prohibited. We are never told, either directly or indirectly, where the princess gets her sexual knowledge from. Her mother has been dead since she was born, so clearly she has had no instruction from her, and in any case we have no idea if girls did receive any kind of sexual education, even from their mothers, before very recent times. This princess cannot be regarded as ignorant: does narrative have an auxiliary function as sexual education?

In a culture that makes the female body a site of conflict, an object of shame, of lust, a means of transmitting one's ownership of land or title, how is the girl to discover a sexual identity for herself? Where are adolescent sexual desire and exploration articulated? Narratives, though, can introduce such topics, and while exempla have a clearly didactic function (hence the presence of incestuous mothers in such tales as a way of demonstrating and damning female lust), romance may also be a means of codifying publicly acceptable behaviour. What is hidden from public view provides a kind of sub-text; one can read the tale of a hero, or one can read the tale that produced him.

Thus between traditional readings of the tale, those that focus on the male heroic, and an alternative reading, which foregrounds the princess, the gaps/absences/discontinuities that I argue for in this tale, allow for a different reading.[19]

As a number of critics have suggested, this tale lends itself to a Freudian reading and the talismans provide an egregious example of the ease with which such a reading can be achieved; in fact James Simpson has remarked: 'This sequence, whereby the hero is literally armed, is also, quite obviously, a sequence whereby he is sexually armed (were it not for the date of the texts, one would have sworn that this was written by Freud).'[20] Other critics have also demonstrated recognition of the textual evidence, which suggests that the tale may be read through its obliquities.[21] The sword is given to the princess by the fairy knight immediately after he has raped her; he instructs her to give it to the child when he is 'of elde'

---

[19] See also W. C. Stokoe, 'The Double Problem of *Sir Degarré*', PMLA 70 (1955), pp. 518–34; H. Kozicki, 'Critical Methods in The Literary Evaluation of *Sir Degarré*', MLQ 29 (1968), pp. 3–14; G. V. Smithers, 'Story Patterns in Some Breton Lais', Medium Ævum 2 (1953), pp. 61–92.

[20] 'Violence', p. 128.

[21] Cheryl Colopy writes: 'While a literal reading of the story yields a poem that is rude, sudden, muddled – full of bizarre events that seem to defy explanation – a psychological one shows the poem's events to be connected thematically and symbolically. The muddle becomes a pattern when we identify the language which the poem speaks: the visual symbolic language of the unconscious which is shared by dream and fairy tale' ('Fairy Tale Oedipus', p. 32). I would also draw attention to C. H. Slover's comment: 'Its [the poem's] literary quality is not high; in fact, the author is so inept in putting together his materials that he has left *unconsciously* [my emphasis] a number of direct clues to his sources and methods' ('*Sir Degarré*: A Study in A Medieval Hack Writer's Methods', *Texas Studies in English* 11 (1931), pp. 5–23, p. 5). Criticism of *Sir Degarré* has often been reductivist, as Bruce Rosenberg remarks, but the vocabulary that such

(119). The sword, though, has part of its point broken off, and the fairy knight reveals to the princess that he will keep the point, which will provide a recognition token: 'Be mi swerd I mai him kenne' (131). Broken swords are, really, useless (what is the point of a sword that you cannot stick into someone?); I would argue that they may indicate some type of transgression.[22] This matter has been largely neglected by criticism; W. C. Stokoe comments: '[the sword] is an appropriate gift for a fairy knight's son and since the principals in this story fight fully armed, is a safer recognition token than the commonly used ring'.[23] This is an issue that is discussed by Elizabeth Archibald, who comments:

> The symbolism of the broken sword tip is striking: the unifying of the sword pieces can be seen as symbolising not only Degaré's establishment of his identity and reputation, and his sexual maturity, but also the unifying of his family which is necessary to legitimise the erstwhile foundling. The masculine and martial nature of the symbol makes the priorities of the writer crystal clear, as does the fact that the heroine is marginalised once she has had her baby, and spends twenty years as an unclaimed tournament prize before being handed over to an unknown youth who has won her in battle.[24]

Degarré fights the princess's father (his grandfather/father) without a sword; this is clearly a jousting contest, with the old king calling for 'a schaft þat wil nowt breke!' (564); he is not given the sword until he has proved himself to be the heir. Foundlings are legitimated because they are proved to have been, all along, the rightful heir; that is how they are enabled to win the contest, as James Simpson remarks.[25] Stokoe's use of the word 'safer' strikes me as interesting; there seems to me to be nothing 'safe' about a sword that has no point; it can really only be said to be safe from the point of view of those who might be on the receiving end, most obviously here, the father himself.

The other recognition token, the gloves, are also worthy of comment. Cheryl Colopy has commented that 'like Cinderella's slipper [the gloves] appear to be a female symbol'.[26] The gloves, which we first see when the princess puts them with her baby as she is about to have him exposed (194-5), will fit no person other than the princess herself; they are identifiers of the child's mother and as such, may be equated with her womb. What the gloves also do is to link this tale with other father–daughter incest tales. 'Handless maiden' tales, as Elizabeth Archibald (and others) note, reflect narratives where the incestuous desire is that of daughter for father and where in earlier forms the girl was punished for desiring her father.[27]

---

criticism employs also acknowledges that there is more to this tale than meets the eye (see 'The Three Tales of *Sir Degarré*', NM 76 (1975), pp. 39–51).

[22] Perhaps the broken sword is analogous to the mutilated hand (discussed below); the rapist leaves the damaged sword with the body of the girl he has transgressed – possibly a displaced version of castration for rapists.

[23] 'The Double Problem', p. 532.

[24] 'Imagination', p. 130.

[25] 'The challenger, however, does not at all present himself on a randomly meritocratic basis. He turns out to be the king's own grandson, who acts according to the ineluctable demands of the identity he possesses by virtue of birth . . .' (Simpson, 'Violence', p. 131).

[26] 'Fairy Tale Oedipus', p. 31.

[27] See Archibald, 'Flight', and T. Fenster, 'Beaumanoir's *La Manekine*: Kin D(R)ead: Incest, Doubling and Death', *American Imago* 39 (1982), pp. 41–58.

The hand remains one of the most potent symbols of sexual knowledge because it signifies knowledge through touch, physical, sensual, knowledge of the body.

However, a child's – sexual – knowledge of its parents is proscribed, so the gloves must be given away when the heir is produced, only to be returned to the princess as a means of preventing further incest. The narrative consistently works to make the princess's illicit pregnancy acceptable. Whose interest does this serve? Clearly the production of a male heir serves the interests of the father, of an ideology that seeks to maintain its power through challenging and fighting any man who might seek access to that power. The dominant concern is to maintain linearity; but it is also the case that a king's lineage is diluted by marriage, for he is always better born than his wife; however, the infusion of his blood into hers improves the stock, so to speak. This is a matter on which the subjects of Chaucer's Walter are unwittingly eloquent when he is feigning to marry his own daughter (*The Clerk's Tale*, 988–90).

Father–daughter incest has a role that is justified in terms of breeding, so in *Sir Degarré*, the princess's rape is, as Saunders remarks, rewritten in a way that makes the union the right thing to have done.[28]

The same cannot, of course, be said of mother–son incest. Such unions are far rarer and the model for them tolls its message of punishment and despair down the ages.[29] Thus, in this tale, Degarré's mother has her hands covered before she is allowed to touch her son. The prevention of incest also effects another kind of recognition than that between mother and son, for it forces the princess to reveal her motherhood to her father. Once her father has his heir, he no longer needs to fight to keep his daughter and she is acknowledged as a grown woman.[30] She is only recognised as such, though, because she says that she is: while physically we know her to be (at least) thirty-two, she has remained a child, although a mother, because she has not previously spoken of her sexual experience except to keep it hidden.

The second part of the story, that which is concerned with Degarré's quest to find his father, provides some mirror images of the first part, and in doing so, it presents us with a woman who is confident, articulate and in control of her own body and lineage, with her own sexual life. Here, Degarré becomes the object of the gaze while placed in an enchanted sleep and silence/speechlessness (itself an important feature of the Middle English Breton lays) is reinvented as a form of power. Now, the silence serves to isolate the man and Degarré is seen as the object here, lying on the bed in a sleep conjured by women, while they, awake, look at him. The dynamics of vulnerability is very clearly at work. The well-dressed dwarf also inverts the power-relations we have seen in the first half of the narrative. The

---

[28] *Rape*, p. 216.
[29] For the most extensive and authoritative discussion of incestuous relations, see Archibald, 'Medieval Imagination', pp. 104–33.
[30] The editors comment: 'Brides are conventionally young. The poet has forgotten that this one is by definition old enough to be the bridegroom's mother' (p. 245, n. 663). To think of the tale this way (that the poet is inept and keeps getting things wrong) is not unusual, but of course if this is an incest story, then she must be old enough to be his mother: it is not the poet who has 'forgotten' that the princess is old enough to be a mother; rather, the princess's father has failed to recognise the fact that his daughter is no longer young.

dwarf acts as a direct contrast to the figure of the powerful male father/suitor; he is a man whom one can look down upon, both literally and figuratively, for dwarves are servants, not masters, their stature makes them subject, however powerful and masculine they might otherwise be.[31] In this part of the narrative the men are rewritten; no longer all-powerful fathers or brutal rapists, they are rendered not just harmless but even helpless: the maiden tucks Degarré up in bed like a mother, covering him warmly, while he is unconscious of what is going on; the dwarf may be ignominiously stuffed under the arm and himself carried off. There is also ambiguity surrounding the maiden's sleeping arrangements; it seems possible that she got into bed with Degarré, for the narrative says:

> Þe levedi wreiȝ him warm apliȝt
> And a pilewer under his heved dede,
> And ȝede to bedde in þat stede. (854–6)

If fathers and lovers are consistently conflated in the narrative, so, too, are mothers and wives. Simpson has remarked that 'seeking mother and wife amount to provisionally the same thing'.[32] This conflation works insofar as the maiden's narrative reflects that of the princess on both a structural and a verbal level. This is the tale that she recounts to Degarré:

> 'Mi fader was a riche baroun
> And hadde mani a tour and toun,
> He ne hadde no child but me –
> Ich was his hair of þis cuntre.' (881–4)

The father enters and disappears from the narrative here; the next thing we are told is that there is a knight, the strongest in Brittany, who has loved her long, but whom she cannot love in return (889–95). This knight attempts to abduct her and he has been engaged in killing her knights and squires one at a time, as though it were a contest: 'þe best he slowgh þe first dai,/ And seþen anoþer, par ma fai,/ And seþen þe þridde, and þe ferþe' (901–3).[33] We are never told that her father has died defending her, and she is very clearly in charge in this castle of maidens: where is he now? The father remains a shady figure, but he is startlingly familiar. This isolated woman, though, has strengths that the girl, the princess of the first part, did not. Firstly she has defied the powerful man who wishes to ravish her; the helpless girl in the woods is a woman in her own castle; no brutal rape outdoors for her.[34] Secondly, she engages her own champion; when Degarré says that he will

---

[31] In Malory's *Tale of Sir Gareth of Orkney* (*Works*, p. 202), Gareth is incensed when his dwarf is stolen. The dwarf knows the secret of his lineage, which is why he has been taken, but what seems to me interesting is the way in which he is picked up and carried off underneath someone's arm, like an unruly child. Such a posture literalises the dwarf as childlike, powerless.

[32] 'Violence', p. 130.

[33] For a discussion of abduction and rape and the confusion and conflation that surrounds this issue, see Saunders, *Rape*, Chapter 1, esp. p. 20.

[34] The privacy of outdoors is a Gothic inversion, because of course it isn't really private: one is vulnerable to exposure, in both senses of the word, when outside; but what this Gothic inversion also tells us is that our expectations of being safe when *at home* are misplaced. In this rewritten half of the tale, home has again become safe for the girl.

fight the attacker for her, she says that she will give him her land and her body (921–4) if he succeeds. Not only is she able to act as her own agent, but we know that she has spent the night with him while he was in an enchanted sleep; women are attacked by demons when they are thus vulnerable: what happens to men? Certainly we can say that sleeping men can be sex objects for women; one has only to think of Lady Bercilak to know that

Degarré's fight with the would-be ravisher leaves the latter dead (968–7). What is remarkable is that this section of the narrative effects a resolution to the problems of the first section, and most particularly when it comes to the problems confronting an heiress approaching puberty and marriage. The hidden rape, the hidden pregnancy, the covertly articulated readiness for sexual experience are translated into overt acts of power over the masculine world; the sleeping man, the absent father, man as inferior. Degarré's triumph over the shady father prefigures his successful quest for his own father. But a search for his own father is a search for a partner for his mother (as critics have pointed out, the fairy rapist becomes a normal sexual partner here, thus a figure who is a substitute for the father, rather than the father himself).

James Simpson has argued that the tale seeks to re-establish the proper order that has existed all along,[35] and Corinne Saunders observes that 'the second half of the narrative structurally rectifies the violation of the start through the mysterious episode of Degarré's rescue of a beautiful maiden from a "ravisser" '.[36] This is an order where the heiress is able to renegotiate her position; we are presented with a woman who has a good look, and then decides whom she will give herself to. The movement of the narrative is from child (subject to father and society) to woman (mistress of her own fate, fortune and body), from hiding the body to bestowing it. Saunders comments: 'Rape is reversed, a hero is created and the faery knight is reclaimed for the woman: the narrative is a female fantasy as well as a male one.'[37]

If the tale is to be read as a female fantasy, then I would argue that what makes it so are the possibilities for sexual adventure, for the exploration of the body, both male and female, which the tale allows. The princess of the first half, while being aware of sexual difference and obliquely inviting the sexual encounter with the father, is portrayed as victim; however, the second princess rejects the shady suitor in favour of the man whom she treats as an erotic object and whom she chooses as her sexual partner. When you're grown-up, sex doesn't literally have to be a bit of how's your father.

---

35 'Violence', p. 131.
36 *Rape*, p. 216.
37 *Rape*, p. 218.

The Female 'Jewish' Libido in Medieval Culture

ANTHONY BALE

IT IS ALMOST a commonplace that in its stereotypes a society articulates its deeply held desires; through strategies of symbolic violence medieval English people could express precious, secret and fragile thoughts.[1] In identifying these desires there is necessarily a degree of speculation, a filling-in of the gaps in what is said and unsaid: what did people, from whom we are now distant, desire? How was this desire mediated? How do texts speak for the desires of their authors and audiences?

In answering these questions contemporary criticism has perceived sexual desire to be latent in medieval Christian portrayals of Jews. Jacob Press has argued that Chaucer, in 'The Prioress's Tale', uses antisemitic fictions of Mariology and corporeality to stage a homoerotic encounter.[2] Kathleen Biddick's work on circumcision and temporality has likewise placed genitalia at the symbolic centre of Christian attempts to move beyond Judaism; for Biddick, via Freud, the prepuce is primarily an anxious sexual signifier.[3] Steven Kruger has 'queered' the *topos* of Jewish–Christian religious conversion, using Judith Butler's conceptualisation of 'gender as a kind of melancholy, or as one of melancholy's effects'.[4] Robert Mills, examining images of the Passion, has described the extravagantly phallic modes of 'Jewish' torturers versus the feminised body of Christ.[5] For Ruth Evans, the Jewish presence in virgin martyr narratives is part of a 'violent production of Englishness' connecting sexuality, nationalism and torture.[6] Lisa Lampert has argued for a parallel reading of gender difference and Jewish difference (to which I shall return).[7] Perverse erotics are an anxious, usually inexplicit, 'cause' of, or parallel animus to, antisemitic expression. In particular, attention has focused on the figure

---

[1] See Miri Rubin, *Gentile Tales: The Narrative Assault on Late Medieval Jews*, 2nd edn (Philadelphia, 2004).
[2] ' "You Go, Figure": the rape of a trope in "The Prioress's Tale" ', *Queer Theory and the Jewish Question*, ed. Daniel Boyarin, Daniel Itzkovitz and Ann Pellegrini (New York, 2003), pp. 285–310.
[3] *The Typological Imaginary: Circumcision, Technology, History* (Philadelphia, 2003).
[4] 'The Spectral Jew', *New Medieval Literatures* 2 (1998), pp. 9–35 (p. 33), quoting Butler, 'Melancholy Gender/Refused Identification', *Constructing Masculinity* 11 (1995), pp. 21–36 (p. 21).
[5] 'A Man is Being Beaten', *New Medieval Literatures* 5 (2002), pp. 115–53.
[6] 'The Jew, the Host and the Virgin Martyr: Fantasies of the Sentient Body', *Medieval Virginities*, ed. Anke Bernau, Ruth Evans and Sarah Salih (Cardiff, 2003), pp. 167–86 (p. 173).
[7] *Gender and Jewish Difference from Paul to Shakespeare* (Philadelphia, 2004).

of the adult Jewish male, his phallic nose, his wounded penis, his menstruating body.[8]

In this essay I shall build on this work but focus on the image of the Jewish woman rather than that of the Jewish man. I shall introduce several texts that have largely been passed over, even though they treat 'Jewish' sexuality and sensuality explicitly.[9] These are texts about the Jew's daughter, fantasised in medieval culture as at once sexually available, physically dangerous and open to conversion. This figure has gained an enduring cultural importance as the medieval ancestor of Marlowe's Abigall in *The Jew of Malta* (c. 1592) and Shakespeare's Jessica in *The Merchant of Venice* (c. 1598), and cognate characters of the 'beautiful Jewess' appear throughout the post-medieval period.[10]

It is necessary, briefly, to adumbrate the general gender dynamics of medieval antisemitic writing. Where medieval Christian texts present 'a Jew' they generally present an adult, male Jew, or groups of adult male Jews; these figures are marked, through both circumcision and physiognomy, as different from Christians. As Ronnie Po-Chia Hsia has suggested, 'late medieval Judaism, characterised by its Christian detractors as a rabbinic religion, was by definition a male-centred rival religion'.[11] In many instances, female Christian intermediaries (in particular wet-nurses) were said to be in league with the Jews;[12] conversely, in the texts and images in which the Jews' wives and children are depicted, they are seen as being open to conversion and capable of pity. Miri Rubin has convincingly argued that this is derived from an idea of women and children, be they Christian or Jewish, as 'pliant and impressionable'.[13] In general, the tortures to which Jews are said to subject Christians are enacted by men and have a sexualised subtext or purchase on a quasi-erotic Passional imagery, usually concerned with pleasure, pain, genitality and physical penetration.

Maculate Conceptions

A story that speaks clearly, if confusedly, of an 'English' and 'Jewish' female libido appears in the fifteenth-century English *exempla* collection, the *Alphabet of Tales*; it is taken from Caesarius of Heisterbach's well-known Latin miracle collection, the

---

[8] Steven Kruger, 'The Bodies of Jews in the Later Middle Ages', *The Idea of Medieval Literature: New Essays on Chaucer and Medieval Culture in Honor of Donald R. Howard*, ed. James Dean and Christian Zacher (Newark, 1992), pp. 301–23; Willis Johnson, 'The Myth of Male Jewish Menses', *Journal of Medieval History* 24:3 (1998), pp. 273–95; D. S. Katz, 'Shylock's Gender: Jewish Male Menstruation in Early Modern England', *Review of English Studies* 50 (1999), pp. 440–62.

[9] For a preliminary discussion, see Ivan G. Marcus, 'Images of the Jews in the Exempla of Caesarius of Heisterbach', *From Witness to Witchcraft. Jews and Judaism in Medieval Christian Thought*, ed. Jeremy Cohen (Wiesbaden, 1996), pp. 247–56.

[10] See Sander L. Gilman, 'Salome, Syphilis, Sarah Bernhardt, and the "Modern Jewess"', in Gilman's collection *Love + Marriage = Death, and Other Essays on Representing Difference*, Stanford Studies in Jewish History and Culture (Palo Alto, 1998), pp. 65–90.

[11] 'Witchcraft, Magic, and the Jews in Germany', *From Witness to Witchcraft*, ed. Cohen, pp. 419–33 (p. 427).

[12] This seems to have been this case in the ritual-murder story of Robert of Bury St Edmunds; see Anthony P. Bale, ' "House devil, town saint": Antisemitism and Hagiography in Medieval Suffolk', *Chaucer and the Jews*, ed. Sheila Delany (New York, 2002), pp. 185–210.

[13] *Gentiles Tales*, pp. 40–5, 73–8.

Dialogus Miraculorum (c. 1220).¹⁴ These tales were used, mainly by preachers, to illustrate key points of Christian doctrine, in accessible and sometimes salacious terms. Such tales may reflect 'popular belief', but also led and inculcated popular belief. It is worth quoting the whole of this remarkable *exemplum*.

> Cesarius tellis how som tyme in þe cetie of London a clerk gatt a Iewis doghter with childe; & he was ferde for grevans of hur fadur & hur moder, & he gatt hym a long rede & come on þe night to þe wall þer hur fadur & hur moder lay within. & he put up þe vpper end of þe rede in at a hole, & he spakk in att þe toder end & said; 'O! ye rightwus folk, in God wele-beluffid!' & callid þaim be þer names & bad þaim be merie, for þer doghter had conseyvid Messias & yit sho was a mayden. And with þat þe man was estonyd & askid his wife if sho hard þis voyce, and sho said nay; & þai made þer prayers at þai myght here it agayn. And þe clerke stude still & harde þaim; and as he did befor, he spakk agayn. And when þai hard hym þai war passand fayn, & trowid þat it had bene trew; & vnnethis þai abade a day vnto þai grapid þer doghter bodie & fand at sho was with childe. & þai askid hur how sho conseyvid, and sho answerd as þe clerk had bedyn hur, & sayd, 'I wote neuer wheþer I be with childe or nay, bod I know wele I am a mayden & had neuer at do with man.' And þer was hur fadur & hur moder so ioyfull þat onone þe noyse ran þurgh þe cetie þat þer doghter was with childe with Messias. So tyme come sho sulde be delyver, & þer come vnto hur many Iewis with grete myrth & ioy, & abade to sho war delyver at þai mot se what sho had born. And in hur travellyng sho had grete payn, & at þe laste with grete sorow & cryiing sho bare a doghter, þat cryed & grete & made mekyll mornyng. And when þai saw þis þai all war confusid passynglie, to so mekill þat ane of þaim in a tene tuke þis childe be þe legg & threw it agayn þe wall & killed it. etc.¹⁵

In the present context, the aspects of this fascinating text upon which I wish to concentrate are those of generative and non-generative sex and the erotic space enabled by the Jewess's body. To a modern audience one hopes that there is little humour in the story; however, the *exemplum* is a medieval version of what we might now call a 'dirty joke'. For the joke to work, that is in order that we 'get the joke', we must apply a variety of doctrinal and gendered beliefs.

The narrative is a moral parody of the Annunciation (Luke 1:26–38), with the clerk as mock-Gabriel and the Jewess as anti-Virgin. The text does not attempt to deny that the clerk has had sex with the Jewess, and indeed this copulation is that which enables the *exemplum* to proceed. The *exemplum* has parallels in medieval lyrics in which a clerk makes pregnant a young naïve, and in *fabliaux* and *chansons de geste*.¹⁶ The clerk and the Jewess are both 'guilty' of non-marital, lustful sex but, as the story goes on, difference is made into hierarchy and subordination through the social and religious outplaying of the sexual act and its consequences. The narrative shows that the clerk had sex with the Jewess either in order to humiliate

---

¹⁴ On Caesarius, see Marcus, 'Images of the Jews'.
¹⁵ Ed. Mary McLeod Banks, *An Alphabet of Tales*, EETS OS 126–7 (London, 1904–5), 2.277–8.
¹⁶ E.g. 'Ladd y the daunce a Myssomur Day' and 'As I went on Yol Day', both in *Medieval English Lyrics*, ed. Theodore Silverstein (London, 1971). A further parallel is the libidinous but evil Saracen woman, on which see Jacqueline de Weever, *Sheba's Daughters: Whitening and Demonizing the Saracen Woman in Medieval French Epic* (New York, 1998), pp. 75–80.

her and her co-religionists, or simply through mutual concupiscence.[17] That the Jewess would wish to have sex is also not commented on, but rather her sexual appetite is a given. The point is that the two are complicit ('sho answerd as þe clerk had bedyn hur') and both are sinful; the text transforms this complicity into control. The Jewess experiences a normal rather than divine labour, 'sho had grete payn . . . with grete sorow & crying', contrasted with the Virgin's painless labour.[18] Like Eve, the London Jewess is cursed to feel libido and to procreate. Within the exemplary tradition, the *exemplum* complements both antisemitic material, in which Jews are said to dispute or deny the Virgin Birth, and Talmudic material, in which the Virgin Birth is indeed traduced.[19] Within Christian thought, something that was neither pure nor virtuous (like the Jewess) cannot be corrupted; St Augustine argued that corruption is always voluntary, so in effect the Jewess cannot be violated.[20]

The clerk mocks the Jews' sense of their own chosen-ness, the ' "rightwus folk, in God wele-beluffid!" ' Jewish belief is an empty space, configured around something that does not happen (the arrival of the Messiah). Yet the Jewess's parents make exactly the same 'leap of faith' as must Christians in accepting the Virgin Birth, tied neither to Body nor to the literal (as we might expect from other antisemitic fictions), but eager to embrace a metaphysical absence of proof, which itself constitutes an exceptional, indeed miraculous, event.[21] The logic of the *exemplum*, in which bodies can be familiar and incredible, is neither 'irrational' nor 'ignorant', but succinctly and coherently Christian.

The scene in the *exemplum* in which the girl is examined by her parents also purchases on secular rather than clerical literary culture, in which the 'ordeal' of tested or proven chastity, 'the ritualized inspection of the virgin's body', is a well-known stock episode.[22] As in the medieval romance or *lai*, the woman's chastity 'is ornament and testimony to the honor of the . . . community'.[23] The Jewess fails the ordeal although, crucially, in this context she 'passes' the ordeal in her parents' eyes ('þai grapid þer doghter bodie & fand at sho was with childe'); for they are easily convinced by *physical* proof that the girl is both pregnant and yet

---

[17] On the euphemistic 'at do', see *MED*, s.v. 'don' 9b(e), 'haven to (at, a) do with', 'to have sexual intercourse with'. The idiom is used elsewhere in the *Alphabet of Tales*.

[18] On this tradition, see Leo Steinberg, *The Sexuality of Christ in Renaissance Art and Modern Oblivion* (Chicago, 1996).

[19] Famously discussed by Martin Luther in his *Von Den Juden*. See too Joan Young Gregg, *Devils, Women, and Jews* (Albany, 1997), pp. 226–7; Israel J. Yuval, '"They tell lies: you ate the man": Jewish Reactions to Ritual Murder Accusations', *Religious Violence Between Christians and Jews*, ed. Anna Sapir Abulafia (Basingstoke, 2002), pp. 86–106. Joseph Dan noted the reciprocity between Christian and Jewish *exempla*; see 'Rabbi Judah the Pious and Caesarius of Heisterbach: Common Motifs in their Stories', *Scripta Hierosolymitana* 22 (1971), pp. 18–27.

[20] See Corinne Saunders, *Rape and Ravishment in the Literature of Medieval England* (Cambridge, 2001), p. 89.

[21] A dominant representation of Jews, from Paul, held them to be tied to the 'letter' rather than the 'spirit' of the Law, in understanding figures such as circumcision and kashrut literally. See Jeremy Cohen, *Living Letters of the Law: Ideas of the Jew in Medieval Christianity* (Berkeley, 1999).

[22] Helen Solterer, 'At the Bottom of Mirage, a Woman's Body: *Le Roman de la Rose* of Jean Renart', *Feminist Approaches to the Body in Medieval Literature*, ed. Linda Lomperis and Sarah Stanbury (Philadephia, 1993), pp. 213–33; Kathleen Coyne Kelly, *Performing Virginity and Testing Chastity in the Middle Ages* (London and New York, 2000), pp. 63–90.

[23] Kelly, *Performing Virginity*, p. 64.

virgin (even though we know, in a kind of invasive dramatic irony, that the girl's hymen cannot be intact) and, joyfully, they 'announce' the chaste pregnancy to their community: 'þe noyse ran þurgh þe cetie'. In discussing similar texts Kathleen Coyne Kelly has argued that homosocial anxieties inform the chastity-test, 'a commentary on the precarious status of the husband, a status which is paradoxically dependent upon his wife's behaviour'.[24] Yet in our story of Jewish–Christian antagonism, rather than marital antagonism, a different kind of homosocial work is facilitated in which the husband's prestige is no longer an anxiety: this *exemplum* celebrates the clerk's potency in humiliating the Jewish father through intercourse with his daughter. Unregulated by a husband, the Jewess misreads her own genital 'proof', just as her parents misunderstand the chastity test. In doing so, the text invites its audiences to imagine and consider the actuality of intercourse, the Jewess's genitals and the clerk's familiarity with these genitals. Moreover, the text fantasises a kind of intercourse that has consequences only for one party, an expression of sexuality without responsibility. Rather than using familiar figures of blood, excretion and menstruation to probe the borders of body and community, the autonomy and integrity of Christianity is probed and then consolidated through sexual commingling.[25]

Yet even with its didactic impulse the *exemplum*'s morality is disordered and its moral *telos*, the Jew's murder of the infant, is difficult to read. The story is not explicitly moralised, and many of the details given are surplus, excessive and unclear. The levity with which the *exemplum*'s medieval authors and translators treat the infant's murder does not preclude its serious functions and meanings. That a Jew (presumably male) seizes the baby by the leg and kills her ('ane of þaim in a tene tuke þis childe be þe legg & threw it agayn þe wall & killed it') is perhaps the most shocking and perverse part of the story, even as it makes sense within medieval ontologies of ritual murder, blood sacrifice, violence against the Christ child and associated narratives.[26] This conclusion extends and literalises sentiments of Jewish vengeance: 'Happy shall he be, that taketh and dasheth thy little ones against the stones' (Psalm 137:9). The violence of rivalry encoded within the sexual act that produced the baby is manifested as the violence against the baby, a violence said to be enacted by a Jew but, in this context, a Christian fantasy of halting Jewish regeneration. That another Jew, rather than the Jewess, seizes the infant returns us to the *ur*-image of the Jew in medieval popular religion, standing in opposition to Marian or maternal pity, that of infanticide. Moreover, the infanticidal Jew is the 'full moral agent' (unlike the weak Jewess) through which contrasts in Jewish and Christian behaviour are presented.[27]

It might be said that the narrative relies on the audience's acceptance of the humiliation of the Jews as a valid reason, or excuse, for the clerk's initial copulation (and the ensuing, if short-lived, miscegenation). Yet the clerk himself would,

---

[24] Kelly, *Performing Virginity*, p. 65.
[25] See K. Theweleit, *Male Fantasies I. Women, Floods, Bodies, History*, trans. Stephen Conway, Erica Carter and Chris Turner (Cambridge, 1987), pp. 385–435, on the erotics of contamination.
[26] On analogous material, see Leah Sinanoglou, 'The Christ Child as Sacrifice: A Medieval Tradition and the Corpus Christi Plays', *Speculum* 48 (1973), pp. 491–509; Bonnie Millar, *The Siege of Jerusalem in its Physical, Literary and Historical Contexts* (Dublin, 2000), Chapter 3.
[27] Lampert, *Gender*, pp. 143–5.

in the eyes of a medieval audience, have been guilty of serious sexual misconduct. The clerk is guilty of the sin of lust (although this might be excused as it has an anti-Jewish imperative); the clerk has certainly broken clerical vows of celibacy, a transgression more, rather than less, serious for being with a Jewess. Moreover, the clerk is guilty of the crime of *struprum*, 'the defloration of virgins . . . outside the context of abduction and irrespective of consent', a crime that demolished the woman's 'value' as virgin and demonstrated the man's lack of control over his desire.[28] The *exemplum* stands in stark contrast to similar religious stories in which saintly men are able to maintain their chastity in the face of brazen female sexual temptation.[29] Is this morality to be suspended if the sexual partner is a Jewess? If not, the clerk is maculate, like his sexual partner.

In a similarly shocking story, Christian sexual morality is indeed suspended if it leads to Jewish humiliation. In a Latin *exempla* collection that survives in three manuscripts (two of which are English), there is an *exemplum* about a spendthrift who takes a job as a servant to a Jew.[30] He decides to steal the Jew's money and 'ruin' (*pereo*) the Jew's daughter (by which rape has been understood), then flees to a forest. The servant confesses his sins while the Jewish master, warlock more than merchant, calls up his demons who fail, on account of the servant's confession, to avenge him. Again the Jewess's body is a site of competing jurisdictions, Christian and Jewish, with the rivalry between men articulated through controlling the Jewess. Sexual integrity, the aspiration to the wholeness of virginity, does not apply to Jewish women, even if in this case rape rather than libido is to blame.

In the Latin source of the *Alphabet of Tales exemplum*, Caesarius' *Dialogus Miraculorum*, the novice says, upon hearing the miracle of the Jewess who gave birth to a baby girl:

> It was a miserable ending, that an infidel maiden, who had been seduced and ruined by a Christian man should not have been brought to baptism . . .[31]

The novice's spiritual guide responds that the lack of conversion might have been owing to the Christian man's lack of effort, or that he 'rejoiced rather in the confounding of the Jews than in the enlightenment of the maiden'.[32] This *coda* is omitted in vernacular versions. The miracle is not always the aim or target of the miraculous narrative; instead, there is pleasure in the licentious narrative.

Such *exempla* are then both transgressive and canonical, laden with desire and yet pretending to orthodoxy. The Jewish woman was useful as a sexual fantasy on which both doctrine and desire might be tested (as is indeed the case with Marlowe's Abigall and Shakespeare's Jessica); she is the place where miscegenation can be performed in a way that provides safe erotic and transgressive pleasure. In the context of later medieval England, itself a world without Jews, there is an

---

[28] Saunders, *Rape*, p. 87. *Struprum* was regarded as a lesser crime to *raptus*.
[29] John H. Arnold, 'The Labour of Continence: Masculinity and Clerical Virginity', *Medieval Virginities*, ed. Bernau et al., pp. 102–18, esp. pp. 104–5.
[30] London, British Library Royal MS 7.D.i, f. 79 (s. xiii); Harley MS 2385, f. 65 (fragmentary; s. xiv, from ?Cambridge/Norwich); Add. MS 33956, f. 83 (English).
[31] *The Dialogue on Miracles*, ed. and trans. H. Scott and C. C. Swinton Bland (London, 1929), 1:106.
[32] Scott and Bland, *Dialogue*, 1:106.

added measure of exoticism and impossibility to the fantasy. The Jewish woman is that which licenses an unsettling – but useful – alliance of sex and violence within normative codes of Christian conduct, an imaginary Jewish body for the self-regarding gratification of the Christian devotional body.

The Jewish Daughter's Pedigree

The *exemplum* from the *Alphabet of Tales* is a story about pleasures: of sexual intercourse, of humiliation, of righteousness. The *exemplum* is not a freakish or isolated text, and in this section I will sketch a history of the Jewish daughter. As Lisa Lampert has persuasively argued, antisemitic texts dramatised the 'logic of [Christian] supercession' as the triumph of youth over age, Christian clerk over Jewish father, Abigall over Barabas, Jessica over Shylock.[33] The texts featured in the present discussion are not simply about Jews, or Jewish women, but about the particular figure of the Jewish daughter – that is, the Jewish man and his daughter – troping a particular kind of genealogy, which is pious, gendered and erotic.

As sketched above, Eve's presence is felt in the *Alphabet of Tales exemplum*, in the anti-heroine's libido and painful delivery. More generally, Jewish traditions of 'useful' and 'good' (heroic, valorised) female eroticism (figures like Esther, Judith, Susannah and Jael (Judges 4:1–24)) may have informed the tale in providing a contrast, at once seductive and repulsive to medieval Christians, to the medieval cult of the pristine Virgin.[34] Figures like Dinah (Genesis 34:8–31) and Tamar (2 Samuel 13:1–39), Jewish women whose defloration is a transaction between men, may also inform the medieval texts.

The association between the Jewish daughter and erotic carnality was evidently well established by the later Middle Ages; in a range of ballads associated with the medieval cult of Little Hugh of Lincoln (d. 1255), the Jewish daughter becomes the (im)moral agent at the story's centre. The Hugh of Lincoln affair has been outlined and scrutinised elsewhere;[35] in this context one need only offer a short synopsis of the incident. The Jews of Lincoln were accused of murdering a little local boy, Hugh, whose corpse had been found. Eighteen Lincoln Jews were put to death. Hugh's shrine stood in Lincoln Cathedral until the Reformation (faint traces can still be seen), although his cult gained most currency in vernacular literature rather than through general ecclesiastical approval or widespread devotion. In English and continental *exempla* and chronicles, including those written in the mid-thirteenth century, the story is fairly static: Hugh was murdered by Jews in a mockery of the Passion, his body discarded. The corpse then miraculously reappeared, cast forth from its place of concealment, usually a well or cess-pit.[36]

However, in a separate and later vernacular ballad tradition ('Sir Hugh, or, The

---

33 *Gender*, esp. p. 144.
34 Piero Boitani, 'Susanna in excelsis', in his *The Bible and its Rewritings* (Oxford, 1999), pp. 58–76.
35 The best account is Gavin I. Langmuir, 'The Knight's Tale of Young Hugh of Lincoln', in his *Toward a Definition of Antisemitism* (Berkeley, 1990), pp. 237–62. Langmuir, in his historical enquiry, is little interested in the ballads.
36 See Langmuir, 'The Knight's Tale'.

Jew's Daughter'), which originated late in the medieval period, Hugh's murderer is the Jew's daughter, who entices the little boy into her garden through affectionate language, using an apple with which to tempt him.[37] She murders him, often in such a way as to suggest that she is preparing his body as food, and drains his blood. The ballad's theme is the perverse erotics of the Jewess's body.

The ballad is not sexual in an explicit way, but rather casts the Jewess as a new Eve engaged in a solitary physical ritual of blood that unites a range of forbidden desires and appetites: sexuality, paedophilia, autonomy, unaccompanied and unofficial worship, cannibalism. The Jew's daughter is imagined in the 'Jew's castell', 'at the window looking out', an inverted lady in the tower.[38] When beckoned to the Jewess's chamber to get his ball, Hugh replies, ' "For as ye did to my auld father,/ The same ye'll do to me" ', indicating his typological and Christological role and his willing, passive assumption of martyrdom. Indeed, the Jewess is described *as* the Jew's daughter and it is in 'her father's garden' that the anti-heroine, a Lincoln Eve, takes an apple, 'to entice [Hugh] in'.[39]

Having cast the Jewess as temptress, the ballad then takes a shocking direction, a bald pleasure in excessive bloodiness:

> She's led him in through ae dark door,
> And sae she has thro' nine;
> She's laid him on a dressing table,
> And stickit him like a swine.
>
> And first came out the thick thick blood,
> And syne came out the thin;
> And syne came out the bonny heart's blood;
> There was nae mair within.
>
> She's row'd him in a cake o' lead,
> Bade him lie still and sleep;
> She's thrown him in Our Lady's draw-well,
> Was fifty fathom deep.[40]

Here a range of beliefs about gender, sexuality and difference coalesce, serving to mark out the Jewess as physical and transgressive. The reference to the pig is an antisemitic commonplace, suggesting a further place of sexual transgression; the blood may propose a faulty Eucharist or menstruation (found in cognate *exempla*, as discussed below).[41] The Jewess's attempt to hide the body in a well dedicated to

---

37 For a survey of the texts see F. J. Child, *The English and Scottish Ballads* (New York, 1957), #155.
38 On this well-known romance and folkloric trope, see Diane Bornstein, *The Lady in the Tower* (Hamden, CT, 1983).
39 A parallel is in the medieval ritual-murder *exemplum* of Adam of Bristol where the Jews use a Eucharistic meal and fruit to tempt the little boy. See Christoph Cluse, '"Fabula ineptissima": Die Ritualmordlegende um Adam von Bristol nach der Handschrift London, British Library, Harley 957', *Aschkenas* 5 (1995), pp. 293–330.
40 Quoted from the Scots 'Four and twenty bonny boys', Child, *Ballads*, 3.421.
41 See Claudine Fabre-Vassas, *The Singular Beast: Jews, Christians and the Pig*, trans. Carol Volk (New York, 1997).

the Virgin reveals her misconceived femininity, as well as calling to mind the rite of baptism.

Blood is central to the ballad's idea of Jewish difference. The ballad derives from another *exemplum* found not only in the *Alphabet of Tales* but in other preeminent collections: Caesarius' *Dialogus*, the *Gesta Romanorum*, *Jacob's Well*.[42] This story, of the bishop's cousin who has sex with a Jewess, likewise conflates the Hugh of Lincoln story with the erotic image of the Jew's daughter.

This *exemplum* tells of 'a clark þat was a chanoun in Lincoln Mynster, and he was nere sybb cussyn vnto þe bisshopp'. The clerk 'laburd at' the 'fayr doghter' of a Lincoln Jew, persuading her to have sex with him. The Jewess responds that, because of her father's protection of her, the only time she would be able to have sex with him is on Good Friday; the text explains 'ffor þan þe Iewis hase a bludie flux, & þai vse little to be occupyed or com forward'. Sexual union is achieved but the next morning the lovers are discovered by the Jew. That evening, it happens that the clerk is due to serve as deacon for the bishop and, in a panic of shame, prays contritely, just as the Jewish father and a number of other Jews arrive at the minster, 'ffor to make complaynt vnto þe bysshopp of his cussyn'. The Jews are struck dumb, and the clerk, seeing this miracle, is shriven by the bishop; the clerk goes on to become a monk 'in Ceustus ordur' (the Cistercians). As for the Jewess, 'þai garte cristen þis damysell, & made hur a non of þe same ordur'. The text concludes, 'afterward þai bothe wer gude halie liffers'.[43]

This was an exceptionally widespread story and its several versions would well repay a more substantial analysis. Once again, while the theme (contrition) is orthodox, the basis of the narrative expresses perverse desire, based around the Jew's faulty conjunction of blood and libido. Other scholars have explored the epistemology of male Jewish 'menstruation' mentioned here (the text suggests that it is male Jews who suffer the flux);[44] the image I would like to foreground is of the 'fayr' Jewess and her sexual availability to a Christian cleric. In his remiss approach to Easter the cleric communes with the incorrect bloody body, a passion enabled by the bloody flux of the Jewish body rather than the Passion of Christ. Again, to have sex with a Jewess is a means of humiliating the Jewish father; the gap between Jewish father and Jew's daughter is suggested in the corrupted nature of the father's body and the desirable nature of the daughter. In this story, the Jewess is brought to faith, although once again the conclusion jars with the narrative as libido becomes chastity. I suggest that the Little Sir Hugh ballads are informed by this *exemplum* of blood, sex and subservience at Lincoln.

Such medieval representations of the Jewish daughter – showing a fallen, sexy, secret and yet open body, engaged with the most precious symbols of Christianity – have an avatar in the later medieval and early modern figure of the witch. As recent study has shown, the witch, like the Jew, was not so much a gendered construct but a sexual construct, which in turn took a gendered form.[45] That is,

---

[42] *The Early English Versions of the Gesta Romanorum*, ed. Sydney Herrtage, EETS ES 33 (London, 1879), #61; *Jacob's Well*, ed. Arthur Brandeis, EETS OS 115 (London, 1900), p. 177.
[43] Ed. Banks, *Alphabet of Tales*, pp. 143–4. This perhaps suggests Abigall's fate in *The Jew of Malta*.
[44] Johnson, 'Male Jewish Menses'; Katz, 'Shylock's Gender'.
[45] See Walter Stephens, *Demon Lovers: Witchcraft, Sex and the Crisis of Belief* (Chicago, 2002), pp. 2–3.

both men and women could be witches – as they could be 'Jews' – and it was through faulty sex and faulty religion that witchcraft (like 'Judaism') was practised. The witches' *sabbat*, suffused with ideas of Jewish ritual, took as its main themes fantasies of flagrant demonic copulation and bloody infanticidal cannibalism.[46] Texts detailing witchcraft are lewd and salacious while defending sacramental religion (not least baptism, matrimony and contrition) but differ from the *exempla* of the Jew's daughter in that the witches' *sabbat* remains a thing apart, Other, un-negotiated. That is, the *sabbat* creates and confirms the divide between Christian and witch; what is striking about the figure of the Jew's daughter is that she exists in order for her Otherness to be enjoyed by the Christian male, for her body to be probed. Whereas witches have sex with each other, or with the devil, Christian men have sex with Jewish women.

These stories are neither simply clerical amusements nor records of erotic desire. As Paul Strohm has commented, '[b]loody beds are rife in late medieval literature'.[47] Sex with the Jew's daughter involves contempt and humiliation; in the first *exemplum* sex leads to an act of violence against the baby; in the second, sex is bound up with the Jews' faulty blood. According to Strohm, medieval texts – in concatenating sex and violence, in presenting sexuality as a wound – struggle with what Freud would later call the 'primal scene', the child's confusion about witnessed parental sexual intercourse, seen (by the child) as an act of violence and a stimulus to rivalry.[48] Strohm's insight is useful here, for these *exempla* are not only about sexuality and violence, but also about defining identity and rewriting origins. These narratives' Christian imperative comes from their depiction of rival typology, rival messianism: sexuality merges with and emerges from an impulse to interpretative competition and an act of humiliation, for it is in the Virgin Birth – the unspoken parallel to the Jewess's sexuality – that the Church Fathers sought 'to deny the origins of Christianity as an outgrowth of Judaism'.[49] In so presenting sexuality, these narratives ask audiences to interrogate the truth of Christian symbols; they mark a leaving behind of Jewish misinterpretation and Jewish bodies.

Thus several popular medieval *exempla* make cognate the physical desirability of the Jewish girl and her ripeness for conversion to Christianity. In one, again with a disordered morality, a Jewess converts to Christianity during her labour. A parish priest kills the child, but it is revived by the Virgin thanks to the mother's prior conversion.[50] In yet another story by Caesarius of Heisterbach, a Jewess converts and, in the face of torments inflicted by her father, refuses to renounce

---

46 See Stephens, *Demon Lovers*, pp. 56, 241; Ginzburg, *Ecstasies*, pp. 63–80.
47 *Theory and the Premodern Text* (Minneapolis, 2000), p. 202; on blood, sacred and profane, see Nicholas Vincent, *The Holy Blood: King Henry III and the Westminster Blood Relic* (Cambridge, 2001); Peggy McCracken, *The Curse of Eve, the Wound of the Hero: Blood, Gender and Medieval Literature* (Philadelphia, 2003).
48 *Theory*, p. 202.
49 See Kathleen M. Hobbs, 'Blood and Rosaries: Virginity, Violence and Desire in Chaucer's "Prioress's Tale" ', *Constructions of Widowhood and Virginity in the Middle Ages*, ed. Cindy Carlson and Angela Weisl (Basingstoke, 1999), pp. 181–98 (p. 182).
50 See *Beiträge zur lateinischen Erzählungsliteratur des Mittelalters 3: Das Viaticum narrationum des Henmannus Bononiensis*, ed. Alfons Hilka (Berlin, 1935), #39.

her faith.[51] In these stories the Jewess must be brought to appropriate authority; this authority is Christianity but also, in most cases, it takes her away from the Jewish father and obliges her to submit to a Christian man. Both 'woman' and 'Jew' are unstable categories of belief.

Conclusions

Lisa Lampert has recently read Shakespeare's *Merchant of Venice* as a debate on Christian traditions of 'woman' and 'Jew'; Lampert has highlighted not only how miscegenation is a central concern of the play – crucially, 'successful' intercourse between Jessica and Lorenzo, 'foiled' intercourse between Portia and Morocco – but how miscegenation can have a happy outcome if 'read' in a Christian way by its protagonists.[52] As Lampert points out, Morocco is unable 'to read like a Christian, to discern inner wealth';[53] Jessica, conversely, stops being an alien when she learns to interpret 'correctly', as a Christian. She is absorbed into the physical and matrimonial matrices of the play when she abandons her religion: 'I shall be sav'd by my husband, – he hath made me a Christian!' (III.v.17). In becoming Christian, Jessica thus also restores the heterosexual balance of the play, with Bassanio no longer the belovèd of Antonio but rather the active male defender of the faith. Likewise, in *The Jew of Malta*, Abigall is introduced in contradistinction to the Nunnery, which threatens to displace her (I.ii.253–5); by the play's close, she has fled to a friar ('Know, holy Sir, I am bold to sollicite thee', III.iii.57) to be admitted to a nunnery.

Naturally, attraction is a part of the same logic as repulsion and the texts under discussion knit these impulses. But, going further than this, these texts seek to connect the sexual impulse with religious conversion and to connect sexual difference with religious antagonism. In essentialising the Jewish body as something that is erotic because it is alien and because it is dangerous and yet also desirable, these stories fantasise and fetishise (and reify) Jewish difference; in seeking to probe the erotic self, these medieval Christian writers and preachers turned to a figure of alterity that articulates unbounded sexuality while rendering it impossible: 'Precisely because this cannot be, I desire it all the more.'[54] The Jewess's impossibility works at several different levels: as an absent presence in medieval England; as an impossible version of femininity; as an impossible version of sexual appetite; as an unacceptable miscegenation. The body of the Jew's daughter is one that is no less tangible, accessible, desirable, fantastical and incredible than Christ's body; both bodies perform desire, teach difference, bridge time and, perhaps most importantly, both bodies establish and integrate pain and pleasure. Finally, within a homosocial configuration, the Jewish daughter embodies the pleasure of attacking the Jewish male. The Christian cleric desires the Jew's daughter; sex with her is pleasurable because it affirms the humiliation of the Jewish father, so affirming Christian masculine identity through erotic pleasure.

---

[51] Caesarius II 25, 26.
[52] *Gender*, pp. 153–6.
[53] *Gender*, p. 155.
[54] Judith Butler, *Bodies That Matter: On the Discursive Limits of 'Sex'* (New York, 1993), p. 171.

Eros and Error:
Gross Sexual Transgression in the Fourth Branch of the Mabinogi

MICHAEL CICHON

ELEMENTS of the erotic appear in much medieval Welsh literature, such as the romantic heroic exploits depicted in the three Welsh Arthurian Romances and more playfully shocking themes, as evidenced by Dafydd ap Gwilym's complaint to his penis and Gwerfel Mechain's response in praise of her genitals.[1] The *Fourth Branch* of the *Mabinogi* is no exception to this penchant for the passionate, replete with its references to sexual encounters that both spark the erotic imagination and serve an instructive social purpose. Recounting erotic situations in and of themselves is not the redactor's primary objective: he uses the erotic potential of his tale to convey the message that misapplied passion and lust result in the breakdown of society. Suggestive rather than descriptive, the erotically charged passages in the *Fourth Branch* illustrate some sort of failure of social order, and this is no surprise: transgressive love is a staple of medieval literature.

The *Fourth Branch*, with its symbolic interpretations of everyday social obligations, communicates the necessity of maintaining social bonds and suggests that trespass of social and familial obligations requires redress and reparation. Myth communicates a number of sentiments – rules for social interaction, ethical conduct and even religious beliefs – and enforces a moral order necessary for group survival.[2] As Roberta Valente notes in her *Merched y Mabinogi*, the *Four Branches* contain guidelines of behaviour that depend on both an individual's obedience to such codes and that individual's ability to interpret difficult situations where principles conflict or are non-existent.[3] Valente also identifies a tripartite division of the *Fourth Branch*: the rape of Goewin, the humiliation of Aranrhod and the birth of Lleu, and Blodeuwedd's adultery.[4]

---

[1] See *Medieval Welsh Poems*, ed. Joseph P. Clancy (Dublin, 2003); *Dafydd ap Gwilym: His Poems*, trans. Gwyn Thomas (Cardiff, 2001); *Women and Writing in Medieval Europe*, ed. Carolyne Larrington (New York, 1995).
[2] Joseph Campbell, *Creative Mythology* (London, 1968), pp. 4–5, 48.
[3] '*Merched y Mabinogi*: Women and the Thematic Structure of the Four Branches' (Ph.D. Dissertation, Cornell University, 1986), p. 97.
[4] '*Merched*', p. 242.

In each case – rape, disgrace owing to the revelation of premarital sex, and adultery – the sexual transgression, made all the more interesting because the author uses animal transformation as a consequence of illicit sex, endangers civilisation and must be punished. The nature and function of the sex scenes in the *Fourth Branch* of the *Mabinogi* offer an example of the medieval Welsh literary treatment of *eros* and illustrate the social and legal expectations of female sexuality in that society.

Holding the honoured position of foot-holder to Math ap Mathonwy of Gwynedd, Goewin is the ill-starred obsession of the magician Gilfaethwy. The narrative recounts that 'ac yn yr oes honno Math vab Mathonwy ny bydei uyw, namyn tra vei y deudrot ymlyc croth morwyn, onyt kynwryf ryvel a'y llesteirei' (at that time Math son of Mathonwy could not live except while his feet were in the lap of a maiden, unless the strife of war prevented him).[5] Gilfaethwy's condition echoes descriptions of love-lorn knights in romance: 'a nachaf y liw a'y wed a'y ansawd yn atueilaw o'y charyat' (p. 67: and behold his colour and appearance and condition were declining because of love).[6] Consumed by an overwhelming passion for her, Gilfaethwy seeks the help of his brother Gwydion, also a magician. At this point, the story departs sharply from more usual descriptions of medieval romances. Rather than a conventional courtship and seduction, the two devise a ruse that embroils Math in a war, allowing Gilfaethwy the opportunity to satisfy his lust. When Math goes to rest his feet on Goewin's belly – a gesture itself charged with sexual potential because the redactor deliberately chooses the word *crowth*, 'womb', rather than the more common *arfedd*, 'lap', when describing this gesture[7] – Goewin announces that an open assault had been made against her, that she did not bear it quietly, and that the perpetrators were none other than the king's nephews Gwydion and Gilfaethwy. Promising to seek redress for Goewin and then for himself, Math takes the girl as his wife and grants her authority over his realm.[8]

The magicians' punishment is unique in medieval literature. Math asserts that it would be impossible for the wizards to make good the dishonour to his person, his loss of men and arms, and the loss of Pryderi of Dyfed against whom he was tricked into warring. Math's retribution transcends the realm of everyday law into something more mythological: with a magic wand, Gilfaethwy is transformed into a hind and his brother into a stag. They are banished to the forest and ordered to return in a year with whatever offspring the one has engendered on the other. At the end of the year, they are transformed into a sow and a boar to repeat the process, this time with Gwydion as female and Gilfaethwy as male. The third and final year of their punishment is spent in the guise of wolves, with Gilfaethwy as

---

5 *Pedeir Keinc y Mabinogi*, ed. Ifor Williams, 2nd edn (Cardiff, 1951), p. 67. Unless otherwise stated, translations of Welsh texts throughout are my own.
6 A cursory glance at other heroes of medieval romance, Chrétien's Lancelot, Owein/Yvain, Chaucer's Troilus, shows that such symptoms were widely acknowledged as an indication of love-sickness.
7 See *Math uab Mathonwy: Text from the Diplomatic Edition of the White Book of Rhydderch*, by J. Gwenogvryn Evans, ed. Patrick K. Ford (Belmont, MA, 1999), p. 21.
8 *Pedeir*, pp. 70–5.

bitch and Gwydion as sire. After this time, the wizards are returned to their human forms, and Math offers them peace and friendship.

This punishment is quite unlike the penalty for rape delineated in the Law of Women, according to most variants of the Law, a financial one. The *Cyfnerth* text states: 'Y neb a dycco treis ar wreic, talet y hamobyr y'r arglwyd a'e dirwy, a'e dilystaut a'e hegwedi a'e sarhaet a tal idi hitheu' (he who rapes a woman, let him pay her *amobr* to the lord and her *dirwy*; and her *dilystod* and *agweddi* and *sarhaed* he pays to her).[9] This version of the Law declares that because the king did not keep the maiden from rape, he loses his *amobr*.[10] The Latin redactions of *Cyfraith Hywel* proclaim that the rapist owes the lord the woman's *merces* and *dirwy*, and the woman her *iniuria*, *egweddi* and *dilysrwydd*.[11] Moreover, the rapist was to pay the king a silver rod as high as his mouth, and as thick as his middle finger; and a gold cup that could hold a full draught for the king, as thick as the thumbnail of a ploughman who had been at the plough for seven years.[12] The *Iorwerth* text is explicit in noting that rape brings shame and insult to a woman, her kin and her lord.[13] According to this text the rapist is to pay twelve cows to the lord and the woman's *amobr*; if the woman is a virgin he pays 'y chowyll a'e hegweddi yn y veint vwyhaf y dylyo, a'e hwynebwerth, a'e dilyssrwyd' (her *cowyll* and *egweddi* according to the greatest amount to which she may be entitled, and her face-value and her *dilysrwydd*).[14]

The medieval legal concept of rape was that it was a crime against the victim's male kin or husband.[15] Math recognises that the deflowering of Goewin is a direct affront to himself as king and guardian, and acknowledges this in his vow to seek redress.[16] That the rape of a maiden violates the protection of the king is clearly stated in the Law of Women, and the symbolic payment of rod and cup that is levied for the rape of a virgin and nearly identical to that for the *sarhaed* of a king further substantiates this link.[17] In the Law, the failure of the king to protect his

9 All references to the Law of Women are taken from *The Welsh Law of Women*, ed. Dafydd Jenkins and Morfydd E. Owen (Cardiff, 1990). *Amobr* is the fee payable to a lord with respect to a sexual union and is rendered *merces* in the Latin redactions of the Law. It was likely originally levied as a virginity-fine, but came to be claimed for second unions as well. *Amobr* was part of the income of the territorial lord. *Dirwy* is a fixed penalty for the more serious offences against state and society. *Dilystod* and *dilysrwydd* are interchangeable and refer to the payment made for the rape of a virgin. *Agweddi* or *egweddi* refers to the specific share of the common pool of matrimonial property to which a woman was entitled upon justifiable separation from her husband. This sum was calculated according to the status of her father. For fuller definitions, see Jenkins and Owen.
10 Jenkins and Owen, *Welsh Law*, pp. 139, 143.
11 Here *iniuria* is used in place of *sarhaed*. The *sarhaed* of a woman was always calculated in terms of her male kin or guardian: one-half the value of her brother or one-third that of her husband.
12 Jenkins and Owen, *Welsh Law*, p. 155.
13 *Llyfr Iorwerth*, ed. Aled R. Wiliam (Cardiff, 1960), p. 171.
14 Wiliam, *Llyfr Iorwerth*, pp. 170–1. *Cowyll* is the 'morning-gift' given to a virgin-bride by her husband, cognate with the English 'cowl', and literally refers to a head-cloth. Technically, it was the maidenhead fee owed to a woman from her husband. Presumably the payment of *cowyll* in the case of rape is to atone for the fact that if the victim afterwards was married, she would not be eligible to claim this gift.
15 James Brundage, *Law, Sex and Christian Society in the Medieval West* (Chicago, 1987), p. 209.
16 *Pedeir*, p. 74.
17 *The Law*, ed. and trans. Daydd Jenkins (Llandysul, 1986), p. 154; see also Valente, 'Merched', p. 250, n. 353.

subject from rape is marked by the denial of *amobr*. In marrying Goewin, Math both acknowledges and accepts responsibility for his failure to defend a maiden under his protection.[18]

Legally in medieval Wales, women had a relatively passive role. A woman's social identity and worth were defined in terms of her male kin or husband, and her nature defined as shameful. Morfydd Owen explains that this innate shame has no ethical connotations and does not imply dishonour. Shyness, blushing and timidity are the physical manifestations of this characteristic and are proper to a woman. As soon as the bonds of propriety are broken, however, shame becomes associated with dishonour and a loss of status.[19] This latent shame appears only when a woman is assaulted.[20] In raping Goewin, the brothers flaunt her shame; it is therefore appropriate that a similar shame be made manifest in them.

Gwydion and Gilfaethwy violate the honour of their king as well as their uncle; thus, the crime is an assault on the sanctity of kinship. Placing the desires of his brother over the security of his social group, Gwydion embroils all of Gwynedd in a war with Dyfed.[21] The rape is particularly heinous: it is not only an assault on an officer of the court[22] and dishonourable to Math, but also because by taking the maidenhead of Goewin, Gilfaethwy has jeopardised the life of Math. Insofar as it threatens his life, the rape might even be read as an attempted coup.[23] No thought was paid to protecting their kin from dishonour, nor have the obligations owed to their uncle the lord of Gwynedd been taken seriously.[24]

The transformation of Gwydion and Gilfaethwy is suitable to their crime and is unique in that it forces incest on them.[25] The punishment is mythical rather than strictly legal, but it does reflect a symbolic enforcement of tractates in the Law. The bestial nature of the criminals is emphasised by their transformation into wild animals.[26] Moreover, their expulsion from society symbolically suggests legal banishment. The animals into which the brothers shape-shift are themselves of note: the stag and boar denote cunning and savagery and, being horned, by extension phallic imagery. The wolf is predatory and associated with exile and outlawry in many cultures.

The metamorphosis itself is a mythological reflection of the law. By turning the rapists into females, Math symbolically castrates them. The *Cyfnerth* redaction of the Law of Women reports: 'Ony eill y gwr y thalu dyker y dwy geill' (if the man cannot pay [the stipulated fines] let his two testicles be taken).[27] That they are

---

[18] *Pedeir*, p. 74.
[19] 'Shame and Reparation: Women's Place in the Kin', *Welsh Law*, ed. Jenkins and Owen, pp. 40–68 (p. 45).
[20] Jacob Black-Michaud, *Cohesive Force: Feud in the Mediterranean and the Middle East* (New York, 1975), p. 218.
[21] Roberta Valente, 'Gwydion and Aranrhod: Crossing the borders of gender in *Math*', *The Mabinogi: A Book of Essays*, ed. C. W. Sullivan III (New York, 1996), pp. 331–45 (p. 335).
[22] Jenkins, *The Law*, p. 32.
[23] Katherine Millersdaughter, 'The Geopolitics of Incest: Sex, Gender and Violence in the Fourth Branch of the Mabinogi', *Exemplaria* 14:2 (2002), pp. 271–316 (p. 288).
[24] Valente, 'Crossing', p. 334.
[25] Andrew Welsh, 'Doubling and Incest in the Mabinogi', *Speculum* 65:2 (1990), pp. 344–62 (p. 359).
[26] Elizabeth Archibald, *Incest and the Medieval Imagination* (Oxford, 2001), p. 198.
[27] Jenkins and Owen, *Welsh Law*, pp. 142–3.

struck with a rod to effect this change recalls the rape itself.[28] Gwydion and Gilfaethwy are literally made female to illustrate to them the vulnerability of women to men.[29] Certainly, the fact that they are forced to copulate and present their offspring at court illustrates this unstated yet integral aspect of medieval Welsh society. The redactor of the *Fourth Branch* has very deliberately taken an instance of erotic potential and used it to demonstrate the consequences of uncontrolled *eros*.

The second instance of gross sexual transgression in the *Fourth Branch* also involves Gwydion and is a direct result of the first. After the rape of Goewin and the termination of the war with Dyfed, Math requires a new virgin footholder. Gwydion, restored to his human self and back in favour with his uncle, nominates his sister Aranrhod for this office. When summoned to court and asked if she is a virgin, Aranrhod replies, ' "ny wynn i amgen no'm bot" ' (*Pedeir*, p. 77: 'I know not but that I am'). Faced with such an ambiguous answer, Math tests Aranrhod by having her step over his magic wand, whereupon a young, blond boy and a so-called 'little thing' drop from her body. Aranrhod flees the scene, and Gwydion scoops up the 'little thing'.[30]

The episode relates another instance of sexual impropriety that endangers the social order and reinforces many of the same social and legal concerns revealed in the punishment of Gwydion and Gilfaethwy. Aranrhod has lied about her virginity, which prolongs the vulnerability of, and could possibly result in the death of, her uncle. Aranrhod, presumably aware of her true condition,[31] would certainly have known about Math's vital need for a virgin foot-holder; her equivocal answer is a lie by which she privileges her own reputation over the life of her uncle and sovereign.

Medieval Welsh Law did not look favourably upon women who lied about their virginity, and Aranrhod's sexual activity has potentially harmful ramifications for her kin over and above the threat it poses to Math. Nerys Patterson observes that in law, the central element in the punishment of a false virgin is exposure of her genitals. This happens to some extent when Aranrhod gives birth openly, revealing her promiscuity to the court. Because public shaming exposes what was concealed and provides some redress for a kin-group stripped of its dignity,[32] the narrative conforms to the spirit of the law while sparing Aranrhod the legal punishment of holding a shaved, greased bull's tail. Interestingly, Aranrhod, a strikingly forthright woman and the most independent woman in the tale,[33] does not seem answerable to Math:[34] Math does not receive *amobr* once her promiscuity is revealed, nor does he undertake to punish her when she ignores her

---

[28] Valente, 'Crossing', p. 335.
[29] Valente, 'Crossing', p. 335.
[30] *Pedeir*, p. 77.
[31] C. W. Sullivan, 'Inheritance and Lordship in *Math*', *The Mabinogi*, ed. Sullivan, pp. 347–66 (p. 359). For an alternative reading, see Sarah Larrat Keefer, 'The Lost Tale of Dylan in the Fourth Branch of *The Mabinogi*', *The Mabinogi*, ed. Sullivan, pp. 79–97, passim.
[32] Nerys Patterson, 'Honour and Shame in Medieval Welsh Society', *Studia Celtica* 16/17 (1981–2), pp. 73–103 (pp. 74–9).
[33] Fiona Winward, 'Some Aspects of the Women in *The Four Branches*', *Cambrian Medieval Celtic Studies* 34 (1997), pp. 77–106 (pp. 83, 88).
[34] Winward, 'Some Aspects', p. 88.

maternal obligations.³⁵ Aranrhod is never named in reference to a man, which implies independence from rules of conventional behaviour.³⁶ Perhaps she succeeds here because she maintains her own dominion,³⁷ or indulges in sex without submitting to love or marriage. Nevertheless, her wantonness and subsequent disavowal of motherhood have lasting repercussions, which seem to interest the redactor more than the erotic potential of her liaisons.

Confronted with the 'little thing' that Gwydion has raised to boyhood, Aranrhod exclaims: ' "Oy a wr! Ba doi arnat ti uyg kywildaw i, a dilyt uyg kywilyd, a'y gadw yn gyhyt a hynn?" ' (*Pedeir*, p. 78: 'Oh man! What came over you to put me to shame, and to strive for my shame, and to keep it as long as this?'). She then utters three 'destinies' for the boy: he will not have a name and weapons unless they are granted by her, and when Gwydion cunningly circumvents these curses, she pronounces that Lleu will not have a wife ' "o'r genedyl yssyd ar y dayar honn yr awr honn" ' (*Pedeir*, p. 83: 'of the race that is on this earth at this time'). Roberta Valente argues that fertility and motherhood allow women to exert power, but failure in these qualities could imperil the community.³⁸ In law, a mother is protected if her child is legitimate but shames the whole kin if she conceives outside acceptable circumstances.³⁹ 'Aranrhod is manipulated by her brother into demonstrating her fertility publicly, and he fosters the product of her female power to her everlasting shame.'⁴⁰ The situation is more complex than the legal examples, for although Gwydion as brother should be shamed by his sister's promiscuity, as an uncaring magician he has consistently demonstrated a lack of responsibility towards his own kin; moreover, by fostering Lleu, he ensures that Aranrhod's shame continues to be explicit. Given that Gwydion and Math forcibly expose Aranrhod's private life,⁴¹ one might be inclined to treat Aranrhod more sympathetically. Beyond her concern for shame, 'Aranrhod seems to understand that a woman's power lies solely in her potential as heir-bearer and that to accept her children would be to compromise her independence and individuality.'⁴² In this light, her refusal to embrace motherhood is a bid for independence, for once a woman fulfils her reproductive function, the focus of the narrative inevitably shifts to the children.⁴³ Although Gwydion might be within his rights as Aranrhod's kinsman to question and censure her sexual activity, he repeatedly exposes her to the very shame from which he is obliged to protect her. The narrative perhaps suggests that men who do not care about the reputation of their kin-group except when it suits them do not have the right to enforce obligations involving honour.

Humiliated because of her brother's impulsive actions and angered by his interference, Aranrhod attempts to deny her son a social identity.⁴⁴ In his study of

---

35 Winward, 'Some Aspects', p. 88.
36 Valente, 'Crossing', p. 336.
37 Winward, 'Some Aspects', p. 88.
38 'Merched', pp. 11–12.
39 Valente, 'Crossing', p. 334.
40 Valente, 'Crossing', p. 335.
41 Valente, 'Merched', p. 257.
42 Winward, 'Some Aspects', p. 100.
43 Winward, 'Some Aspects', p. 105.
44 Valente, 'Merched', p. 62.

Welsh kinship, T. M. Charles-Edwards shows that a child was technically a foetus until baptised or named, and that naming implied public recognition of kinship.[45] Aranrhod's refusal to name denies her son his place as an adult in the kin.[46] Furthermore, naming was a public event and announcement of kin relationships.[47] Keeping her son out of the social order, Aranrhod veils her shame and also maintains the secret of the father's identity.[48] On an anthropological level, Jacob Black-Michaud reports that 'the sexual integrity of a woman is vested with extreme value, since the misuse of the reproductive powers of women results in the "waste" of an affinal tie and, if progeny ensues, a potential misappropriation of manpower'.[49] Illicit sex here compromises social order, blurs the bonds of kinship, and the mother's response severely disadvantages the resultant offspring.

Aranrhod's and Gwydion's conflicted relationship merits further attention with regard to the hint that Lleu is the product of their incest. Although many critics assume this, the text is ambiguous.[50] In their translations of the *Mabinogi*, Jeffrey Gantz and Patrick Ford both point out that obviously more than one tradition about the Children of Dôn circulated before the *Four Branches* were written down, which might explain this uncertainty.[51] The independent tradition that Lleu is as much Gwydion's son as Aranrhod's[52] makes possible a contemporary audience's accepting the incestuous relationship, which further complicates the already delicate social problem engendered by Aranrhod's active sex life. Katherine Millersdaughter argues that Gwydion rapes Aranrhod, and that Gwydion is 'arguably the man to whom she lost her viriginity'.[53] She is perhaps over-forceful here, especially because in the text of the *Fourth Branch* there is no explicit indication that the two have any kind of sexual relationship. Even if she did have intercourse with Gwydion, this may not have been her first sexual experience. Sarah Keefer argues convincingly that Dylan, the first-born twin, is in fact the product of Aranrhod's relationship with a sea-divinity, and, as Andrew Welsh observes, the birth of twins was considered 'a classificatory embarrassment'.[54] That sex with one person was believed to yield only one child is further substantiated by Marie de France's lai *Le Fresne*,[55] so we might at most have evidence of multiple partners.

Throughout this essay I link sexual impropriety with animal transformation. Upon first glance this pairing seems to be absent from the narrative of Dylan's and Lleu's birth; however, Keefer, following W. J. Gruffydd, points out that after his birth and baptism, Dylan changes from human into a nameless sea creature appar-

---

45 Charles-Edwards, *Early Irish and Welsh Kinship* (Oxford, 1993), p. 177.
46 Charles-Edwards, *Kinship*, p. 178.
47 Valente, 'Merched', p. 133.
48 Valente, 'Merched', pp. 263–4.
49 *Cohesive Force*, p. 226.
50 Welsh, 'Doubling', p. 356.
51 Jeffrey Gantz, trans., *The Mabinogion* (Harmondsworth, 1976), introduction passim, esp. p. 10; Patrick Ford, trans and ed., *The Mabinogi and other Medieval Welsh Tales* (Berkeley, 1977), introduction passim, esp. p. 29.
52 See W. J. Gruffydd, *Math vab Mathonwy* (Cardiff, 1928), where Gruffydd posits an independent tradition for Gwydion's and Aranrhod's affair. See also T. Gwynn Jones's tale of Huan in *Welsh Folklore and Folk-Custom*, 2nd edn (Woodbridge, 1979), pp. 16, 28.
53 'Geopolitics', p. 303.
54 'Doubling', p. 350.
55 See *Lais: Marie de France*, ed. Alfred Ewert (Oxford, 1947).

ently by his own volition.⁵⁶ If this is the case, and Keefer argues strongly for it, then there is good reason to accept the association of transfiguration with each episode of transgressive sex in the *Fourth Branch*. Furthermore, reading Gwydion's and Aranrhod's relationship as incestuous further reinforces the negative socio-political connotations suggested by forbidden sexual acts. Whether or not we regard Gwydion and Aranrhod as lovers is not central to the argument that illicit sex compromises social order, but such a reading most certainly magnifies the seriousness of an already severe offence.

If the most disturbing episode of sex and transformation in the *Fourth Branch* affects Gwydion and Gilfaethwy, certainly the most heart-wrenching involves the ill-fated trio Lleu, Blodeuwedd and Gronw Pebr. In response to Aranrhod's final curse, Gwydion and Math create a bride for Lleu using 'blodeu y deri a blodeu y banadyl a blodeu yr erwein' (*Pedeir*, p. 83: flowers of the oak-tree, and flowers of the broom, and flowers of the meadow-sweet). Immediately afterwards, Blodeuwedd, the Flower Maiden, is baptised and following a wedding feast, she and Lleu consummate their marriage (*Pedeir*, p. 83). Later when Lleu is away, Blodeuwedd offers hospitality to a travelling hunter, Gronw Pebr. The two become lovers, plot and then carry out the murder of Lleu (*Pedeir*, pp. 84–8).

Once again, the narrative presents a series of events that link illicit sex to detrimental socio-political outcomes. Gwydion's and Math's best efforts to circumvent Aranrhod's third curse literally engender the adultery problem.⁵⁷ Indeed, moulded as the perfect wife, Blodeuwedd becomes the 'sensual deceiver',⁵⁸ proving that while the magicians can create life, they cannot control love. Too many variables are at play for the relationship between Lleu and Blodeuwedd to proceed smoothly.

Blodeuwedd's downfall begins with the best of intentions: she offers hospitality to a wandering hunter. As Valente notes, 'hospitality is a serious responsibility in this world; it is hard to know which is worse – to refuse to accept it or to forget to offer it'.⁵⁹ Offering food and shelter to a passerby, Blodeuwedd behaves as the wife of a respectable lord ought to and until she meets Gronw Pebr, she has no ulterior motives. It is only once the future lovers make eye contact that 'nit oed gyueir arnei hi ny bei yn llawn o'e garyat ef. Ac ynteu a synywys arnei hitheu; a'r un medwl a doeth yndaw ef ac a doeth yndi hitheu' (*Pedeir*, p. 85: there was not a part of her that was not full with the love of him. And he took notice of her, and a thought came to him as it had come to her). This love at first sight has much in common with medieval courtly love narratives, and it also recalls Gilfaethwy's ill-omened lust for Goewin. Like Gwydion's solution, the plan to murder Lleu concocted by the adulterous pair can only end in disaster. Still, the redactor seems sympathetic towards Blodeuwedd who, 'though she is created by men for their own purposes, exercises her own free will in a recognisably and passionately human situation'.⁶⁰ Sioned Davies echoes this sentiment, proposing that although her adultery is an act of rebellion, 'it is no ordinary adultery but rather a wife who wishes to control her own personality and freedom to use her intellect and

---

56 'Lost Tale', pp. 82ff.
57 Sullivan, 'Inheritance', p. 342.
58 Winward, 'Some Aspects', p. 78.
59 '*Merched*', p. 155.
60 Valente, '*Merched*', p. 43.

emotions as she chooses'.[61] Unfortunately, this desire conflicts with the social values expected of medieval Welshwomen – patience, modesty, wisdom, chastity and loyalty. While Aranrhod seems to escape censure by not loving, Blodeuwedd accedes to her desires and crosses the bounds of all propriety. Black-Michaud notes that women are an 'unimpeachable excuse for a feud',[62] and the laws report that if unlawful intercourse happens with a woman, it engenders kin-feud.[63] Julian Pitt-Rivers observes that 'the preoccupation with the sexual purity of women and its protection relates to the belief in the transmission of moral qualities through physical inheritance',[64] and that 'lack of chastity in women places in jeopardy the family honour accumulated by forbears, whereas in men it destroys the honour of *other* families'.[65] Whatever sympathy one might have for a woman who endeavours to control her own destiny, Blodeuwedd's duplicity, sexual transgression and attempted murder of her spouse brazenly defy all accepted social norms and thus necessitate a reprisal equal to or greater than the original offence.

When Lleu returns, Blodeuwedd feigns a protective concern for him in order to learn how he might be killed. This is the first time we see any kind of conversation take place between Lleu and his wife.[66] Elsewhere in the *Four Branches*, loving couples converse regularly. Davies points out that dialogue is an important narrative technique in this text, and also notes that the male characters in these stories highly praise women who are good conversationalists.[67] Valente notes that in literature, Celtic women are admired for abstract qualities such as sweet speech, wisdom, voice and chastity,[68] and as Winward proves, the chief power of women in the *Four Branches* stems from the manipulation of words and understanding how to exploit social dynamics.[69] In Blodeuwedd's case, however, *ymddiddan*, 'conversing', is employed for devious purposes. Blodeuwedd says nothing until she meets Gronw, so 'this intimately detailed moment of meeting is meant to reopen the discussion which had been explored throughout this Branch: the tension which results when one person manipulates social codes and obligations to satisfy his or her own ambitions and desires'.[70] Her relationships, built on plotting and deception, are obviously meant to contrast with other loving relationships in the *Four Branches*. When Blodeuwedd has convinced Lleu to pantomime the conditions under which he might be slain, Gronw stabs him with a poisoned spear. Thus betrayed, Lleu becomes an eagle and flies away.[71]

Much has been made of Lleu's metamorphosis. It recalls Gwydion's and Gilfaethwy's alteration into beasts and without doubt foreshadows Blodeuwedd's change into an owl. To the author of the *Fourth Branch*, transformation is very clearly a theme linked to acts of deception and illicit sex. When Gwydion at last

---

[61] *The Four Branches of the Mabinogi: Pedeir Keinc y Mabinogi* (Llandysul, 1993), p. 80.
[62] *Cohesive Force*, p. 206.
[63] *Llyfr Iorwerth*, p. 24.
[64] Julian Pitt-Rivers, *The Fate of Shechem: On the Politics of Sex* (Cambridge, 1977), p. 78.
[65] *Fate*, p. 78.
[66] *Pedeir*, p. 85.
[67] *Four Branches*, pp. 42–3.
[68] 'Merched', pp. 110–11.
[69] 'Some Aspects', p. 102.
[70] Valente, 'Merched', pp. 273–4.
[71] *Pedeir*, p. 88.

finds his nephew, the 'eagle' is rotting. Pitt-Rivers notes that the cuckold is an object of contempt and in a state of desecration, not because adultery is an issue of right or wrong behaviour but rather one of sanctity and defilement.[72] Lleu's mouldering state is a physical reflection of his desecration and defilement. The form of an eagle is also important, as it is one of three beasts of battle mentioned in Welsh poetry. David Klausner observes that references to eagles often occur in warrior similes, where the idea is that the hero possesses the qualities of the beast to which he is compared.[73] Here, Lleu's form signals what he should be, a warrior, whereas his physical condition indicates what he is, a cuckold.

After Gwydion restores Lleu to human form and arranges for his convalescence, Lleu demands revenge. Not surprisingly, Lleu refuses financial compensation for the insult he has suffered and instead slays Gronw with a spear. Gwydion, for his part, hunts down Blodeuwedd and turns her into an owl:

> 'Ny ladaf i di. Mi a wnaf yssyd waeth it. Sef yw hynny,' heb ef, 'dy ellwng yn rith ederyn. Ac o achaws y kywilyd a wnaethost ti y Lew Llaw Gyffes, na ueidych ditheu dangos dy wyneb lliw did byth, a hynny rac ouyn yr holl adar, a bot gelynyaeth y rynghot a'r holl adar, a bot yn anyan udunt dy uaedu a'th amherchi y lle i'th gaffant ...' (*Pedeir*, p. 91)

('I will not kill you. I will make it worse for you. That is,' he said, 'I will set you free in the form of a bird. And because of the shame you have done to Lleu Llaw Gyffes you are never to show your face in the light of day, because of a fear of all birds, and let there be hostility between you and all birds, and let it be their nature to harass and molest you in the place they may find you.')

Blodeuwedd is punished for a crime that violates the social order and that endangers a future heir to the throne of Gwynedd.

The final incident of shape-shifting in this tale recalls the previous transformations, drawing attention to a sexual transgression and serving as redress for that breach. Blodeuwedd's creator Gwydion was transformed for a comparable crime with similar repercussions, and one might conjecture here a medieval Welsh version of the nature/nurture question. Moreover, her transformation mirrors what happened to Lleu, first in terms of physical change – they both become birds – and second in terms of community. The attempted murder of her husband made him an outcast so she, in turn, is cast out. The transformation into owl form is telling, and the text explains it somewhat:

> 'no chollych dy enw, namyn dy alw uyth yn Blodeuwed. Sef yw Blodeuwed, tylluan o'r ieith yr awr honn. Ac o achaws hynny y mae digassawc yr adar y'r tylluan ac ef a elwir etwa y dyllyan yn Blodeuwedd.' (*Pedeir*, p. 91)

('you shall not lose your name, but you will forever be called Blodeuwedd. Blodeuwedd is "owl" in the language of this particular time. And on account of this birds are hateful to the owl and it is even now called Blodeuwedd.')

---

[72] *Fate*, p. 24.
[73] David Klausner, 'The Topos of the Beasts of Battle in Early Welsh Poetry', *The Centre and its Compass: Studies in Medieval Literature in Honour of Professor John Leyerle*, ed. Robert A. Taylor, James E. Burke, Patricia J. Eberle, Ian Lancashire and Brian S. Merilees (Kalamazoo, 1993), pp. 247–63 (pp. 253–4).

This imagery echoes Biblical literature, especially Psalm 102, which describes an owl in a wilderness, in waste places, as a lonely bird on a rooftop, taunted by enemies.[74] Certainly, as J. K. Bollard notes, the ethos of the *Mabinogi* is consistent with the Judaeo-Christian ethical system within which the audience lived.[75] Notably, one also sees a mythological reflection of the lawcodes here. The Iorwerth Code states that one of the three things for which it is right for a man to beat his wife includes finding her with another man.[76] Both Davies and Valente observe that hostile birds will strike Blodeuwedd just as a cuckolded husband is allowed to strike his wife by law; therefore, the punishment to which Lleu is legally entitled becomes the responsibility of the birds.[77]

Undeniably, the episodes that make up the *Fourth Branch* of the *Mabinogi* reflect a society that placed great stock in strict adherence to well-defined roles and behaviours. In pre-industrial shame-cultures, honour is both a claim to pride and the communal acknowledgement of the right to that pride.[78] Associated with the trespass of social and familial obligations, then, is the necessity for redress and reparation, illustrated here by the interactions between Math and his nephews, Gwydion and Aranrhod, and Lleu, whose first self-sufficient act is to seek revenge. Furthermore, Catherine Byfield characterises the *Fourth Branch* as a series of illicit sexual acts, unnatural offspring, usurpation of roles and kinship transgressions with Gwydion as the pivot.[79] This reading conforms with Andrew Welsh's sense that the narrative is a cautionary tale about too much tampering with nature and social order.[80] Describing romances and erotic situations is not the main purpose of the redactor: his narrative is more related to social situations, although these are all driven by lust. In effect, he uses the erotic potential of his tale to moralise. The various transgressions are rooted in passion, and the strength of passion is directly proportional to the transgression it sets up. With its inevitably punitive outcome, every transgressive sexual act initiates a social exchange that, as in the compensation for any insult, resolves the disruptive pairing. Threatening order, sexual staining can only be contained by being likened to verbal staining and cleansed in the same way. All insult thereby comes to possess a sexual dimension, as indeed does the whole social exchange of punishment for offence. This is literally and figuratively manifest in the *Fourth Branch*, where the redactor explores the interplay between the erotic and violence, and each transgression, although punished by shame and transformation, engenders another.[81]

---

74 Psalm 102, New Revised Standard Version.
75 'The Role of Myth and Tradition in *The Four Branches of the Mabinogi*', *The Mabinogi*, ed. Sullivan, pp. 277–302 (p. 278).
76 Valente, '*Merched*', p. 281.
77 Davies, *Four Branches*, pp. 64–5.
78 Pitt-Rivers, 'Honour and Social Status', *Honour and Shame: the Values of Mediterranean Society*, ed. J. G. Peristiany (Chicago, 1966), pp. 19–78 (p. 21).
79 'Character and Conflict in the *Four Branches of the Mabinogi*', *Bulletin Board of Celtic Studies* 40 (1993), pp. 51–72, passim.
80 'Doubling', p. 360.
81 My thanks to Lisa Erickson, Heather Giles, David Parkinson, Alan Reese and Andrea Schutz for their assistance with this essay.

Perverse and Contrary Deeds: The Giant of Mont Saint Michel and the Alliterative Morte Arthure

THOMAS H. CROFTS

B Y WAY OF introduction, I would like to look again at one of the most well-known words in the alliterative *Morte Arthure*. In the *proem*, just when the poet turns from the Almighty to his earthly listeners, he gives this indication of his subject matter:

> 3e that liste has to lyth or luffes for to here
> Off elders of alde tym and of theire awke dedys,
> How they were lele in theire lawe, and louede God Almyghty.[1]

In apposition to the 'elders' are their deeds, which the poet calls 'awke', in Edmund Brock's gloss 'perverse and contrary',[2] in Krishna's 'strange, perverse'. It is a rare usage, but Malory's employment of the word in his 'Tristram' section is instructive: 'And therewithal sir Trystrames strode unto hym and toke his lady from him, and with an awke stroke he smote of hir hede clene'.[3] In his glossary to Vinaver's edition, G. L. Brooke supplies 'back-handed' for *awke*, and for *awkewarde* (at 230:10, also describing a sword-stroke) 'with a backward stroke'.[4] 'Awke dedys', then, according to the alliterative poem's argument, play out over the total genealogy of the elders in question, which genealogy, we should recall, is not only Arthurian, but, as indicated in the poem's concluding lines, also Trojan:

> Thus endis kyng Arthure, as auctors allegges,
> That was of Ectores blude, the kynge sone of Troye,
> And of sir Pryamous, the prynce, praysed in erthe;
> ffro thethene broghte the Bretons alle his bolde eldyrs
> In-to Bretayne the brode, as the Bruytte tellys. (4342–6)

---

[1] *The Alliterative Morte Arthure: A Critical Edition*, ed. Valerie Krishna (New York, 1976), 12–14. This edition, as AMA, is cited throughout.
[2] *Morte Arthure, or The Death of Arthur*, ed. Edmund Brock, EETS OS 8 (London, 1871).
[3] *The Works of Sir Thomas Malory*, ed. Eugène Vinaver, rev. by P. J. C. Field, 3rd edn, 3 vols (Oxford, 1990), p. 415.
[4] *Works of Malory*, p. 1707.

he audience of the poem is urged at the outset, then, to listen carefully, to be scrutinising deeds (both reported and implied) for things that are 'awke'.

Numerous modern critics have certainly heeded this conjuration, especially with reference to the internal logic (or illogic) of conquest. The word *awke* itself, as many have noted, contradicts the line that follows it. As William Matthews observes, 'the effect of "awke" in this crucial position could only have been to impose some measure of ambiguity upon all the splendor and heroic victories that follow'.[5] Lee Patterson has traced the poem's genealogical memory of conquest and migration to show how the poem, though its hero Arthur, proceeds with 'breathtaking inconsistency' in its delineation of right.[6] Also mindful of the poem's imperial project, Jeffrey Jerome Cohen observes that the epistemology of gigantism thrives in romance, that the eradication of the Giant of Mont Saint Michel is both a political and an erotic problem that reveals uncomfortable truths about the genre: 'Because regnal and monstrous bodies ultimately coincide in the romance, Arthur is implicated in the crimes that the giant commits.'[7] Standing on the shoulders of these and other readings, I will take the course here of investigating the peculiar sex life of the Giant of Mont Saint Michel, who, I shall argue, becomes ever more fully embodied within the tradition until, in the alliterative *Morte Arthure*, he emerges so voluptuously as to render 'awke' the entire enterprise.

The Giant of Mont Saint Michel: From *Topos* to Monstrosity

The Giant of Mont Saint Michel has been a fixture in Arthurian literature since, in Geoffrey of Monmouth's *Historia regum Britannae*, he wandered out of Spain and began terrorising Arthur's subjects in coastal Brittany. Drawing on biblical and historiographical traditions going back to the Old Testament and supported by Augustine, Geoffrey introduced the Giant as a challenge to Arthur's martial prowess at the peak of his imperial ambitions. The creature is found overwhelmingly in chronicle and romance texts that retell Geoffrey's history of Arthur's Roman war, in all of which he invariably does, at least, what Geoffrey made him do: kidnap and murder Arthur's kinswoman Helena, daughter of Hoel, Duke of Brittany, and in turn suffer Arthur's punishment. The Giant's regular, often rote, appearance in many chronicles attests to his integral place in the historiographical tradition. By the time of the alliterative *Morte Arthure*, however, Arthur's gigantomachy has become not just a fixture, a *topos*, but, in Corinne Saunders' words 'a founding event in Arthurian history'.[8] The alliterative *Morte Arthure* loads the giant-episode with meaning as Geoffrey and his two great vernacular followers Wace and La3amon do not. This is due in part to the fourteenth-century poem's more limited historical scope, since treating only Arthur's history allows for more dilation, but it is due also to the alliterative *Morte Arthur*'s own preoccupations. How this giant goes from being a *topos* – rhetorically external and prior to the

---

5 *The Tragedy of Arthur: A Study of the Alliterative 'Morte Arthure'* (Berkeley, 1960), pp. 112–13.
6 *Negotiating the Past: The Historical Understanding of Medieval Literature* (Madison, 1987), p. 215.
7 *Of Giants: Sex, Monsters, and the Middle Ages* (Minneapolis, 1999), pp. 87, 154.
8 *Rape and Ravishment in Medieval England* (Cambridge, 2001), p. 206.

Morte Arthure – to being a fully embodied, lust-ridden and *foundational* rapist and cannibal is the subject of the first part of this essay. I will argue that this movement from rhetorical figment to literal monstrosity may be traced to the convergence within romance of two *topoi* – the *gigantomachia* and the *raptus*. I will preface my reading of the alliterative *Morte Arthure* with a brief look at each *topos* individually.

Gigantomachia

The Giant of Mont Saint Michel's literary and historiographical context is both broad and inherently political. Not only the giant's size, but his existence as a stumbling block to Arthur's continental designs marks him as a descendant of the Anakites, a tribe of giants encountered by Israel in its migration out of Egypt. In Numbers 13:32–3, men sent by Moses to scout out the land of Canaan return with discouraging news:

> They brought up an evil report of the land which they had spied out to the children of Israel, saying, The land, through which we have gone to spy it out, is a land that eats up the inhabitants of it; and all the people who we saw in it are men of great stature. There we saw the Nephilim, the sons of Anak, who come of the Nephilim: and we were in our own sight as grasshoppers, and so we were in their sight.

Apart from the danger represented by the Nephilim, the promised land itself is anthropophagous ('a land that eats men').[9] Giants such as the Anakites, such as Goliath, uncanny leftovers from antediluvian times, are peculiarly omnipresent in Old Testament history. Going further back we find them in Genesis 6:4:

> Giants were on the earth in those days, and also after that, when God's sons came to men's daughters. They bore children to them: the same were the mighty men who were of old, men of renown.

St Augustine takes this to mean that giants were being born before and after this moment, which – since the moment just after this is the flood itself – means that giants are not monstrous, one-off hybrids, products of unnatural coupling between angels and the daughters of men, but part of God's creation and latent in human generations:

> Some people, however, are worried by the statement in the Bible that the mating of those who are called the 'sons of God' with the women they loved resulted in men who were not of our own kind: they were giants. These critics seem to ignore the fact that even in our own time men have been born whose bodies far exceed the normal stature of men today ... Was there not in Rome a few years ago, when the destruction of the city by the Goths was drawing near, a woman, living with her father and mother, who towered far above all other inhabitants with a stature which could be called gigantic? An amazing crowd rushed to see her, wherever she went. And what excited special wonder was the fact that both her parents were not even as tall as the tallest people that we see in our everyday experience.[10]

---

9   See also Deuteronomy 2:20–1.
10 *City of God*, trans. Henry Bettenson (Harmondsworth, 1984), Book XV, Chapter 23, pp. 638–9.

Citing recent history, scripture and Vergil,[11] Augustine is careful to stress that giants (a) exist, and (b) are a category of human being. They were present at, but not participants in, the mating between 'sons of God' and 'daughters of men'. They perished in, but also survived, the deluge and, just as the germ of wickedness somehow survived that flood, so giants could resurface to squat in Canaan or cause a stir in Rome. The humanity, let alone the citizenship, of giants is a counter-intuitive proposition, to say the least, but one intended for the ears of Augustine's own doctrinal adversaries, on whom he would impress the irrelevance of human citizenship. That Augustine's giant girl arises just before the sack of Rome by the barbarians is no accident. She is a sign of Rome's own enormities. Ruminating on Rome's foundation by fratricide, after all, Augustine condemns the avarice of its entire subsequent history thus: 'what would have been kept smaller and better by innocence grew through crime into something bigger and worse'.[12]

In Geoffrey's *Historia*, which is a Vergilian and not an Augustinian history, Brutus receives a prophecy about Britain from Diana that runs as follows:

'Brutus, beyond the setting of the sun, past the realms of Gaul, there lies an island in the sea, once occupied by giants. Now it is empty and ready for your folk. Down the years this will prove an abode suited to you and to your people; and for your descendants it will be a second Troy. A race of kings will be born there from your stock and the round circle of the whole earth will be subject to them.'[13]

This is essentially the same moment as *Aeneid* I.278-9 – *his ego nec metas rerum nec tempora pono/ imperium sine fine dedi*[14] – and an exemplary witness to the Vergilian subtext of Geoffrey's history. In form, it is a replication as well as a continuation of that 'primary' *translatio imperii*. On arrival in Albion, however, Brutus finds Diana's information to be not entirely good, since now it 'was uninhabited except for a few giants' (*a namine exceptis paucis hominibus gigantibus inhabitabatur*).[15]

Nor can we omit the strange and perverse tale that kicks off the Middle English prose *Brut*, in which Albyne and her thirty-two sisters are married off by their father, the king of Syria, to thirty-three royal husbands. After brief, unhappy marriages, Albyne leads her sisters in slitting their husbands' throats as they sleep. Banished and set on a boat with a year's provisions, they eventually arrive at an unpeopled island, which Albyne names after herself, and where the sisters eat their way through the island's herbs, fruits and beasts, gorging until they 'bycomen wonder fatte', whereupon they develop insatiable sexual appetites (literally insatiable since there are no men on the island). Perceiving an opportunity, the Devil divides himself into thirty-three incubi and lies with the sisters, whereby 'weren born horrible Geauntes in Albion'. These are the very giants, says the *Brut*, which Brutus later 'conqueryd & scomfyted'.[16] As Cohen acutely remarks of this tale, 'a

---

[11] *City of God*, Book XV, Chapter 9, p. 609.
[12] *City of God*, Book XV, Chapter 5, p. 600.
[13] *History of the Kings of Britain*, trans. Lewis Thorpe (Harmondsworth, 1966), p. 65.
[14] 'To them no bounds of empire I assign,/ Nor term of years to their immortal line' (Dryden).
[15] Thorpe, p. 72; *The Historia regum Britanniae of Geoffrey of Monmouth I: Bern, Bugerbibliothek, MS. 568*, ed. Neil Wright (Cambridge, 1984), p. 13.
[16] *The Brut, or Chronicles of England, Part I*, ed. Friedrich W. D. Brie, EETS OS 131 (London, 1906), pp. 1-4.

monstrous feminine origin has been provided for Geoffrey's orderly masculine one'.[17] In any case, British history proper cannot begin until the giants are exterminated.

Raptus

But the Giant of Mont Saint Michel is more than a recalcitrant aborigine: he is a creature motivated by 'filthy lust' (*fedo coitu*) and 'bestial desire' (*detestanda venere*).[18] The historiographical function of the giant – the stumbling block to imperial expansion – so became combined, in romance, with another *topos*: rape and its punishment by a chivalric hero. 'The structure of medieval romance', writes Kathryn Gravdal,

> depends on episodic units that recur systematically but are joined in interchangeable units such as the knight's dubbing, the battle, the journey through the forest, the crossing of water, the hospitality of an unknown squire, the feast day, and many other set pieces. What has rarely been said is that the threat of rape, attempted rape, and the punishment of the rapist also constitute familiar episodic units in the construction of a romance. Sexual violence is built into the premise of Arthurian romance; medieval romance is a genre that by definition must create the threat of rape.[19]

It is important to remark that the *raptores* of romance always *intend* rape in the modern sense, but only rarely accomplish it; rape is indeed 'built into the premise of Arthurian romance' even if it is rarely written into its pages. Still, the rape of the Duchess of Brittany by the Giant of Mont Saint Michel is firmly in the tradition of Guinevere's many abductions by evil knights; of the rape, attempted rape, or imprisonment of many of Chrétien's ladies; and of Arthur's own conception at Uther's rape of Igraine. That Geoffrey named the duchess Helena, of course, suggests her ultimate heritage, suggesting at the same time the importance attaching to her rescue (or attempted rescue). Rape is not simply anathema to chivalry, but necessary to the *matière* itself. In Arthur's story, the king must deal with rape on two fronts: in France, but also at home, where Mordred's retainers 'ravische thi nones' (AMA 3539) and where Mordred himself

> has weddede Waynore, and hir his wieffe holdis,
> and wonnys in the wilde bowndis of þe weste marches,
> And has wroghte hire with childe, as witnesse telles.
>
> (AMA 3550-2)

---

[17] *Of Giants*, p. 50. On the early fourteenth-century origin and development of the Albyne story in Anglo-Norman and Middle English versions of the *Brut*, see Julia Marvin, 'Anna and Isabelle: Regicidal Queens and the Historical Imagination of the Anglo-Norman Prose *Brut* Chronicles: With an Edition and Translation of the Prose Prologue to the Long Version of the Anglo-Norman Prose Brut', *Arthurian Literature XVIII*, ed. Keith Busby (Cambridge, 2001), pp. 143–83; Tamar Drukker, 'Thirty-three Murderous Sisters: A Pre-Trojan Foundation Myth in the Middle English Prose *Brut* Chronicle', *Review of English Studies* 54:216 (September 2003), pp. 449–63; Lesley Johnson, 'Return to Albion', *Arthurian Literature XIII*, ed. James P. Carley and Felicity Riddy (Cambridge, 1995), pp. 19–40; and Lister Matheson, *The Prose 'Brut': The Development of a Middle English Chronicle* (Tempe, AZ, 1998), pp. xvii–xxxvi, 1–49.

[18] Thorpe, pp. 238–9; Wright, p. 118.

[19] 'Chrétien de Troyes, Gratian, and the Medieval Romance of Sexual Violence', *Signs* 17:3 (Spring 1992), pp. 558–85 (p. 564).

But *is* it rape, or is it a generic rhetorical device to heighten suspense or make an allusion? Never in Geoffrey, nor in Chrétien, does a rape, if it is accomplished, receive narrative amplification. Geoffrey spares the duchess and allows rape to be (a) committed on her servant, and (b) reported (thrice) rather than 'witnessed' by the reader. The scene of Chrétien's typical *raptus* is similarly veiled, and Gravdal has a keen eye for what is at stake: 'Chrétien tastefully situates the actual rapes in the past tense. Once the hero arrives on stage, rape is maintained as a constant threat but it is not actually represented. Chrétien does not show the physicality of rape, the blood or tears of a victim, thus precluding any reaction of horror from his audience.'[20] In other words, rape in Chrétien is a cold-blooded *topos* and not the subject of tragedy. I part ways with Gravdal inasmuch as she reads absence of detail as decorous avoidance. In so rhetorically refined a poet as Chrétien, it is the possibility of rape, not its depiction, that is required (and anyway, horror, if it is desired, may lie elsewhere than in *amplificatio*). But Gravdal is right to suspect that, if the rape happens offstage, it must return to trouble the text in other ways, and hers is an observation that could be extended to any of the texts we have been discussing. Quite often, in fact, it is the poets' ever more elaborate avoidance that may alert the reader to that horror that poet and reader must conspire to situate in the visual periphery. But, as if the gaze itself were infected with the crime it seeks to look away from, the thing to which it turns seems always somehow perverted.

Representation of Rape in the Tradition: Parallel Develoment

It is frequently the custom, that is, to look away from the Giant of Mont Saint Michel's rape of the duchess, but to amplify – as a parallel development – either the rape of someone (or something) else, or the giant's repulsive eating habits. We note that the tradition puts the duchess's nurse through worse and worse torture (without ever killing her) and that the pigs that the giant roasts for himself in Geoffrey are in later texts transformed into children.

Geoffrey, of course, preserves the duchess' body from violation. As Cohen writes:

> The monster's sexual intentions in kidnapping Helena are obvious enough, but because the violation of a noblewoman is too indelicate for Geoffrey to include in his narration, Helena dies of fright, and the crime is displaced onto her nurse, an old woman whom the monster (and the text) finds easier to 'befoul'.[21]

In his own version, Wace is vague but does not, as Geoffrey does, rule out at least an aborted attempt at that violation:

> La pulcele volt purgisir,
> Mes tender fud, nel pot suffrir;
> Trop fud ahueges, trop fu granz,
> Trop lai, trop gros e trop pesanz;

---

[20] 'Chrétien', p. 569.
[21] *Of Giants*, p. 37.

> L'alme li fist de del corse partir,
> Nel pot Helyne sustenir.

(He wanted to ravish her, but she was delicate and could not stand it; he was too huge, too large, too ugly, too gross, and too heavy. He made her soul leave her body; Eleine could not endure it.)[22]

So careful is Wace to give the giant his oppressive size and weight, and to characterise them so redundantly (as *ahueges*, *granz*, *gros* and *pesanz*) in relation to the girl's tenderness, that it would seem the giant *began* to violate Helena's body, destroying it in the attempt. The giant therefore moves on to the rape of the nurse herself:

> 'Quant Helyne fud devïee –
> Dunt jo quidai de sens issir,
> Kar a hunte la vie murir –
> Lu jaiant me fist ci remeindre
> Pur sa luxure em mei refreindre;
> Par force m'ad si retenue
> E par force m'ad ci purgëue;
> Sa force m'estuet otrïer,
> Ne li puis mie deforcier.'

('When Eleine expired – which made me nearly lose my mind, for I saw her die in shame – the giant made me stay here, to assuage his lechery. By force he kept me here and by force he raped me. And I have to yield to his strength, I cannot prevent him.')[23]

Wace gives the nurse a most affecting keening. The repetition of 'force' is itself almost mimetic of the repeated brutalising the nurse endures. (The nurse's complaint, as we shall see, is developed in a significantly different way by the alliterative *Morte*-poet.)

Laȝamon then, with epic fullness of expression, makes the physicality of the giant felt all over Brittany. As the nurse relates the abduction, we learn that an entire walled town was sexually violated:

> He uerde to Bruitaine,   to aðelest alre bolde,
> To Howeles castle,   hæh mon inne Brutene.
> Þa ȝaten all he tobrac   and binnen he gon wende;
> He nom þare halle wah   and helden hine to grunde;
> Þæs bures he warp adun   þat heo tobarst uiuen.
> He funde I þan buren   færeest alre burden,
> Eleinen wes ihaten,   aðelest kunnen,
> Howeles dohter,   hæh mon of Brutene,
> Arðures maȝe,   of swiðe heȝe cunne.

---

[22] Text from *La Geste du roi Arthur: selon le Roman de Brut de Wace et l'Historia Regum Brittaniae de Geoffroy de Monmouth*, ed. Emmanuele Baumgartner and Ian Short (Paris, 1993), p. 162; translation from *Wace's Roman de Brut: A History of the British*, ed. and trans. Judith Weiss (Exeter, 1999), p. 287.
[23] Baumgartner and Short, p. 162; Weiss, p. 287.

(He went into Brittany, to the noblest of all dwellings,
To the castle of Howel, the chieftain of Brittany:
He smashed all the gates and squeezed himself inside,
He grabbed the curtain wall and hurled it to the ground,
He tossed down the chamber door and it shattered in five pieces;
He found inside the chamber the loveliest of all young women,
Elaine was her name, of most exalted lineage,
The daughter of Howel, chief man in Brittany,
Relative of Arthur, of the royal line itself.)[24]

If Geoffrey displaces the rape on to the nurse, La3amon displaces it, momentarily at least, on to Howel's castle. The giant's successive penetration of town, castle and chamber are described in order like a Chinese box, at the very centre of which lies the duchess's body. As the giant works his way in, both his size and his violence are at all stages asserted. He tears down the gates, but must still *force* his way in; too big to enter by a door, he tears down a wall. By this time, the enormity of his person having been established by synecdoche (his path of destruction), it is all the more horrifying to find him at the girl's door, which he smashes down. The giant saves the final stage of penetration for later, but his rape has already been described in the gate squeezed through, the door burst open. Brittany itself is erogenised and violated at the same moment. But the 'displacement' has been only temporary, since all that happens to the castle happens also to the duchess and her nurse (in this, La3amon's account follows the 'aborted rape' in Wace's poem). Here, the rhetorical evasion of the rape extends grotesquely into a paraleipsis-like prognostication of it. The Giant-*topos*, in the English poet's hands, is becoming narrative instead of tableau, and so more capable of its own imbalance and horror.

Eating Habits

Food was still more important in the early Christian days than sex. For instance, in the rules for monks, the problem was food, food, food. Then you can see a very slow shift during the Middle Ages, when they were in a kind of equilibrium...[25]

This observation of Foucault's may call to mind a variety of erogenous victuals in medieval literature – Grendel whose 'heart laughed' as he anticipated a man-feast in Heorot; or the carnivorous meals interspersed with bedroom scenes in *Sir Gawain and the Green Knight*. Medieval texts transmitting the Giant of Mont Saint Michel story are likewise consistent in providing some detail of the Giant's food. The author of *Castleford's Chronicle* (1338),[26] who follows Geoffrey quite closely, relates the rape briefly (but violently: the duchess is 'slane and draghen ... al to pece', 22067), spending many more lines on the giant's manner of eating pigs. This is a source of horror – even if it is a somewhat refined horror – since the giant,

---

[24] Text from *La3amon's Arthur: The Arthurian Section of La3amon's Brut*, ed. W. R. J. Barron and S. C. Weinberg (Austin, 1989), 12917–25; translation from *Lawman: Brut*, trans. Rosamund Allen (London, 1992), p. 330.
[25] 'On the Genealogy of Ethics: An Overview of Work in Progress', 1983 interview with Michel Foucault, in Hubert L. Dreyfus and Paul Rabinow, *Michel Foucault: Beyond Structuralism and Hermeneutics*, 2nd edn (Chicago, 1983), p. 229.
[26] *Castleford's Chronicle or The Boke of Brut*, ed. Caroline D. Eckhardt, 2 vols (London, 1996), vol. II.

repulsively, does not cook his meat all the way through. Geoffrey's text – 'He had swallowed bits of [the pigs] while he was roasting the rest over the live embers on the spits to which he had fixed them'[27] – is amplified here as follows:

> Rudeli, certes, he ete of þis fleis,
> Wiȝ salte, þat was so tender and freis –
> He ete þareof bi bites and bites
> Rostande it rathelie on þe spites,
> Sumdel rosted and sumdel ra,
> Ful vnsemelie he fedde him sua,
> Bot on þe spites yitte he tholes,
> Sum rostande better opon þe coles. (22150–7)

Robert Mannyng, with Wace, makes reference in his *Chronicle* (1338) to the terrifying size of the giant as compared with the smallness of the duchess:

> Heleyn he wild haf forlayn
> Scho ne might not with þat payn.
> He was so grate ouer mesure
> & scho was ȝong & might not dure;
> For grete destrisse hir hert braste,
> In his armes scho ȝald the gaste.[28]

And he is equally vague as to specific cause and effect. Again, for visual confirmation of the giant's monstrosity, we are brought to his hideous table:

> Be a mykille fire he sat
> & roste suynes flesc fulle fat,
> Som rosted & som was sothen.
> His bryne, his berde, þerwith was broþen
> & alle solied with þe spike
> (I trow þat sight was loþelik). (12037–42)

Such accounts catch the giant *in flagrante delicto*, and register a corresponding horror and embarrassment. We cannot be sure, however, which is the more embarrassing, his dietary or his sexual behaviour, and so cannot ignore the possibility that the eating was more disturbing – or titillating – than the raping. In all versions, Arthur encounters the giant at supper. In sum, a search for the erotic in Middle English literature must not overlook the repast; it is also a site of the giant's perversion and lubricity, perhaps even of a puerile autoeroticism.

Synecdoche
The horror, however, attaches ever more specifically to the corporeality of the monster, and especially to his penis. Beginning perhaps with the giant's attempted rape in Wace's poem – in which the intended victim may have been 'broken' before she could be violated – the unexpressed principle of the giant is that his

---

[27] Thorpe, p. 239.
[28] Robert Mannyng of Brunne, *The Chronicle*, ed. Idelle Sullens, MRTS (Binghamton, NY, 1996), 11969–74.

penis is larger than a normal man's in proportion to the giant's freakish size. The reader's mind is forced to contemplate this part–whole relation upon learning that, for the duchess, intercourse with the giant is instantly fatal. In order to embody the giant's physicality further and to provide an illustration of what the princess suffered, Laȝamon has added the gruesome, though entirely logical, detail of the old woman's bones being crushed from having the giant on top of her. She remarks twice that 'all my bones are broken' – 'mine leomen he haueð tobroken' (12907); 'Nu hafeð he mine ban alle ladliche abroken' (12940) – adding that the violence of the giant's rape 'disjointed all my limbs' ('mine leomen al toleðed', 12941). Again, we are made to understand a sexual act that bends joints backwards, destroys tendons. This very act, which the nurse has – presumably through working-class hardihood – managed to survive, is, in the reader's mind, retroactively visited on the delicate body of the fifteen-year-old Helena, now a (mercifully hidden) corpse. Laȝamon, between the rubble of Howel's castle and the ruined body of the nurse, comes as close as we have seen to imagining, in time, the exact circumstances of Helena's death. It is possible, however, that the alliterative *Morte*-poet comes even closer.

The Alliterative *Morte Arthure*

Though the *Morte*-poet will amplify the giant's foul supper in novel ways – making him a cannibal and a decadent gourmand – his account of the rape scene merits special attention. Like Wace and Laȝamon, the alliterative poet employs synecdoche, but whereas Laȝamon first shows the reader how big the giant is by means of his penetration of the castle and town, and then the nurse, the *Morte*-poet trains the violence primarily on to the body of the duchess, and in so doing creates a more concentrated, indeed more fetishistic, effect: a duchess-specific *amplificatio*, a vision of the body *having been* penetrated and destroyed. By this monstrous synecdoche the alliterative poem makes even more marked reference to the giant's giant-size penis.

Here, Arthur himself (albeit incognito) spies out the top of the mount, and so it is to Arthur himself that the poor nurse must narrate the following:

> 'Loo, here the duchez dere – todaye was cho takyne –
> Depe doluen and ded, dyked in moldez;
> He hade morthirede this mylde be myddaye war rongen,
> Withowttyn mercy one molde – I not watte it ment.
> He has forsede hir and fylede, and cho es fay leuede;
> He slewe hir vnslely and slitt hir to the nauyll.
> And here haue I bawmede hir, and beryede þeraftyr;
> For bale of þe botelesse, blythe be I neuer.' (974–81)

The alliterative poet chooses not to preserve the sanctity or privacy of the duchess's body, but to make it a carnal sign of the giant's size and violence, and also a record of how the giant, so clumsily (' "vnslely" '), killed her. Though her body is now covered, it behaves – in the act of the nurse's narration – like a *tabula* on which may be read the dimensions of the giant's body, and the details of his crime.

The nurse's embalming of the duchess, the sweetening the corpse, is a required part of this story, a component of the horror: the duchess's body has been not only raped but *fylede* (978), defiled, which is not a physical but a spiritual condition.

The nurse's body itself, as traditionally, is also part of the tableau. Though she is not reduced to a corpse, her body, by its very survival, also tells a story, and a different one than in the earlier poems. As Corinne Saunders observes:

> the old woman is not allowed the release of death, but lives to tell the tale and to suffer repeated rape, perhaps as a result of her lower class status, but also, we presume, because of her sexual experience. A physiological contrast between virginity and sexual experience is implied, whereby virgins are 'slit' by rape and matrons are not. Laʒamon's version adds to the account of the rape of the old woman a disturbing quality of voyeurism and public shame, for here the rape is enacted with Arthur and his men looking on, but without intervening. The poet of the alliterative *Morte*, by contrast, removes the detail of the old woman's rape, an alteration that suggests the unacceptability of portraying so graphic an act in romance, and the potential detraction from Arthur's reputation.[29]

Saunders here registers an important fact: that the nurse in the alliterative *Morte* is granted something like the dignity of a protagonist. This is only fair, since it is she who, though clearly traumatised, narrates the crime and makes the lament over the dead duchess. Note the difference between her lament in Wace (cited above) and that in the alliterative *Morte*:

> 'Of alle þe frendez cho hade, þere folowede none aftyre,
> Bot I, hir foster modyr of fyftene winter;
> To ferke of this farlande, fande sall I neuer,
> Bot here be founden on felde till I be fay leuede.' (982–5)

There is no mention here of the giant's forcing her to stay, no protestation that she is kept here against her will. In the alliterative *Morte* the nurse stays put for Helena's sake, doing homage to the corpse. Wace's nurse would go if she could, leaving the duchess's body to the four winds. This would be in perfect accordance with Augustine's notion of the Christian corpse. For Augustine, all bodies are generic and expendable, nothing to be sentimental about; the real ethical questions lie beyond them.[30] The nurse in the fourteenth-century poem seems to have no consciousness of this doctrine. Her attention, like the giant's, is focused on the girl's body. That the nurse cannot leave the site of the horror, cannot repose in Augustine's future repository of bodily restoration, the restoration of parts, beauty and proportion – of innocence, above all – may suggest that, in the world of this poem, no such repository exists. The embalming speaks of burial but not resurrection.

Perhaps the alliterative *Morte*-poet spared the nurse some of Laʒamon's tortures

---

[29] *Rape*, p. 209. I do not find that, in Laʒamon, the nurse is raped with Arthur and his men looking on, but rather while they stand below the mount, hearing Bedevere's tale and considering what to do (cf. 12954–94). Nevertheless, Laʒamon lets the *reader* look on, which the alliterative *Morte*-poet does not, and that in itself is, for the reasons Saunders gives, a noteworthy development.

[30] *City of God*, p. 22.

so that she might be thus eloquent, but it remains difficult to say whether he thought graphic violence 'unacceptable'. I would suggest, inasmuch as the Giant 'slitt her to the nauyll', that the alliterative *Morte*-poet, however unacceptable graphic violence might be to him, does not fail to deliver it. Nor does he fail to establish – with his grotesque anatomical specifics – an active theatre of perverse enjoyment. The giant's offence against Arthurian values, against chivalry, is secondary; his primary goal is pleasure. He is an eating and fucking machine, and a bodily isolation of these functions from the reality principle. A creature of great size, he is priapism incarnate. The *raptus* of the duchess, then, is imagined by the poem as sex. The giant's sex life is dangerous and hideous, but it is recognisably, nakedly, organised around desire and gratification. The duchess's death wound *is*, perversely, an effect of *eros*.

Even if it is countered that the poet's synecdoche, the visual remove of the duchess's corpse-tabula, spares us having to see the rape and murder itself – having to see the penis – the poet does not spare us elsewhere. His *amplificatio* is still at work when the nurse describes the Giant's diet:

> 'He sowppes all þis seson with seuen knaue childre,
> Choppid in a chargour of chalke-whytt syluer,
> With pekill and powdyre of precious spycez,
> And pyment fulle plenteuous of Portyngale wynes;
> Thre balefull birdez his brochez þey turne,
> Þat byddez his bedgatt, his byddyng to wyrche;
> Siche foure scholde be fay within foure hourez,
> Are his fylth ware filled that his flesch ȝernes.' (1025–32)

A more horrible picture of the appetitive self could hardly be imagined. The ogre likes his food dainty and wines suited to his Iberian palate, but the food is children on a spit and the spit is turned by girls reserved for post-prandial coitus, a carnal dessert in keeping with Foucault's idea of the medieval 'equilibrium' between the erotics of food and sex. When Arthur approaches this scene, he beholds with disgust

> How vnsemly þat sott satt sowpand hym one;
> He lay lanand on lang, lugand vnfaire,
> Þe thee of manns lymme lyfte vp by the haunche;
> His bakke and his bewschers, and his brode lendez
> He bekez by þe bale-fyre, and breklesse hym semede.
> Þare ware rostez full ruyd, and rewfull bredez,
> Beerynes and bestaile brochede togeders,
> Cowle full cramede of crysmed childyre,
> Sum as brede brochede, and bierdez þam tournede. (1044–52)

The stage could not be better set for a righteous extermination. It is here, however, that the Giant of Mont Saint Michel has become – for the *Morte Arthure* poet – most problematic. The nature of the problem is suggested, I think, by what comes next in the monster fight, a sequence that is wholly the invention of the alliterative poet:

> He folowes in fersly and festenesse a dynte
> Hye vpe on þe hanche with his harde wapyn,
> That he hillid þe swerde halfe a fote large –
> The hott blode of þe hulke vnto þe hilte rynnez;
> Ewyn into inmette the gyaunt he hyttez,
> Iust to the genitales, and jaggede þam in sondre. (1118–23)

If this passage does not bring us to the end of the fight, it does bring us to the end of the Giant. Whatever rhetorical structures have up to now shielded the Giant of Mont Saint Michel from so tragically necessary, so classically articulate, a cleansing – synecdoche, parallel development, topological convention – they are now nowhere to be found. The fight goes on for many more lines, but the climax is the castration: Arthur cannot simply kill the giant, but must visit on his body the reversal of that body's excess. And it is not simply a castration, but a great carving-out of the lower body. Arthur starts his incision 'high up on the haunch', that is, just beneath the last ribs, 'hiding' half a foot of his sword in the flesh. His sword goes to the 'inmeat' or intestines; then, without being removed, it goes 'evenly to the genitals' and cuts them away. This language bespeaks not a clean stroke, but the prying off of a great side of meat: hard, sawing work.[31] Again, the castration of the giant is the fourteenth-century poet's contribution to the Mont Saint Michel episode, and one wonders whether it was not meant to be the *coup de grâce* of the entire convention.

But inasmuch as the giant is an entirely libidinal creature, Arthur's grievous penetration and severing must be understood to take place *within* that giant's sex life; Arthur's desire, in other words, is perversely calculated as an exchange for the giant's own desire. Anne Clark Bartlett observes with great subtlety the poet's mingling of military- and erotic-conquest tropes 'into a rather sadomasochistic variety of sexual imagery',[32] whose details include a wrestling contest worthy of D. H. Lawrence: Arthur and the giant 'wrythyn and wrystill togederz/ Welters and walowes ouer within þase buskez,/ Tumbellez and turnes faste and terez þaire wedez' (1141–3). Arthur and the giant tumble in the bushes, tearing each other's clothes off, *even after the giant has been castrated*. If, as I suggested above, the castration was the symbolic end of the giant as a foe, then this grappling episode is indeed excessive, and indicates a desire other than that for Arthur's victory, the giant's death, a desire the poem has not yet satisfied and may not be able to satisfy. It is at this moment, as Cohen writes, that the *unheimlich* nature of the giant, on which the poem and the genre rely, is 'subtly eroded by conflating [the giant] with Arthur, and by the text's investing a perverse enjoyment in the celebration of his atrocious excesses'.[33] In this poem, not only must you kill, but you must embrace, and be embraced by, the monster; there must be a phase of combat unmediated by weapons and armour. One could also argue, of course, that this very conflation is

---

[31] This is poetic work but also physical work: giants are big. When Arthur kills another one, at line 2087, the same verb is used: the king 'Enjoynede with a geaunt, and jaggede hym thorowe'. Again at 2908–9: 'Gyawntis forjustede with gentill knyghtes,/ Thorowe gesserawntes of Iene jaggede to þe herte'.

[32] 'Cracking the Penile Code: Reading Gender and Conquest in the Alliterative *Morte Arthure*', *Arthuriana* 8:2 (Summer 1998), pp. 56–76 (p. 65).

[33] *Of Giants*, p. 153.

what is most *unheimlich*: what becomes 'eroded' is not the Giant's alterity, but Arthur's exemplary humanity. The king does kill the monster, but not before becoming grotesquely interchangeable with him.

Violent Sex and Arthur's Imperial Claims

This monster has now become more than just a token giant or token rapist, but a fully articulated nightmare. The additive proliferation of monstrous features and crimes attaching to it make it impossible to predict its movements. He stands like an Old Testament giant, blocking the way into Canaan, but he is also a wanderer, a foreigner; he not only exceeds the generic requirements of romance by *actually* raping and killing the maiden, but he also eats children. As Laurie Finke and Martin Shichtman observe, the Giant, even before his incarnation in the alliterative *Morte Arthure*, serves the poems of Wace and Laȝamon as a multiply-encoded 'nodal point' which

> 'quilts' together networks of ideological relations these histories were designed to produce, while itself producing a certain excess (Žižek calls this 'surplus-enjoyment') that exceeds the rape's ideological and structural function. The event coalesces several anxieties about the maintenance of boundaries during times when they are being redrawn in potentially disturbing ways. The particular ideological field being quilted by the rape is attempting to shore up the boundaries between those born to wealth and those born to poverty, between those trained to fight and those who are not, and, most significantly, between familiar and foreign.[34]

Part of this anxiety – an anxiety planted there by Geoffrey – is that there is no one to rescue. Chivalric ideology must be content to derive its credentials from avenging, instead of preventing, rape and murder. As this problem is confronted, the poem becomes excessively violent and highly sexualised; this gigantomachy is not a *topos* but a narrative of multiple atrocities. It is an occasion for the poet to remind the reader of this poem, this war poem, that war also intends the grievous penetration and dividing of the body. The alliterative *Morte*'s Giant is foundational because *this* rape – this violent, hyperbolically non-reproductive sex – bears a thematic relation to Arthur's justification for war: 'Myne ancestres war emperours' (276). Reasoning thus, Arthur will perversely march back along the genealogical path to Rome, into the matrix of the Trojan *translatio*, and, contrarily, the Giant of Mont Saint Michel will prepare him a womb: one that is virginal, dead and grotesquely breached. In this Arthur might have read a sign of his whole enterprise, an indication that matter cannot bear the conflation of right and conquest. If the king cannot read it (it is embalmed and buried after all), the poet can. The moral is that neither on campaign nor in the homeland can Arthur uphold the law, but only avenge its violations. The king does not quell outrage, that is, or 'awke

---

[34] 'The Mont Saint Michel Giant: Sexual Violence and Imperialism in the Chronicles of Wace and Laȝamon', *Violence against Women in Medieval Texts*, ed. Anna Roberts (Gainesville, 1998), pp. 56–74 (p. 68).

dedys', but deals back the same; and this is a simple binary negation, not a genealogy, not *translatio* at all. So, in the alliterative *Morte Arthure*, it is not only the penis, but the *loins* themselves – that universal metonym for generative, genealogical potency – that are breached and voided. It is a fitting midway point for a tale that results in Arthur's and Mordred's mutual penetration; if that final combat is sexualised, it too is non-reproductive. Of course, the point of sex in this poem is not reproduction, but penetration; just as the net victory of conquest is not imperial, but homicidal.

Epilogue

'But how', Freud asks (innocently enough), 'can the sadistic instinct, whose aim it is to injure the object, be derived from Eros, the preserver of life?'[35] Doers of *awke dedys* are emphatically not thinking about preserving the species, but they are, equally, blind to the possibility of extinction. In fact, the Mont Saint Michel episode bears a relation to Arthur's Roman war similar to that between the Abu Ghraib prisoner-abuse scandal to the United States' ongoing Iraq war. The butchering by (and of) the giant and the torture of Iraqi POWs are incidental, not integral, to their respective campaigns; on the other hand both incidents are entirely symptomatic. Let us not forget that the giant, too, was an invader and an occupier, and that his acts also belong specifically to the heady moment of sudden licence, of 'conqueste fulle cruelle' wherein one – as Arthur in Scotland – 'skyftys as hym lykys'.[36]

Torture of detainees at Abu Ghraib by American soldiers was, overwhelmingly, conducted in the erotic register: rape, bondage, electrical wires attached to genitals, manipulation of prisoners' bodies into sexual positions, and other elaborate humiliations, have all been documented. And we must include in that list the documentation itself: not only the (involuntary) photographing of victims, but the trade in these photographs among the soldiery; even photographs not explicitly sexual in content – such as those depicting the defilement of prisoners' corpses – drove a pornographic market. In addition, these facts shade harrowingly into more obscure reports of murders and disappearances.

It is clear that the atmosphere within the American-held Abu Ghraib prison was ungoverned – in the sense of *unchecked*, and deliberately so – by the United States government. In that environment – not only the inside of the prison but the lawlessness of a newly toppled regime – it is unsurprising that the reality principle is nowhere to be found, or that the capital of superior force is so quickly converted into sexual enjoyment. And, deplorable and monstrous as torture is, we must admit that we can scarcely imagine the exhilarating frontiers of cruelty which those

---

35 *Beyond the Pleasure Principle*, trans. and ed. James Strachey (New York, 1961), p. 65.
36 'Skathyll Scottlande', 'dangerous Scotland', is a place where Arthur 'disposes as he likes' (32), and where there is a dubious distinction between Arthur's claim and that of the Romans, who, as King Aungers complains, 'rauyschett oure wyfes,/ Withowttyn reson or ryghte refte vs oure gudes' (294–5).

American soldiers occupied. Theirs was the mastery of the absolute creditor in Nietzsche's metaphor, who may exact unheard-of forms of compensation:

> Let us be clear as to the logic of this form of compensation: it is strange enough. An equivalence is provided by the creditor's receiving, in place of a literal compensation for an injury (this in the place of money, land, possessions of any kind), a recompense in the form of a kind of *pleasure* – the pleasure of being allowed to vent his power freely upon one who is powerless, the voluptuous pleasure 'de faire le mal pour le plaisir de le faire' [of doing evil for the pleasure of doing it], the enjoyment of violation. This enjoyment will be the greater the lower the creditor stands in the social order, and can easily appear to him as a most delicious morsel, indeed as a foretaste of higher rank. In 'punishing' the debtor, the creditor participates in *the right of the masters*: at last he, too, may experience for once the exalted sensation of being allowed to despise and mistreat someone as 'beneath him' – has already passed into the 'authorities,' to see him despised and mistreated. The compensation, then, consists in a warrant for and title to cruelty.[37]

As with Nietzsche's creditor, the torturers' creditorship, their 'injury,' was borrowed, freely lent them by the war. Nevertheless, it 'elevated' them, briefly, to that bad eminence, a god-like status, allowing them to operate exclusively on the pleasure principle. The Giant of Mont Saint Michel and the torturers of Abu Ghraib were equally plunged into the latent dream – not yet a nightmare – which Nietzsche identifies, and which the Arthur of the alliterative *Morte* must face as he advances upon his own frontier, since this dream-effect is a real potential of conquest.

Again, this potential represents a brave new world that is difficult enough to conceive. The GIs committing rape and torture in Abu Ghraib were, like the Giant of Mont Saint Michel, living on the edge.

---

37 *On the Genealogy of Morals*, trans. Walter Kaufman and R. J. Hollingdale (New York, 1967), pp. 64–5. William Pfaff comments: 'In the whole affair, the real if unavowed appeal of sadism and nihilism is at work; this cannot be ignored, and it functions not only at the individual level. Certainly the pathetic reservists whose souvenir photos of torture in the Abu Ghraib prison were early evidence of these practices found themselves unexpectedly in circumstances that evoked or even licensed perverse impulses that otherwise would have remained suppressed' ('What We've Lost: George W. Bush and the price of torture', *Harper's* (November 2005), pp. 50–6 (p. 56)).

Her Desire and His:
Letters between Fifteenth-century Lovers

KRISTINA HILDEBRAND

THE FIFTEENTH century contains many examples of expressions of erotic desire, in genres ranging from romances to hagiographies. Whether the texts aim at sexual arousal or pious horror in the reader, these genres were intended for publication. Even the most explicit depiction of private life in the fifteenth century available to us, Margery Kempe's *Life*, was intended for the public. However, this is not the case with the private letters in collections such as the Paston, Stonor and Plumpton papers.[1] In these letters, we encounter men and women expressing erotic desire in what they perceived as private communications – as evinced by the occasionally stated request that the recipient burn the letter. This essay investigates the gendered voices of desire in fifteenth-century letters between spouses or prospective spouses, and suggests a new reading of the discourse of dominance/submission.

Reading these letters today, we encounter a number of limitations. Firstly, the preserved letters of the fifteenth century spring from a small social group, mainly from the strata of clerical and upper-class correspondents. Although the clerical letters may well contain comments on erotic love, for letters between spouses, where erotic love was permitted and practised, we must turn to the nobility, gentry and merchant classes. Thus, the understanding of erotic love inside marriage we draw from the letters is limited to those social strata, to which the writers of the three collections all belong. The Pastons were a rising family acquiring – and losing – property and influence during the turbulent years of the late fifteenth century; the Stonors, who are still living in their ancestral house, were a typical gentry family with a great deal of local influence, who avoided participation in the Wars of the Roses; the Plumptons differ from the Pastons and Stonors mainly by originating in the north of Britain.

Secondly, while a number of letters between spouses have been preserved, we are still at the mercy of the vagaries of the survival of papers and the later tran-

---

[1] *Paston Letters and Papers of the Fifteenth Century*, ed. Norman Davis (London, 1971); *Kingsford's Stonor Letters and Papers 1290–1483*, ed. Christine Carpenter (1919; Cambridge, 1996); *The Plumpton Letters and Papers*, ed. Joan Kirby (Cambridge, 1996). References will be shown as (family name page number).

scription of the texts. Many letters have been lost through the centuries, as we see from references in the surviving texts. Moreover, the Plumpton letters were all transcribed in the early seventeenth century, and may have been subject to errors or censorship.

Furthermore, we are frequently forced to attempt to read between the lines. There are various ways in which the letters may have been rendered opaque already when written down: the letters between men and women, even when married or negotiating marriage, were constrained by many things. The letters have been filtered through the standard forms and formulae of letter writing; even though, as we shall see, such formulae could be turned to erotic use. As the letters were generally written down by a scribe, especially when it comes to women's letters, we have no way of telling if they were changed in writing or if, as may well be imagined, the person dictating them was hesitant in voicing sexual desire in front of the scribe. Still, with all these factors taken into account, we see that men and women managed to convey erotic desire, at least implicitly, in their letters.

The selected letters are between current or future spouses, with a few to prospective spouses or lovers (exact figures may be found in the appendix). Interestingly, this is a woman-dominated genre, with women's letters either more numerous or better preserved – it may be that since these letters were for men, and would appear in the papers of the heads of families, they were kept to a greater extent than letters appearing among women's papers. We know of letters from husbands that have not been preserved, as we have references to them in the existing letters, but it is not clear whether there were originally as many letters from men as from women, or if the different number to some extent mirrors reality. In the Paston letters, there are nine letters from husbands to wives, three with multiple recipients including a spouse, two for lovers or prospective spouses; there are seventy-six from wives to husbands and two from fiancée to future husband. The vast majority of these were sent from Margaret Paston to her husband John Paston I. The Stonor letters contain one letter from husband to wife, one to a fiancée; there are sixteen letters from wives to husbands and one to a future husband. The Plumpton letters provide us with two letters from husband to wife and eight from wives to husbands.

Most of the letters are very far from love letters. These men and women discuss matters related to their current situation: politics, finances, household affairs. They are exchanging information, not discussing philosophy or, with few exceptions, their love for each other. There is nothing here like the touching love letters of Lord and Lady Lisle a century later. Still, it is evident in these letters that love, including intimacy and eroticism, may be present in the fifteenth-century marriage.

In the social class with which we are dealing, marriage was of course largely a matter of economics and social standing. Dowries and settlements ascertained that money would always be an important part of what was deemed a good match; also, the social standing, future prospects and influence of the prospective spouse's friends and family were essential. The prospective spouses also had at least not to object to each other, as we can see in Agnes Paston's hopeful letter: 'as for þe furste aqweyntaunce be-twhen John Paston and þe seyde gentilwomman, she made hym gentil chere in gyntyl wise and seyde he was verrayly yowre son. And so I hope þer shal nede no gret treté be-twyxe hym' (Paston 26). Although the partners could reject the match, considerable pressure was brought to bear on recalcitrant offspring, and more than one young woman seems to have married mostly to end the constant harassment. An undesirable match, contracted in secret, might sever all bonds, temporarily or permanently, between parents and children, as the story of Margery Paston's marriage to Richard Calle shows (Paston 341–4).

It should be noted, however, that not all marriages were arranged by parents. Many were widowed and remarried. Men or women remarrying might well have established themselves financially and socially with their first marriage, leaving them free to apply their own choice the second time. At this point, it is unlikely that parents, even if they were still living, would arrange the marriage; still, assistance was sometimes sought, as we can see from Agnes Wydesdale's letter declaring that she will, as promised, conclude no marriage agreement without having spoken to the unknown recipient (Stonor 356).

Marriage was the only state where sexual intercourse was, as Margery Kempe puts it, 'leful onto hir in leful tyme'.[2] Sexual satisfaction of one's spouse was an obligation, referred to as 'the marriage debt', and could not be avoided. That the duty to participate in marital intercourse was taken for granted can be seen in Margery Kempe's inability to deny her husband sexual access; even though 'the dette/ of matrimony was so abhominabyl to hir . . ./ . . ./ He wold have hys wylle, and sche obeyd wyth greet wepyng and sorwyng/ for that sche mygth not levyn chast' (3.256–7, 261–2). Also, in *The Franklin's Tale*, Chaucer's character comments on the folly of loving 'another mannes wyf,/ That hath hir body whan so that hym liketh'.[3] However, Kempe also refers to 'the gret delectacyon that thei haddyn eythyr of hem in/ usyng of other' (3.264–5), clarifying that for both parties, married sexuality could be a pleasure as well as a duty.

Married sexuality and intimacy were not necessarily the same experience for the husband and the wife. On a closer reading, the letters evince a clear gendering of voices. While male and female voices of desire do exhibit similarities – both genders are inclined to express themselves discreetly and even obscurely – the dissimilarities are striking. Men express both extra- and intramarital desire, women express intramarital desire only; vocabulary and expressions also exhibit differences along gender demarcations.

Gender-differentiated Writing

The letters exhibit varying degrees of intimacy. Many of the writers sign themselves in terms that clearly denote the intimate nature of their relationship, such as 'bedfellow'. While this term is not unambiguous, and could refer to the habit of sleeping two to a bed, it is clearly used to denote a sexual partner in the Middle Ages, being listed in several dictionaries as meaning spouse or consort as well as

---

[2] *The Book of Margery Kempe*, ed. Lynn Staley, TEAMS (Kalamazoo, 1996); citations from the online version (stable URL: <www.lib.rochester.edu/camlot/ teams/kemp1frm.htm>), 4.339.
[3] Geoffrey Chaucer, *The Canterbury Tales*, ed. F. N. Robinson, *The Complete Works of Geoffrey Chaucer* (London, 1933), 1004–5.

mistress.⁴ Some letters exhibit a very intimate tone, even where the writers are not yet married, such as Thomas Betson's letter to his fiancée Katherine Ryche. This letter is unusual in that the recipient is still very young, and Thomas's letter, addressed to 'My nowne hartely belovid Cossen Kateryn', employs both amusing comments and references to their married future (Stonor 262–4). Betson's language vacillates between treating Ryche as a child and as a woman: 'whanne I remember your ffavour and your sadde loffynge delynge to me wardes, ffor south ye make me evene veray glad and joyus in my hart: and on the toþyrsyde agayn whanne I remember your yonge youthe' (Stonor 263). After asking her to 'be a good etter off your mete allwaye, that ye myght waxe and grow ffast to be a woman', he also refers to her as 'ffull womanly and lyke a loffer' (Stonor 263).⁵ The informality and intimacy of this letter may be explained by the recipient's youth, but it also agrees with the general tone in men's letters to wives and fiancées. Unfortunately, we have no preserved letter by Katherine Ryche for comparison.

A notable difference between male and female writers is the much greater formality in the letters by women. Thomas Stonor addresses his wife as 'myne oone good Jane', and as 'lemman' and 'goode swete lemman' (Stonor 97); the term 'lemman' denotes a sexual partner, and indeed often an extramarital partner.⁶ In the light of this, it seems slightly surprising that Jane replies in an entirely formal manner, addressing him as 'goode syr', commencing with 'syr, I recommande me unto yow as lowly as I cane', and signing herself simply 'your awne Jayn Stonor' (Stonor 62, 110). A similar situation can be observed in the Plumpton letters, where Robert Plumpton, although using the standard form 'I recommend me unto you', addresses his wife Agnes as 'deare hart' and 'best beloued', endorses the letters 'to my entyrely and most hartily beloued wife', and refers to himself as 'your owne louer' and 'your louing husband' (Plumpton 152, 169–70). Agnes, in her turn, replies formally, using standard formulae and signing herself 'your wyfe'; so does his second wife Isobel, although she uses the signature 'your bedfellow' (Plumpton 156, 158–9, 170–4, 181).

The Pastons are the most formal of the letter writers discussed here. With few exceptions, letters between spouses are formal to the point of coldness, conveying an interesting picture of marital life. In her only preserved letter to her spouse, Agnes Paston addresses him as 'Dere housbond' and signs herself 'yowres' (Paston 26), using a level of informality that will not be seen again until her grandson John Paston III woos Margery Brews. Her daughter-in-law Margaret Paston with few exceptions addresses John Paston I as 'Ryght worshipfull husbond', or with some variety thereof (Paston 215–86, 289–306, 310–23, 329). That this is not simply a

---

4   Julie Coleman, 'The Treatment of Sexual Vocabulary in Middle English Dictionaries', *Middle English Miscellany*, ed. Jacek Fisiak (Poznán, 1996), pp. 183–206 (p. 186). While this text primarily discusses the selection of the sexual terminology found in various Middle English dictionaries, it also lists and explores such terminology.
5   In the 1919 edition, Kingsford states in his introduction that '[t]he playful letter which . . . [Thomas Betson] wrote to his future wife, as a child of twelve or thirteen, is amongst the most charming of all private letters of the time that have survived' (Stonor 56), displaying a marked lack of problematisation of a love letter from a grown man to a child.
6   Coleman, 'Treatment', p. 190.

scribe's standard opening can be seen in her letters to her sons, where she writes 'I grete you wele and send you Goddes blissyng and myn', sometimes including the address 'Ryght welbelouyd son' (Paston 287, 308–9, 333–69, 371–6, 380). While this is still a formulaic address, it is considerably warmer and indicates a mother's authority rather than a wife's submission. Margaret Paston also rarely expresses any warmer feelings in the letters themselves, although there is the comment, when John Paston I is ill in London, that 'Yf I mythe have had my wylle I xulde a seyne yow er dys tyme. I wolde ȝe wern at hom ... lever dan a new gounne, þow it were of scarlette' (Paston 218). Considering how much space new gowns take up in Margaret Paston's letter, this seems to be a strong sentiment. John Paston I writes to her using, with one notable exception, 'I recommaund me to yow' and signs himself, if at all, with 'yowr' or 'yowr own' (Paston 91–3, 95–8, 125–6, 134–5, 138–9). Despite the chilly formality of John Paston I, we may note that the only occasion of warmer expression is on his side, while his wife never deviates from her polite phrases. John Paston III, in the only preserved letter to his wife Margery, addresses her politely as 'Mastress Margery' and wishes earnestly for a plaster to cure his friend, as he 'is the man that brought yow and me togedyrs' (Paston 628), implying his own lasting pleasure in that fact. Margery, on the other hand, writes him in the most humble tone employed by any of the Paston women (Paston 662–7).

The formality of the women writers may be because of their unwillingness to express erotic desire through a scribe. Men more often wrote their own letters, and, even when writing through a scribe, were able to express sexual desire without stepping out of their expected gender role.[7] We may note that Elizabeth Stonor chooses to include the more intimate parts in postscript in her own hand, thus keeping them private from the scribe. Still, the gender differentiation cannot be understood without the power differentiation. Diane Watt points out that '[t]he greater the social divide between writer and recipient, the more exaggerated the formality of the language and the more extreme the writer's appeal to the condescension of the recipient'.[8] The use of different registers of formality mirrors the position of the husband as his wife's social superior. However, as we shall see, there are other subtexts to be considered in the formality of women's letters.

---

[7] All male members of the Paston family wrote at least some of their letters themselves; the majority of the letters by John Paston III are in his own hand. All the identifiable hands of the Paston letters are men's, while unidentifiable hands might, of course, be women's (Paston lxxv–lxxix). Among the Stonors, the situation is slightly different. Sir William Stonor wrote his own letters, as did his father, his brothers and his mother, Jane Stonor. William's wives generally dictated their letters: Elizabeth wrote at least one letter herself (Stonor 9), but the majority are dictated, often with a last paragraph added in her own hand; Agnes and Anne seem to have dictated theirs (Stonor xlvi–xlvii, 99–101, 140). In the Plumpton letters, which have been transcribed, the original hand cannot be determined.

[8] Diane Watt, ' "No Writing for Writing's Sake": The Language of Service and Household Rhetoric in the Letters of the Paston Women', *Dear Sister: Medieval Women and the Epistolary Genre*, ed. Karen Cherewatuk and Ulrike Wiethaus (Philadelphia, 1993), p. 127.

Sexuality

As mentioned above, men use intimate and erotically charged terms such as 'lemman' and 'your own lover' when writing to their wives. John Paston III, in his letter to a Mistress Annes, also employs erotic references, this time in an extramarital situation. This woman may have been a prospective wife, and may have been the 'Stoctonys doghtre' who was married off in haste to someone else (Paston 479). John Paston III comments 'in faythe I trowe ye be in bed' and hopes that, in reading his letters, 'yow aqweynt yow wyth thys my lewd hand, for my purpose is that ye shalbe more aqweyntyd with it' (Paston 591). This may refer to his letter arriving late and his desire to keep writing to her; but the comments are, indeed, sexually suggestive. 'Lewd' may, of course, refer to the real or pretended clumsiness of Paston's writing, but the term already had the connotation of sexuality for which it is now primarily used.[9]

Although, in these letters, men seem more free than women to use terms, such as 'lemman' and 'lover', and, indeed, 'lewd', which imply love and sexuality, a few women do express their desire for physical and erotic contact. Margery Paston writes to her husband: 'Ser, I prey you if ye tary longe at London þat it wil plese [you] to send for me, for I thynke longe sen I lay in your armes' (Paston 665). Elizabeth Stonor is also one of the exceptions to the normal formality. A remarried and wealthy widow, she may have been able to make her own choice of husband, and consequently felt freer to address him as she pleased. Her letters were dictated to a scribe, but often contain a last clause or postscript in her own hand. She addresses her husband as 'cousin', and warms her formal phrases with additions: 'Right Reverent and Worshippful and enteirly best beloved Cosyn', 'Right Interly and beste belovyde Cosyn, I recomaunde me unto you in the moste loving wyse' (Stonor 265–8). Her postscripts contain messages about medicines she sends him, but also cryptic references to marital life: 'My owne good [husb]ond I se well ye [re]membre þe puttyng at . . . out off þe bed when you and I lay last togedyr' and 'My good Cosen, I am crassed in my baket: you wat what I men' (Stonor 271, 274, 279).[10] While many of these phrases defy interpretation, their very opacity suggests that they refer to sexuality, and also points to the intimacy of a marriage where hints like these would be understood. Possibly Sir William Stonor, whose letters to his wives have not been preserved, was not a formidable or intimidating husband. His second wife, Agnes Wydesdale, also a widow, writes to him cheerfully before their wedding and signs herself 'your tru lover' (Stonor 100–1). His

---

9 Coleman, 'Treatment', p. 189.
10 The last sentence in particular defies interpretation. The notes suggest that 'crassed' means either 'sick' or 'increased', and that 'bakyd' may refer to her back. Either she has had pains in her back or she has grown wider over the back, which may refer to a pregnancy. Elizabeth Stonor uses the phrases 'crised and besy' (275) and 'I was crasyd at the makyng off thys letter, but I thanke God I am ryght well amendyd' (298), which seems to indicate the meaning 'ill'. If, like many women, she experienced pain in her lower back during menstruation, that may be what she refers to in such secretive terms. It has also been suggested that 'bakyd' is a term for 'head', making the phrase 'my bucket is cracked', and that the phrase refers to things getting out of hand or her being overworked (private e-mail from P. J. C. Field, 25/10/04).

third wife, Anne Neville, is also less than formal, expressing her wish to see him and signing herself 'your new wyf' (Stonor 140).

It should be noted that all the women above were, in one way or another, exceptions to the rule of fifteenth-century marriages as parental arrangements. John Paston III and Margery Brews fell in love, and managed to marry despite the need for intense negotiations about marriage portions.[11] Sir William Stonor's first two wives were wealthy widows, with the ensuing freedom, and his third, while not a widow, was a Neville and socially much above her husband. The formality and polite phrases of Jane Stonor, Agnes and Isobel Plumpton, and Agnes and Margaret Paston are perhaps more typical of the relationship between wives and husbands in the fifteenth century.

However, the easily recognised terms of affection or erotic love are not the only erotic terminology used in these letters; through them runs what we may call an erotic subtext employing terms of dominance and submission. Watt notes what she calls 'the rhetoric of service' in the texts and refers to Margery Brews's usage of petition and submission to her future husband's sovereignty.[12] I would argue further that this rhetoric, when used between spouses, expresses the power imbalance of medieval marriage and implies the sexuality for which marriage was the permitted outlet.

Fifteenth-century Britain was, of course, a patriarchal society. In a patriarchy, the genders are positioned hierarchically; where a woman may have higher status than a man of a lower social class, she will always have lower status than a man of her own class. It has been pointed out by various scholars that patriarchal society eroticises this power imbalance between the genders: as Sheila Jeffreys puts it, '[s]ex as we know it under male supremacy is the eroticised power difference of heterosexuality'.[13] This erotisation is inextricably linked to the gender hierarchy: 'the erotisation of dominance and submission creates gender, creates woman and man in the social form in which we know them'.[14] The power imbalance is thus perceived not only as right, natural, or divinely ordained, but as necessary to gender difference and sexual attraction: male sexuality is seen as dominant, and is expressed through dominance and control, whereas female sexuality is associated with and enacted through submissive behaviour.

However, the eroticised power difference is not clear cut along a gender divide: although the association of male/dominance and female/submission is the most common form, I would claim that the power imbalance in itself constitutes an erotic subtext. Power, in a patriarchy, is sexy: the courtly love imbalance between serving man and adored lady contains the same erotic charge as the submission of wife to husband. The division of power is the essential part, and such power looks

---

[11] In John Paston's memoranda we find: 'Memorandum to kepe secret from my moder that the bargayn is full concluded', even though she had been of considerable help with the marriage negotiations (Paston 608).
[12] Watt, ' "No Writing" ', pp. 126–30.
[13] *Anticlimax: A Feminist Perspective on the Sexual Revolution* (New York, 1990), p. 3. Also, 'heterosexual desire is eroticised power difference' (Jeffreys, *Anticlimax*, p. 299).
[14] Catharine A. MacKinnon, *Feminism Unmodified: Discourses on Life and Law* (Cambridge, MA, and London, 1987), p. 50. See also: 'heterosexual desire is defined here as sexual desire that eroticises power differences' (Jeffreys, *Anticlimax*, p. 2).

remarkably similar regardless of the gender of the wielder. The knight's unquestioning obedience to an unreasonable lady or Patient Griselda's submission to an equally unreasonable husband may not appear to all of us as erotic discourse, but if one of them is, surely so is the other.

Nevertheless, the medieval and Renaissance erotisation of the powerful lady seems rarely to have stretched beyond the wedding. A powerful lady to serve and obey was undoubtedly an erotic image for many, but a wife was expected to be submissive and obedient. Late medieval writers were not unaware of the inherent contradiction between wooing a lady with the discourse of courtly love and expecting her to become a submissive wife; Chaucer's *Franklin's Tale* discusses this particular dichotomy at length, but begins the discussion by stating what must have been the general understanding of such matters: 'Thus hath she take hir servant and hir lord,/ Servant in love, and lord in marriage' (792–3). We may note that this text, too, here constructs love explicitly in terms of power. Fifteenth-century men may have been servants in love, but they were certainly lords in marriage.

While it is by no means certain that the late medieval gentlemen generally wooed their future or current wives in any way that resembles contemporary romances, they do occasionally use the language of courtly love; we have one preserved letter where John Paston I, usually so businesslike, addresses his wife as 'my owne dere sovereyn lady' and signs himself 'yowr trew and trusti husband' (Paston 140–5). Similarly, John Paston III, when writing to two ladies, neither of whom he married, addresses them entirely in the language of courtly love as 'Mastresse' and 'myn owne fayer lady', speaks of his service and refers to himself as their servant (Paston 590–1, 603–4). The discourse of serving knight and sovereign lady was by no means unknown to these men, even though it seems to have been employed only rarely. However, as John Paston III asks his mistress Annes to burn the letter (Paston 591), there may have been other instances of such letters that were destroyed.

Much more common is the woman's voice as subordinate. The wives' letters are generally indistinguishable in phrasing from letters by servants and children; as we have seen, they address their husbands as they would an overlord, and sign themselves humbly. While this leaves the modern reader with a sense of chilly distance, we may approach this style not as a sign of coldness but of sexuality, using the letters of Margery Paston, née Brews, as examples.

Margery Paston is one of the most explicitly formal and humble writers, calling her future husband 'Ryght reuerend and wurshypfull and my ryght welebeloued Voluntyne', and even before the wedding signing herself 'youre seruaunt and bedewoman' (Paston 662–4). The formality of her letters is intriguing, as we know that her marriage was actually a love match. Her forms of address cannot, then, be explained by any coldness between the couple. Watt argues that 'Margery happily accepts the sovereignty of her future husband'.[15] However, at the point when the famous valentine letters were written, the dowry was not agreed on and there was no certainty that the marriage would ever be contracted. Margery Brews, whose

---

[15] Watt, ' "No Writing" ', p. 130.

letters testify to her earnest desire to marry John Paston, may have been expressing not just love but sexuality. She refers to herself as already obliged to obey his commands: 'yf ye commande me to kepe me true where-euer I go, Iwyse I will do all my myght ȝowe to love and neuer no mo' (Paston 662). In her second letter, she tells him a higher dowry is impossible, and portrays herself as a petitioner: 'yf þat ȝe cowde be content wyth þat good and my por persone, I wold be þe meryest mayden on grounde' (Paston 663). She clearly states her subordinate position when appealing to him to be satisfied:

> yf ȝe thynke not ȝowre-selfe so satysfyed, or þat ȝe myght hafe mech more good, as I hafe vnderstonde be ȝowe afor, good, trewe, and lovyng Volentyne, þat ȝe take no such labure vppon ȝowe as to come more for þat mater; but let it passe, and neuer more to be spokyn of, as I may be ȝowr trewe louer and bedewoman duryng my lyfe. (Paston 663)

The letter reminds John Paston III that if he settles for the dowry her parents will give, he will have a woman whose submission promises all that can be desired in a wife, as well as the access to her body that marriage will entail. In both her premarital letters Margery Brews refers to her body – 'I am not in good heele of body ner of herte', 'my por persone' (Paston 662–3) – keeping it almost as a bait before her lover. The phrases serve as a reminder of her female body and the comment about her dowry being 'ryght far fro the acomplyshment of ȝowr desyre' (Paston 663) as a reminder of the desire he may accomplish, provided he is willing to forgo a larger dowry.

Once married she does once use the less formal address 'Myne owyn swete hert', but returns to 'Right reuerent and worchyspfull syr', and consistently signs herself 'your seruaunt' (Paston 665–7). Even before the wedding she seems to be implying, through her submission and her use of the terms 'my por persone' and 'trewe louer', with all their connotations, that their marriage will be erotic and not just businesslike. After the wedding, she continues to use a more humble language than any of the other women studied here. In employing a subtext of dominance/submission, she is actually expressing erotic desire in a form permitted to a woman, even when not yet married. She may also be aiming at arousing her future husband's desire: one cannot help wondering if this explicit and erotic submission may have been part of the attraction.

Fifteenth-century letters between lovers show us a world of concealed and unstated sexuality. Even in private letters between spouses, erotic love is hidden and has to be found between the lines, although men are more free than women to express affection and sexuality. Still, the erotic charge contained in the use of terms which are explicitly extramarital, such as 'lemman', and even more, in the language of dominance/submission, is very clearly present. As we come to an understanding of the erotisation of gendered power imbalances, the private letters of the Paston, Stonor and Plumpton families shed new light on erotic love in the fifteenth century.

Appendix

The PASTON FAMILY
William Paston I 1378–1444, married (1420) Agnes Berry ?–1479
John Paston I 1421–1466, married (1440?) Margaret Mautby ?–1484
John Paston III 1444–1504, married (1477) Margery Brews ?–1495
   married (1495?) widowed Agnes ?–1510

The Paston Letters and Papers contain:
Agnes Paston (to William Paston I)	1	
John Paston I (to Margaret Paston)	11	(3 with multiple recipients)
Margaret Paston (to John Paston I)	69	
John Paston III (to Mistress Annes)	1	
(to unknown lady)	1	
(to Margery Paston)	1	
Margery Paston (to John Paston III)	6	

The STONOR FAMILY
Thomas Stonor 1424–1474, married Jane or Joan, natural daughter of William, Duke of Suffolk ?–1493
William Stonor 1449–1494, married (1475) widowed Elizabeth Ryche ?–1479
   married (1480) widowed Agnes Wydesdale ?–1481
   married (1481) Anne Neville ?–1486

The Stonor Letters and Papers contain:
Thomas Stonor (to Jane Stonor)	1
Jane Stonor (to Thomas Stonor)	2
Elizabeth Stonor (to William Stonor)	13
Agnes Wydesdale (to William Stonor)	1
Anne Stonor (to William Stonor)	1
Thomas Betson (to Katherine Ryche)	1

The PLUMPTON FAMILY
Robert Plumpton, ?–1523, married (1477) Agnes Gascoigne ?–1504
   married (1505?) Isobel Neville ?–?

The Plumpton letters and papers contain:
Robert Plumpton (to Agnes Plumpton)	2
Agnes Plumpton (to Robert Plumpton)	7
Isabel Plumpton (to Robert Plumpton)	1

Sex in the Sight of God:
Theology and the Erotic in Peter of Blois'
'Grates ago veneri'[1]

SIMON MEECHAM-JONES

> Item, si, sicut tota clamat divina scriptura, tantum tres sunt ordines salvandorum, virginum, continentium, et conjugatorum, simplices autem fornicatores in nullo reperiuntur ordinum istorum, non itaque sunt in ordine salvandorum.
>
> (Now, as all the Sacred Scriptures attest, there are only three classes of people who will be saved: those who are virgins, those who are continent, and those who are married. And since fornicators are by no means found among these groups, they certainly will not be saved.)[2]

THROUGHOUT the Middle Ages, theologians had drawn on the strictures of St Paul to bolster and reanimate the Church's veneration of virginity as an ideal state of human life.[3] In the twelfth century, the Church's full acceptance of the centrality of this theology of virginity was witnessed by the imposition of the rule of clerical celibacy at the Second Lateran Council of 1139. It is the more surprising then that the twelfth century should also have produced a rich crop of lyrics written in Latin that are notable for a level of sexual explicitness that renders them as provocative to twenty-first-century sensibilities as they must have been to readers or listeners when they were first written. It should not be thought, either, that these surviving poems comprise fortuitously preserved remnants of an invisible or *samizdat* clerical culture. Unlike some of the apparently 'occasional' erotic verse that survives in Medieval Welsh, for example, these poems have not generally been preserved on loose scraps of paper, or scrawled on to the margins of

---

[1] The text of this lyric, with an English translation, is presented in an appendix at the end of this chapter.
[2] Giraldi Cambrensis, *Opera*, ed. J. S. Brewer, Rolls Series 21, vol. II (London, 1862), pp. 175–6; Gerald of Wales, *The Jewel of the Church*, trans. John J. Hagen, Davis Medieval Texts and Studies (Leiden, 1979), Second Distinction, Chapter 2 (p. 136).
[3] In the chapter quoted above, for example, Gerald quotes as doctrine extracts from Hebrews 13:4, Ephesians 5:5, Colossians 3:5 and the First Book of Corinthians 6:9 as well as extracts from the Revelation of St John 21:8, the Second Gospel of Peter 2:9–10, Genesis 38:24–5, Leviticus 21:9 and Ezechiel 14.

other texts.[4] Many of these poems survive in verse compilations that were compiled and preserved in disparate areas of Christendom, and a number of the most striking lyrics survive in more than one autograph.[5]

Furthermore, it seems clear that, in their own time, these lyrics were often associated with, and distributed under, the names of leading intellectuals within the Church, such as Hugh Primas, Peter of Blois and Walter of Châtillon. These lyrics, written (or believed to have been written) by leading figures of Authority in the Church, and read by a clerical and clerically educated audience, are notable for their direct and unembarrassed engagement with the experience of sexual contact. That such lyrics should be written and circulated widely across Europe in a period when the Church did not hesitate to claim and to exercise immense power in both the spiritual and political spheres requires explanation, raising the question of whether accepted interpretations of medieval piety need to be reconsidered. The most pressing question must be: to what degree should these poems be understood as explorations of their ostensible subject, physical intimacy, or should we expect to interpret the representation of sexual acts as poetic figurations, being used metaphorically to comment on philosophy, theology, politics or literary history? The (presumed and actual) distance between accepted sexual mores in the twelfth and twenty-first centuries acts to focus attention on the extent to which current readings of these poems are necessarily coloured both by a sense of the shifting and contingent nature of ethical judgments across the centuries in matters concerned with the expression of sexuality, and also by a realisation that any reading cannot avoid being shaped by preconceived expectations of what a medieval lyric should, and should not, be able to depict and discuss.

These difficulties are seen to be both immediate and acute in critical readings of one of the most sophisticated and ambitious collections of medieval erotic verse in Latin, the poems that have become known as the Arundel Lyrics. Seventeen love-songs were written out as the major part of a collection of twenty-eight lyrics, surrounded by religious and moral prose extracts in the manuscript British Library MS Arundel 384. Read as a cycle, these lyrics undertake a remarkable drawing together of mythological symbolism, literary tropes and the description of erotic encounters, in which the poet (or poets) recounts a series of amorous pursuits and conquest, while also displaying his mastery of imagery and motifs from the classical erotic tradition.

The authorship of the Arundel love lyrics has proved the subject of scholarly debate and controversy. Despite the appearance of Walter of Châtillon's satirical lament 'Licet eger cum egrotis' among the satirical verses in the manuscript, the

---

4   The wide variety of erotic poetry surviving in Medieval Welsh is surveyed by Dafydd Johnston (*Canu Maswedd yr Oesoedd Canol* (Bridgend, 1998)).
5   The lyric 'Grates ago Veneri', which appears in the Arundel lyrics, also appears as one of the Carmina Burana; the lyric 'Sevit aure spiritus' is similarly found in both collections, while two other of the Arundel lyrics are also found in MS Vat. Lat. 4389 ('Iam vere fere medio' and 'De grege pontificum'). *Carmina Burana: Die Lieder der Benediktbeurer Handschrift: Zweisprachige Ausgabe*, ed. A. Hilka, O. Schumann and B. Bischoff (Munich, 1979); *The Oxford Poems of Hugh Primas and the Arundel Lyrics*, ed. C. J. McDonough, Toronto Medieval Latin Texts (Toronto, 1984); B. Bischoff, 'Vagantenlieder aus der Vaticana', *Zeitschrift für romanische Philologie* 50 (1930), pp. 76–97.

possibility of Walter's authorship was soon felt to be improbable, in view of the stylistic difference from Walter's other surviving lyrics.[6] Nonetheless the 'formal and verbal parallelism found within the group'[7] has encouraged the belief that the love lyrics are the work of a single writer. Spanke's diagnosis of the presence of an acrostic spelling the name Petri within the seventh lyric caused him to identify this single poet with the figure of Peter of Blois, the moralist and indefatigible letter-writer who served for many years at the court of Henry II. A more sustained attribution of the lyrics to Peter of Blois was offered by Dronke.[8] Nonetheless, the identification of the author of such flamboyantly outrageous lyrics as 'Sevit aure spiritus' and 'Grates ago Veneri' with the rather more staid and conventional moralist delineated in Peter's copious letters remains controversial. Southern's attempted rebuttal of Dronke's identification requires the identification of another writer, contemporary with Dronke's Peter, and also (self-)identified as Peter of Blois. Central to the debate between Dronke and Southern is the interpretation of two letters from Peter's collected correspondence. In Southern's view, the Epistles 76 and 77 'illuminate his [Peter's] struggle between a desire for literary fame and his call to a life of serious religious dedication'.[9] The interest of the letters, which Southern dates as being from c. 1184 (Ep. 77) and c. 1192–93 (Ep. 76), lies in 'their contrasting attitude towards the person to whom they are addressed, and the piquancy of the situation arises from the addressee having the same name as the writer: he too is Master Peter of Blois'.[10] Both Southern and Dronke wrote in response to Bezzola's suggestion that in addressing (and preserving for future generations) two letters to 'Master Peter of Blois', Peter was involved in a complex gesture of literary self-examination, which enabled him to distance himself from the classically inspired literary productions of his 'other career'.[11] Where Bezzola identifies the two Peters as representing different periods of the career of a single author, Southern draws on historical detail to put forward his theory of two discrete, and fortuitously named, writers, writing at the same time but in different modes. In contrast, Dronke, developing Bezzola's suggestion, had used the details of Peter's account of his Master's literary productions to identify that projection of Peter's creativity with the poet of the majority of the Arundel lyrics.[12] Certainly the terms of Peter's admonition in Epistle 76 seem to offer a close, if perhaps ironically intended, commentary on the style and themes of many of the Arundel lyrics:

---

[6] The possibility was raised, and dismissed, by Karl Strecker (*Die Lieder Walters von Châtillon in der handschrift 351 von St. Omer* (Berlin, 1925), p. xiii).

[7] McDonough, *The Oxford Poems*, p. 12.

[8] Peter Dronke, 'Peter of Blois and Poetry at the Court of Henry II', *Mediaeval Studies* 28 (1976), pp. 185–235; repr. in Dronke, *The Medieval Poet and his World* (Rome, 1984), pp. 281–339.

[9] R. W. Southern, 'The Necessity for Two Peters of Blois', *Intellectual Life in the Middle Ages: Essays presented to Margaret Gibson*, ed. Lesley Smith and Benedicta Ward (London and Rio Grande, 1992), pp. 103–18 (p. 103).

[10] Southern, 'The Necessity', p. 104.

[11] R. R. Bezzola, *Les Origines et la Formation de la littérature courtoise en occident (500–1200)* (Paris, 1963), pp. 41–2.

[12] Dronke suggests a single author for the first sixteen of the Arundel lyrics, as well as the Easter Hymns 'Flos preclusus sub torpore' and 'O cessent gemitus' and the final lyric 'Quam velim virginem' ('Peter of Blois', p. 219).

Et quae insania est de Hercule et Jove canere fabulosa, et a Deo qui est via, veritas et vita, recedere?

(and what madness is it to sing fantasies about Hercules and Jove, and to draw back from God, who is the way and the truth and the life?)[13]

In fashioning this condemnation of his earlier work, Peter would have been allying himself with a venerable literary tradition dating back to Virgil's (apocryphal?) request that the unfinished *Aeneid* be destroyed. The distancing from his own creativity apparently attempted in Epistle 76 has formal parallels with the gestures of disengagement presented, for example, by Walter of Châtillon in lyrics such as 'Versa est in luctum Cythara Waltheri', 'Dum Galterus egrotaret' and 'Licet eger cum egrotis'.[14] What would seem to make Peter's exercise in creative self-distancing more original is that he chooses to attempt it within the form of the letter, rather than within the conventions of the lyric form. The effect is the same: to articulate an 'orthodox' penitence for the possibly indecorous material of 'mere' literary work without causing that work to cease to exist, as a genuine repentance might.

Curiously, the most recent analysis of Peter's letters defines his practice as an author in terms which prove remarkably appropriate to the poet of 'Grates ago Veneri':

> Indeed there seems to be a developing critical consensus that his creative mind is, as I have suggested, distinctively shaped by conflict – not just in the sense that he conveys his anxieties and self-doubts in ways that are strikingly persuasive, but also in the sense that he deliberately and characteristically seeks out and stylizes oppositions and contrasts, both formally and thematically.[15]

Cartlidge's powerful sense of 'the essential and self-conscious conflictedness of Peter of Blois' as a writer of letters leads him to read aspects of Peter's performance in the Epistles as being 'almost incomprehensible except as part of an ongoing, conscious attempt to define and extend the poetics of contention'.[16] Whether coincidentally or not, it is as the unfolding of a series of poetic contentions that 'Grates ago Veneri' must be understood.

Some of those contentions were inherent in the lyric form itself. In design and in execution, medieval Latin lyric poetry was an exercise in reconciling opposites, stretched on the frames of the expectations of disparate traditions. Writing in an esteemed but ancient language, the medieval lyricist needed both to show his ability to compete with the 'Masters' of the past and to demonstrate the superiority of his own time, which had received the gift of God's enlightenment. The

---

[13] Peter of Blois, *Epistolae*, ed. J.-P. Migne, *Patrologiae Cursus Completus, Series Latina*, vol. 207, 232B–C.
[14] Karl Strecker, *Moralisch-Satirische Gedichte Walters von Châtillon* (Heidelberg, 1929).
[15] Neil Cartlidge, 'An Intruder at the Feast? Anxiety and Debate in the Letters of Peter of Blois', *The Writers of the Reign of Henry II*, ed. Ruth Kennedy and Simon Meecham-Jones (New York, 2006), pp. 122–56 (p. 131).
[16] In reaching this conclusion, he draws on 'Dronke's observation that Peter's artistic methodology connects rather strikingly with the distinctive poetics of medieval debate-poetry' (Cartlidge, 'An Intruder', p. 135).

medieval Latin lyric characteristically combined imitation of its classical sources with a semi-dramatised 'self'-presentation that expressed a critical commentary on that tradition. The texture of the resultant lyric is self-conscious and 'hybrid' – not confined within one time or cultural context but, for that reason, not securely fixed within a reliably supportive living tradition. The choice of the learned language as a compositional medium necessarily restricted the scale of potential audience, and this has perhaps encouraged an interpretation of the development of the erotic mode in medieval Latin poetry as the expression of a wholly literary phenomenon, through which learned and ambitious Christian authors sought to prove their ability to imitate and emulate the styles of classical models.[17] Since the erotic mode was a frequently used weapon in the armoury of Ovid, Martial and their peers, it might seem inevitable that Christian authors would feel obliged to see if they could bend Odysseus' bow in this way. Godman draws attention to the ways in which 'Grates ago Veneri', the tenth lyric in the Arundel manuscript, can be seen as a self-consciously allusive reworking of classical themes, 'where the ancient (notably Ovidian) concept of the *militia amoris* is recast in a fresh and modern mould'.[18] But the value of classical precedent in sanctioning the erotic licence found in the Arundel lyrics, though substantial, should not be overstated. Peter was writing before the discovery of the poems of Catullus,[19] which were to cause the re-evaluation of the scope and importance of the erotic mode in classical lyric. Nor did the existence of classical literature on sexual themes absolve Peter from respecting (in his writing as, presumably, in his life) the Church's teachings on chastity. Ziolkowski reminds us of the dangers of assuming that medieval scholars felt able to read the classical (but pagan) literature of the past with uncritical enthusiasm: 'Yet in no post-classical period were the Classics accepted wholesale without reservation, since they contained licenses in their usage that later writers could or would no longer allow themselves'.[20] Paradoxically it was the incomplete transferability of the classical tradition that enabled poets like Peter of Blois and Walter of Châtillon to adapt and appropriate elements of classical poetry within the texture of their own work to answer the needs of their own intellectual context – as later poets were to adapt from their work also.[21]

---

[17] As, for example, by Moser (Thomas C. Moser, Jr, *A Cosmos of Desire: The Medieval Latin Erotic Lyric in English Manuscripts* (Ann Arbor, 2004)).

[18] Peter Godman, 'Literary Classicism and Latin Erotic Poetry of the Twelfth Century and the Renaissance', *Latin Poetry and the Classical Tradition*, ed. Peter Godman and Oswyn Murray (Oxford, 1990), pp. 149–82 (p. 163). Godman's purpose is to show that the allusive 'Alexandrianism' of Peter's literary technique does not preclude but rather enables Peter's claim to originality and to his poem achieving an equal status to that enjoyed by its sources.

[19] With the exception of Carmina LXII, which is found in a ninth-century manuscript, the codex Thuaneus par. Lat. 8071, it has generally been believed that all of Catullus' poems were lost to late antiquity and the early medieval period. Knowledge of his style and subject matter derived from the discovery of a manuscript in Verona, soon after 1300. Although that manuscript seems to have been lost before the end of the fourteenth century, modern editions draw on three manuscripts (codex Oxoniensis Canon. cl. lat 30, codex Sangermanensis. Par. lat. 14137 and codex Romanus: Vat. Ott. lat 1829), all of which have been dated to the 1370s and which present (partial) copies of the lost Verona original.

[20] Jan M. Ziolkowski, 'The Highest Form of Compliment: *Imitatio* in Medieval Latin', *Poetry and Philosophy in the Middle Ages: a Festschrift for Peter Dronke*, ed. John Marenbon (Leiden, 2001), pp. 293–307 (p. 301).

[21] McDonough (*The Oxford Poems*, pp. 80–1), for example, draws attention to persuasive similari-

Whichever Peter (if two existed) we believe to be the author of the Arundel lyrics, the questions remain to be answered as to why Peter should have written such incendiary and unprecedented lyrics, and why they were not lost or suppressed as, for example, the amorous lyrics of Abelard appear to have been lost.[22] The curious parallelism projected in Peter's Epistles – between two authors, or two facets of a single author's career – paradoxically brings us closer to the constructing fiction that validates the existence of these verses. For, beyond question, one crucial attraction for the Arundel Poet of the imagery of sexual coupling is that it allows the poet to fashion verse that attempts to witness the contemplation of duality – that state of unresolvedness which contemporary philosophy and theology sought to extinguish. The sexual act, with its momentary conjoining of discrete bodies, allowed for the possibility of the resolution of the pains of dualism, even if it also demonstrated the briefness and implausibility of this resolution.

Such contemplation of duality was possible only within a creative context that was both learned and clerical. In the most recent study of the genre Moser reminds us that 'medieval Latin erotic poetry was a poetry of the schools and of clerics trained in classical lore'.[23] In a poem like 'Grates ago Veneri', the classical influence is mediated through two levels of familiarity: through a direct knowledge of the classical texts and through imitation of and allusion to the images and expression of prior medieval poets, like Bernardus Silvestris, who had sought to assimilate and reanimate elements of the literary past.

The relationship of this corpus to other forms of expression in the medieval lyric mode remains unclear. Dronke links the surviving learned material to a lost oral tradition, erased by its own ephemerality: 'any claim that something is new in the twelfth century must be qualified by attempts to fathom the lost literature – and, even more, the lost oral compositions – of the earlier periods . . .'[24] There is little surviving evidence, however, that might prove Dronke's judgement to be correct. Instead critics must reckon with the fact of absence: 'In western Europe generally, erotic lyrics from before the late eleventh century are rare, highly various, and scattered.'[25] The twelfth century was also a period of exceptional fertility in the writing of satirical verse, much of it aimed at the corruptions of Church governance. Again, the relationship of the erotic canon to the corpus of satirical verse has been contested. While Dronke is happy to include the erotic verse under the cloak of 'goliardic' satire, Moser is keen to establish the erotic as a distinct canon: 'Though they can be funny, raucous, and irreverent, the poems under discussion here are not a part of that body of medieval Latin poems loosely called "goliardic".'[26] It is a distinction that seems difficult to maintain since authors regularly straddle the frontiers of Moser's distinction between modes.

---

ties between the imagery of the fourth Arundel lyric 'A globo veteri' and phrases from Gerald of Wales's *De mundi creatione et contentis eiusdem*.

[22] Peter Abelard, *Historia Calamitatum*, ed. Jacques Monfrin (Paris, 1962).
[23] Moser, *Cosmos of Desire*, p. 94.
[24] Peter Dronke, 'Profane elements in Literature', *Renaissance and Renewal in the Twelfth Century*, ed. Robert L. Benson, Giles Constable and Carol D. Lanham (Oxford, 1982), pp. 569–92 (p. 570).
[25] Moser, *Cosmos of Desire*, p. 3.
[26] Moser, *Cosmos of Desire*, p. 9.

Walter of Châtillon, the most trenchant, at times most apocalyptic, of satirists, was also credited with the authorship of the erotic lyric of (unsatisfied) longing, 'Importuna Veneri'. Similarly, eroticism (sometimes implicitly hinted at) appears as one element in the satirical gibes of Hugh Primas. Further, Moser's attempted distinction between the erotic and the goliardic also seems to have been unnoticed by contemporary audiences, if we read the evidence of collections such as the *Carmina Burana* or the Arundel Lyrics, in both of which erotic lyrics such as the 'Grates ago Veneri' and 'Sevit aure spiritus' are found alongside Walter's satiric tirades.[27]

In part, Moser enforces a distinction between the erotic and the goliardic by defining the erotic within a tightly drawn generic prototype that would exclude more apparently 'occasional' (and goliardic) lyrics such as 'Importuna Veneri':

> In its own time, Latin erotic poetry must have had many different audiences and may have competed for a while, particularly in England, with other forms of court entertainment, such as the new songs of the *trouvères*. But it always remained a poetry about a particular sort of clerical experience of eros seen through the lens of Neoplatonism and colored by a humanistic understanding of the aims of an ambitious educational program.[28]

Moser's insistence on the philosophical context once again seeks to read the erotic mode as a means of expressing an abstract state of mind, distanced from the experience of physical desire. But, in choosing a language that necessarily restricted the range of readership, the writers of Medieval Latin erotic verse seem to have felt encouraged to enjoy a greater degree of experimentation in the choice of subject matter. The lyrics found within the Arundel Lyrics are notable for including not merely lyrics of desire and pursuit, but also poems dealing with physical consummation. As such, they take the poetic voice some way beyond the tradition, derived from the Song of Songs, which had long licensed the identification of the pains of physical desire with the desire of the soul, exiled from God.[29] Nor can lyrics such as 'Sevit aure spiritus' or 'Grates ago Veneri' be read in any way as imaginations of a projected consummation with Christ. The shifting inequality in the power-relationship between the figura of the poet/narrator and his beloved that might be considered to be a generic marker of the mode of the erotic lyric would have been wholly inappropriate, if not blasphemous, when applied to a celebration of man's loving relationship with his Creator, in which the relationship of Christ as dominant and always the giver, and man as always both the obligated and the courted party, cannot be gainsaid.

More seriously, Moser's delineation of the intellectual context perhaps distracts

---

[27] A reading of the contrasted aesthetics of 'Importuna veneri' and 'Sevit aure spiritus' is presented in S. Meecham-Jones, 'Resisting Utopia: Temptation and Assertion in the Latin Lyrics of Walter of Châtillon and Peter of Blois', *Utopias*, ed. Francoise Le Saux and Neil Thomas (Durham, 2000), pp. 77–100.

[28] Moser, *Cosmos of Desire*, p. 3.

[29] For example, in the *Eighty-six sermons on the Song of Songs* by Bernard of Clairvaux (trans. Kilian Walsh and Irene M. Edmonds, 4 vols, Cistercian Fathers Series (Kalamazoo, 1971–80), v. 4, 7, 31, 40). The tradition is also referred to a number of times by Peter Dronke in *Medieval Latin and the Rise of the European Love-Lyric* (Oxford, 1965).

attention from the philosophical and ethical incongruity inherent in any project that sought to reconcile and assimilate the competing demands of the terms 'clerical', 'eros' and 'Neoplatonism'. The medieval lyric almost invariably functions as a site of dualistic oppositions, which it is the purpose of the author to surf with a playful agility, which displays his mastery of, and refusal to be contained within, contrasted traditions of thought and expression. The poet's ability to remind the reader of the contrasting expectations of clerical asceticism and erotic affirmation marks out the opposition of irreconcilable values as a structural motif, which invests the verse with a palpable, but subcutaneous, tension. It is an effect that, in 'Grates ago Veneri', the Arundel Peter magnifies through the apparent confidence of the narrative voice, which might be characterised as a display of courtly cockiness. The orthodox Christian notions of chastity are not absent in the poem, but are merely silent, like the poet's unspeaking lover.

The opposition of the demands of virginity and the flesh offers a template that is echoed in parallel oppositions of clashing values. The poetic contention of Christian and Neoplatonic themes offers related, but subtler, and more aesthetic, pleasures. In the Philosophical Schools of the twelfth century, philosophers had laboured to mark out the limits of the compatibility of Christian-revealed Truth with inherited Neoplatonic methods of discourse. For the poet, these terms were marked temporally as well as ethically – Neoplatonism engaging the poet in a dialogue with the past where Christianity offered a reminder of his present status, and a promise for the future. The balancing of Christian and Neoplatonic elements is often a crucial element in the strategy of the medieval Latin lyric to celebrate and exploit the temporal dualism that characterises the poetic form – created, yet experienced as if still happening, simultaneously asserting its dualistic nature as a present reflection of past experience.

For twenty-first-century readers the strenuous interrogation of the limits of classical logic by the philosophers of the Schools of Paris and Chartres can seem alienated from the concerns of everyday lived experience – finally no more than an exercise, albeit an absorbing one, in intellectual discourse. But the far-reaching consequences of the disputation between Berengar of Tours and Lanfranc over the nature of the Eucharist in the late eleventh century had shown the powerfully disruptive, if perhaps also creative, power released by the (perceived) misapplication of dialectic procedures to theological questions. Writing from a viewpoint that embraces the Church's claim to Authority, Sheedy dismissed Berengar's work as being vitiated by a failure of process:

> In applying the science of logic to theology he was merely continuing an established principle. But in *building* his theology on logic, in placing dialectics as the foundation and first principle of his theology, he inverted the order beyond all question, and thus separated himself from the pre-scholastic stream. That is the basic position of this study: that the error of Berengar of Tours lay at a deeper level than any aspect of Eucharistic theology which was involved. He was a heretic on principle before he touched the Eucharist.[30]

---

[30] Charles E. Sheedy, *The Eucharistic Controversy of the Eleventh Century Against the Background of Pre-Scholastic Theology* (Washington, DC, 1947), p. 33.

In Sheedy's judgement, Berengar's attempt to show that there was no distance between the knowledge of God and the processes of pagan intellectualism that could describe it was inherently misplaced. Berengar's attempts to fuse two antithetical traditions was, in the view of the Church, vitiated by his failure to distinguish between these traditions – to mark out one as privileged by divine grace and therefore not to be compared with a merely human tradition.

The Eucharistic debate raised serious and troubling issues about the relationship of Learning to Authority, and of the crucial role of Faith as the mediator between the symbols of Language and an abstract concept of truth. 'Grates ago veneri' is a poem that displays the psychological backwash of this disputation, sublimated from the contention of theological Truth with philosophical method to the less perilous issues raised by the 'merely' literary mode of the lyric.

In 'Grates ago Veneri' Peter uses the formal dualism that constitutes the aesthetics of the learned lyric as a weapon against a conceptual dualism of a different order, a dualism inherent in much of the philosophical discourse that might be considered Neoplatonic – that of the dualism of the soul and the body, as described in the writings of Proclus, Iamblichus and their followers. 'Grates ago Veneri' was written at a time when the Authority of the Church was being increasingly challenged by the spread of 'heretical' sects, whose rejection of the physical world grew from the overlapping of Late Classical, Neoplatonic, Jewish and Gnostic philosophies. The processes of textual contact and transmission that played a role in this fusion remain obscure, and it may be that the simultaneous development of seemingly parallel ideas in disparate communities was often merely fortuitous, but the physical and spiritual hardships of medieval Europe made attractive to many the notion that the (suffering) body was the prison of the spirit: 'The Book of Wisdom (9:15) echoes Phaedo 81C, "For a perishable body weighs down the soul, and the earthy tabernacle is a burden to the thoughtful mind".'[31] It was an idea that can seem close to many expressions of Patristic asceticism, and which at times shadows the thought of Saint Paul himself, but which ran counter to one of the Church's most crucial but most paradoxical teachings, that of the Incarnation, the doctrine that declared that Christ on Earth was simultaneously fully human and fully divine. To assert that the doctrine of the Incarnation was beyond the rules of classical logic offered no answer to the problems raised by the doctrine: that if Christ-as-man was fully human, then his body must have shared the physical properties of human bodies (even if not their taint of original sin). The disputation between Berengar of Tours and Lanfranc about the physical properties of the host and wine in the Eucharist had shown how potent a spiritual weight could reside in a debate about physical 'accidentals' – at the moment of the Eucharistic miracle, did the bread and wine lose their prior physical properties, and were the qualities of the Body of Christ created in their place (which must be impossible, since the Body of Christ was eternal, without beginning)? These were heavy questions, and Lanfranc was obliged to counter Berengar's attempts to answer them through dialectic by invoking the extra-dialectical powers of

---

[31] Arthur Darby Nock, 'Gnosticism', *Harvard Theological Review* 57:4 (1964), pp. 255–79, repr. in *Gnosticism in the Early Church. Studies in Early Christianity: A Collection of Scholarly Essays*, Vol. 5, ed. David M. Scholer (New York, 1993), p. 9.

Authority and Faith. It was the exercise of Faith, sanctioned by Authority, which required and enabled the Christian to *know* as true a conclusion that could not be experienced by the intellect or the senses alone.

If the refutation of Berengar had the effect of reinscribing the exercise of Faith at the centre of Christian theology, it may seem mischievous of Peter to fashion a poem that offers a veiled critique of the reliability of Faith, when not guided by charity or wisdom. The certainty of judgement, which Sheedy lauds as orthodoxy, is recalled and parodied in the experience of the narrator of 'Grates ago Veneri', whose belief in the evidence of his senses leads him to recount an experience, the certainty of which the reader experiences more questioningly, coloured by what Godman describes as 'a note of sophisticated ambiguity'.[32] Admittedly, the suggestion of a 'sophisticated ambiguity' proves expedient, reassuring the unease of modern readers confronted with a sexual experience to which the female partner's consent is (at best) not explicitly voiced. But a poem that seems to declare the primacy of sensual experience also deftly, if implicitly, defines the gap between physical experience and true understanding – as the narrator shows himself, in Godman's phrase, to be 'in physical conquest and in imaginative defeat'[33] – even if that 'defeat' may be discernable to Godman and to the reader, but not to the narrator himself. For all that the 'sophisticated ambiguity' of the poem can tell us is that the exercise of Faith must remain mysterious – maybe the girl consents, maybe not – but a state that is internal (even when its consequences are physical) must remain unverifiable, even to those who know or believe themselves to experience it.

'Grates ago Veneri' is a lyric that purports to shock as a means of demonstrating the playful and paradoxical orthodoxy of its depiction of the primacy of Faith over intellect – an orthodoxy that explains its apparently baffling circulation and survival. The Arundel poet explores several unexpected levels of apparently paradoxical orthodoxy in the construction of the poem. Central to this purpose is the detailed physicality with which he describes his encounters in the lyrics of the cycle, a physicality that is signalled by Godman as being central to their purpose:

> But Peter, in Grates ago Veneri, was no more attempting to depict a scene of seduction than he was seeking, in Sevit aure spiritus, to compose a *descriptio pulchritudinis*. The simpler strategy of imitation was one he rejected in order to create something more complex. With Ovidian boldness, the ancient amatory metaphors of *militia amoris* are invested with new literal meaning.[34]

But the value, if any, of that 'new literal meaning' – to readers in the twelfth or the twenty-first centuries – demands fuller explanation. That value cannot lie solely in the 'note of sophisticated ambiguity' that, for Godman, distinguishes Peter's lyrics from their classical (and, in particular, Ovidian) sources. The evocation of a narrative ambiguity might be seen as a necessary revision to the model to render its ostensible subject containable (if only just) within a Christian context, but some

---

[32] Godman, 'Literary Classicism', p. 168.
[33] Godman, 'Literary Classicism', p. 167.
[34] Godman, 'Literary Classicism', pp. 167–8.

part of the true Christianity of the lyric lies in its surprising engagement with physicality.

At a time when the development of scholastic Neoplatonism sought to emphasise the division of body and soul, the erotic lyricists sought to re-establish the corporeal experience as being worthy of respect – if it were not so, why did Christ agree to take on a human body? With a logic as audacious as that of his narrator, the Arundel Peter presents the seduction of women as a parallel that confirms (if it cannot prove) the theory of the incarnation of Christ – of the mutually dependent coexistence of the bodily and the spiritual. The idea is shocking not merely because it is unexpected, but also because it allows Peter to frame a mocking and pragmatic, but finally orthodox, riposte to the dualistic heresies of the asceticism of the Cathars and others who denied the humanity of Christ. It was a figuration that reveals much about the philosophical and theological fears of its own time, perhaps as much as it reveals about the poet's opinions on or experiences of the physical act of consummation.

But if the poet hoped that, as in the miracle of the Eucharist, his materials would be transformed by Faith into something eternal, paradoxically it is the 'accidental' properties of his chosen imagery of sexual contact, rather than its theological message, that has returned the poem to the notice of a new readership. The sexual act, so often framed in the imagery of religious and philosophical discourse as an unanswerable guarantee of an expression of Truth in action, is reinterpreted through a narrative that questions the possibility of emotional, spiritual and psychological 'surrender', beyond reservation, even at the moment when two bodies are joined in union.[35] At once mocking and celebrating the physical, emotional and spiritual uncertainties that sex cannot resolve, in 'Grates ago Veneri', Peter's narrator offers the sexual act as an ambiguous image of the (often-misled) triumph of Faith over experience in human affairs.

Appendix*

1a	1b
Grates ago veneri,	Dudum militaueram
que prosperi	nec poteram
michi risus numine	hoc frui stipendio;
de virgine	nunc sencio
mea gratum	me beari,

---

[35] In a tradition harking back to exegesis of *The Song of Songs*, the sexual act was often figured allegorically in the imagery of religious and philosophical discourse as an unanswerable guarantee of an expression of 'truth' in action. It was an image that was to be alluded to or experienced repeatedly in visionary and in mystical writings, and which reached its epitome in the imagery of the mystical marriage of Christ the bridegroom with the Holy Church. But there is nothing mystical about the figuration of physical contact in 'Grates ago Veneri'. Instead, the imagery of sexual intimacy is invested with a perhaps comic, perhaps tragic valency, through the pivotal space it occupies within a narrative that undermines the potency of the image through its questioning of the possibility of emotional, spiritual and psychological 'surrender', beyond reservation, even at the moment when two bodies are joined in union.

* Text of 'Grates ago Veneri' from McDonough; the translation is my own.

et optatum
contulit tropheum

serenari
nutum Dyoneum

2a
Visu colloquio
contactu basio
frui virgo dederat;
set aberat
linea posterior
et melior
amoris.
Quam nisi transiero
de cetero,
sunt, que dantur alia,
materia
furoris.

2b
Ad metam propero;
set fletu tenero
mea me sollicitat,
dum dubitat
soluere virguncula
repagula
pudoris.
flentis bibo lacrimas
dulcissimas;
sic me plus inebrio,
plus haurio
feruoris.

3a
Delibuta lacrimis
oscula plus sapiunt;
blandimentis intimis
mentem plus alliciunt
ergo magis capior
et acrior
vis flamme recalescit
set dolor Choronidis
setumidis
exerit singultibus
nec precibus
mitescit.

3b
Preces addo precibus
basiaque basiis;
fletus illa fletibus,
iurgia conuiciis.
meque cernit oculo
nunc emulo,
nunc quasi supplicanti.
nam nunc lite dimicat,
nunc supplicat
dumque prece blandior,
fit surdior,
precanti.

I give thanks to thee, Venus, who by the power of her kindly smile, has just granted to me a pleasing and welcome victory over my girl.

For a long time now I had fought, nor was I able to enjoy this success. Now I feel that I am making progress and that the face of Dione is smiling upon me. My girl has allowed me to enjoy her face, her speech, her touch, her kiss, but the final stage was beyond my grasp, and the better stage of love. Unless I pass it, as for the rest, what is given to me is but another source of madness.

I hasten to the goal but my girl begs me with tender weeping, while she hesitates to loosen the virgin bands of her shame. I drink up her sweet tears while she weeps so I drink up more eagerness, the more I am intoxicated by her in this way. Her lips which are moistened with tears have more taste. They entice my mind all the more by their intimate attractions. Therefore, I am the more captivated and the more powerful force of the flame of love grows hot within me. But the grief of a Coronis reveals itself with swelling sobs, nor does it soften at my entreaties. I add entreaties to entreaties, kisses to kisses and she [adds] weeping to weeping and curses to re-crimination. She now looks at me with waxy eye which also now entreats me. For now she struggles from the fray, now she begs me and while I press her with my entreaties, she becomes deaf to my prayers.

Boldly, I bring more violence to bear and she lashes me with her cruel nails and tears my hair. She repels my force boldly. She bends herself and entwines her knees, nor is the gate of her shame opened to me. But at last I advance further and I bring triumph to my purpose through embraces; having grasped her firmly, I pin down her arms and I press my implanted kisses upon her, and so the kingdom of Dione is unlocked. The issue was pleasing to us both, and she grudged me less, and more gently giving kisses with no bitterness, sweet as honey.

And swelling with trembling, half-closed eyes, as though with an anxious sigh, she slept.

A Fine and Private Place[1]

JANE BLISS

LESBIAN practice is recognised, proscribed and then euphemised almost to invisibility in the *Ancrene Wisse*.[2] Almost, but not quite: the writer is caught in the dilemma of a confessor who, fearing to put ideas into his penitent's head, yet needs to drag forth and deal with every conceivable sin.[3] After all, it is no use telling her she must not have sex with men if she therefore thinks it is all right to have sex with women – her fellow anchoresses – or even by herself, and still keep her virginity. And so he drops several hints into his text, which are sufficient for a reader as attentive as she is.[4]

These hints have not been examined at all closely by *Ancrene Wisse*'s modern readers – perhaps it is thought that their implications do not add anything to our appreciation of the text. A certain amount of work has been done on female homosexuality in the Middle Ages.[5] But research suggests that theologians, from St Paul onwards, openly recognise it as sin though nobody else does; consequently there are very few documented cases, as if through 'an almost active willingness to disbelieve'.[6] As far as I can discover, nobody studies *Ancrene Wisse* in any detail against this background, because the hints I examine do not, alone, amount to very much. But it is rather remarkable that they are here at all, given the silence in so

---

[1] Of the friends and colleagues who contributed suggestions during my work on this article, I want to thank Chris Cannon especially for his encouragement.
[2] *Ancrene Wisse*, ed. J. R. R. Tolkien, EETS OS 249 (London, 1962); M. B. Salu, trans., *The Ancrene Riwle* (1955; repr. Exeter, 1990). Page numbers following citations and references will be to the former (the text) and then to the latter (the translation). There are several versions of the text; I cite two of the others below.
[3] See e.g. Linda Georgianna, *The Solitary Self: Individuality in the Ancrene Wisse* (Cambridge, MA, 1981), p. 140.
[4] In line with Georgianna and other scholars, I refer to her in the singular, though the original recipients of the text never numbered fewer than three: the writer frequently, but not always, addresses his reader in the singular.
[5] See e.g. Judith C. Brown, *Immodest Acts: The Life of a Lesbian Nun in Renaissance Italy* (New York, 1986), Introduction; Vern L. Bullough, 'The Sin against Nature and Homosexuality', *Sexual Practices and the Medieval Church*, ed. Vern L. Bullough and James Brundage (Amherst, NY, 1994), pp. 55–71. Chapters in Carolyn Dinshaw, *Getting Medieval: Sexualities and Communities, Pre- and Postmodern* (Durham, NC, 1999), and in Karma Lochrie, *Covert Operations: The Medieval Uses of Secrecy* (Philadelphia, 1999), provide valuable context.
[6] Brown, *Immodest Acts*, p. 9.

many texts.⁷ In my view they betray aspects of the writer's anxiety, even desire, which in turn contribute powerfully to the quality of the writing. All the essays in the present volume are concerned with a search for the erotic in medieval literature; my own research leads neither to fabliau nor fairyland but, unexpectedly, to a book of devotion. The women here are not objects of sadistic male desire, nor is their sensuality embodied as sorcery, vanity or lust for power. Yet the writer's interest in erotic sexuality for its own sake is apparent from the hints about what could happen among women shut up together; both powerful imagination and physical sensitivity are suggested by the astonishing quality of his prose. Vivid, colourful, fresh and vital, extraordinary, spirited and articulate, imagistic . . . Most scholars, whatever else they have to say, recognise *Ancrene Wisse* as a remarkable piece of literature.

Before going on to discuss the sensuality, and the rich stylistic variousness, of this Rule for enclosed women, I shall set out the hints that I have mentioned: the first group includes references to masturbation, the second to sex with other women.

The first example is 'bute fere oðer wið' (107: 'with or without a companion' (91)). In this section on Temptations, the writer describes several kinds of lechery (children or 'cundles' of the Scorpion) including incest, which are unfortunately 'to monie al to cuðe' ('all too well known to many'). Then he turns to those other kinds that he dares not name 'leste sum leorni mare uuel þen ha con ꞇ beo þrof itemptet' ('for fear anyone should learn more of evil than she already knows, and should be thereby tempted'), and alludes to lechery with another woman – or with herself: 'wakinde ꞇ willes' ('in a waking state and voluntarily') implies that she can't help it in her sleep). There is another reference to masturbation in the section headed Confession: 'hondlede him i swuch stude: oðer me seoluen' (163: ' "touched him in such a place", or "myself" ' (141)).⁸

The same passage provides the most explicit of my examples: 'hit wes wið . . . a ladles þing. a wummon as ich am' (163: ' "it was with . . . an innocent creature", "a woman such as I am" ' (141)).⁹ Shrift must be 'naked', and not wrapped up in mealy-mouthed euphemisms; she must call herself a stinking whore, a foul mare on heat, and so on. But the writer can hardly bring himself to say just what this 'scheome' might be. A further reference to female homosexuality lurks, I believe, in the External Rules near the end of the book: the anchoress may have two women as servants, but they must not sleep together – 'eiðer ligge ane' (218: 'Let

---

7 'In matters officially declared unmentionable, absence of evidence . . . is not evidence of absence.' Kolve's narrative, while acknowledging valuable feminist studies, ignores female same-sex desire. But he urges that we make ourselves alert to subtleties and submerged images – or risk becoming complicit (V. A. Kolve, 'Ganymede/Son of Getron: Medieval Monasticism and the Drama of Same-Sex Desire', *Speculum* 73:4 (October 1998), pp. 1014–67 (pp. 1065–6)).
8 Salu separates 'him' from 'myself' by placing quotation marks (the words are given the anchoress to say when she confesses); the absence of such marks in the Middle English text suggests that masturbation could be part of intercourse.
9 Bennett notices this passage, but with enormous innocence ignores the tell-tale 'as ich am': 'Has the Master here forgotten whom he is addressing?' (J. A. W. Bennett, *Middle English Literature* (1986; repr. Oxford, 1990), p. 268). Hasenfratz ('apparently a reference to homoeroticism', Robert Hasenfratz, ed., *Ancrene Wisse* (Kalamazoo, 2000), p. 459) makes little of it, especially since Brown's *Immodest Acts* (to which he refers) does not mention *Ancrene Wisse*.

each sleep by herself' (189)).[10] The writer realises that it is easier (not least because he must not say certain things) to protect his charges from predators or lovers outside the anchorhold than it is to prevent them, inside, from enjoying one another's bodies or their own.[11]

My reading is supported by reference to a Middle English version of Aelred's *De Institutione Inclusarum*, one of the works on which *Ancrene Wisse*'s writer drew. Both authors had read Aelred's Latin, and chose not to translate it: 'in oþer wise ... which schal not be sayd now ne ynemned' (in other ways ... which shall not be said now nor named).[12] Aelred strongly condemns both male and female homosexuality, and alludes to loss of virginity through autoeroticism; he does not hide his meaning from his female audience. He is writing this treatise, on ordering the life of an anchoress, at the request of his (blood) sister; his manner, when addressing her directly, comes across (at least in its Middle English version) as admiring and even envious of her blessed freedom from sin. He bewails to her his own sin, asks for her pity, and laments that he cannot hope to be 'euene wit þe in lyf þat is to comen!' (equal with thee in life that is to come).[13] There is a very great difference between Aelred's manner to his sister and that of *Ancrene Wisse*'s writer to his reader(s): the latter is variously avuncular and patronising, affectionate and authoritative, but his discourse is entirely one-sided and he gives away nothing – almost nothing – about himself.

The anchoress is literate: she reads French and English, and probably some Latin; we know she can write because she must not write letters without leave (217, 188). She can write down her Hours, for example (15, 8); even her servants are educated enough to teach ... other girls, of course (217, 188). It is possible that the writer is one of the few people she is allowed to correspond with. Given the intense and quite personal tone that comes through in many parts of the text, it is

---

10 See Brown, *Immodest Acts*, p. 8. The refusal to name certain things, 'lest oþer ben ytempted þere of', is in a later version (A. Zettersten, ed., *The English Text of the Ancrene Riwle*, EETS OS 274 (London, 1976), p. 94); so is the 'wakeand and willes' indulgence. But 'bute fere oðer wið' is not in this passage. In the corresponding passage on Confession neither of the phrases that I have quoted from *Ancrene Wisse* is present (pp. 134–5), nor does the prohibition on servant-women sleeping together appear in the External Rules (pp. 183–4). The dangers perceived by the earlier writer are ignored or suppressed entirely by the redactor of a text addressed to a (larger) group of both men and women (p. xxi). This redactor may have thought those passages dangerous and feared their effect, or simply have considered them to be irrelevant.

11 Dinshaw (*Getting Medieval*, p. 91) mentions the confusion of lesbian sex with masturbation – because 'seipsis'/'hemself' can mean either with herself/themselves or with one another. Both were 'unnatural', but neither 'polluted' in the sense of wasting seed. Note the distinction: not between natural and unnatural (everything except orthodox 'missionary-position' sex – and that only so as to make babies – was unnatural, see e.g. Lochrie, *Covert Operations*, p. 10), but between speakable and unspeakable.

12 Aelred of Rielvaulx, *De Institutione Inclusarum: Two English Versions*, ed. John Ayto and Alexandra Barratt, EETS OS 287 (London, 1984), Vernon manuscript (the other English version does not contain this key passage), p. 27 (translations mine). Notes (to lines 63–4, 65) give what Aelred really said: 'cum detestandum illud scelus quo uir in uirum, uel femina furit in feminam, omnibus flagitiis damnabilius iudicetur' (that crime is to be detested, by which a man goes mad for a man, or a woman for a woman; it is to be judged more damnable than all other vices); 'et absque alienae carnis consortio uirginitatis plerumque corrumpitur' (often virginity is corrupted in the absence of anybody else's flesh).

13 Aelred, pp. 52–4. A note to lines 1102ff. discusses Aelred's youthful sins 'of a homosexual nature'.

surprising that he never speaks of visiting the sisters. He is evidently fond of them: not only does he refer to their life before enclosure[14] as if he were a family friend (though probably not the one who supplies their needs) but he also knows, for example, that they have a tendency to be too hard on themselves (e.g. 211, 183), and he sometimes gives way to emotion: 'ʒe beoð ase wealle . . . A weila ʒef ʒe worið ne bide ich hit neauer' (130: 'You are the spring, as it were. . . Ah, if you were to grow dry, I could not bear it' (113)). Readers have combed the text for rare clues about his circumstances: Janet Grayson notes that his expressions of weariness may be quite natural at the end of a long work and not due to old age;[15] E. J. Dobson's research suggests that he was a secular religious and therefore free to travel around.[16] However, 'In a meldei we seggeð ba. placebo ᛝ dirige efter þe mete graces. I twímel dei efter non . . .' (16: 'We, when we have one meal in the day, say both *Placebo* and *Dirige* after the Grace before and after meat; after None when we have two meals in the day . . .' (9)) sounds as though it comes from within a community (whether enclosed or not). Therefore his freedom of movement may have been restricted. It seems that for whatever reason – age, distance or house rules – he is unable to travel.

Thus the richness of *Ancrene Wisse* may be partly because the writer compensates himself for the absence of his subject. He travels in the mind both for and with the anchoress, giving her journeys and adventures to enjoy, and he visits her imaginatively by means of his text. Because he writes to her and not about her, we seem to be intruding on a private conversation; an uncomfortable feeling of prurience (in the reader who does not wish to be a voyeur) results from the fact that our view of the anchoress is his, and his text is the keyhole through which we peep.[17]

Scholars such as Jocelyn Price and Sarah Beckwith, discussing the problem of 'the body', in *Ancrene Wisse* in particular, recognise the mixture of horror and fascination that we experience as modern readers.[18] I see this as a double effect: we are fascinated by the anchoress' sin (or by the possibility of her transgression) and horrified by the circumstances of her life; the writer, our mirror, is horrified by the sin and fascinated by the circumstances. This mixture in the writer's feelings is betrayed in his vivid, sensual style – which paradoxically encourages vivid, sensual feelings in a reader.

Elizabeth Robertson's controversial book celebrates (or perhaps deplores) the vivid and 'quotidian psychological realism' of a style developed specifically for uneducated (female) readers.[19] Much of the imagery – especially the little inset

---

[14] See Salu's interpolation, pp. 84–5. Jocelyn Wogan-Browne notes his real respect and admiration for his readers ('Chaste bodies: frames and experiences', *Framing Medieval Bodies*, ed. Sarah Kay and Miri Rubin (Manchester, 1994), pp. 24–42 (p. 25)).

[15] *Structure and Imagery in Ancrene Wisse* (Hanover, NH, 1974), p. 3.

[16] *The Origins of Ancrene Wisse* (Oxford, 1976).

[17] Jocelyn Price [now Wogan-Browne] (' "Inner" and "Outer": Conceptualising the Body in *Ancrene Wisse* and Aelred's *De Institutione Inclusarum*', *Medieval English Religious and Ethical Literature*, ed. Gregory Kratzmann and James Simpson (Cambridge, 1986), pp. 192–208 (p. 195)), characterises as prurient our very natural curiosity.

[18] Price, 'Conceptualising', pp. 194–5; Sarah Beckwith, 'Passionate Regulation: Enclosure, Ascesis, and the Feminist Imaginary', *South Atlantic Quarterly* 93:4 (Fall 1994), pp. 803–24 (p. 805).

[19] *Early English Devotional Prose and the Female Audience* (Knoxville, TN, 1990), p. 3. In fact the audi-

scenes used to illustrate moral or practical precepts – is earthy, comic, even risqué. Perilously close to fabliau, these images are all about transgression because they point literally and metaphorically at what not to do. Village-life touches include the fool who shouts about the valuables he is carrying (79, 67), the hayward like the one in 'Mon in the mone' (213, 185),[20] and the gossips at the anchorhold (48, 39);[21] these contribute substantially to our pleasure in the text. They are among the images by which the writer, intentionally or not, encourages sensual thoughts and feelings in his reader(s).

And our curiosity is excited by the glimpses we are offered of the recluse's life inside the anchorhold: the field of vision (as it were) is narrow but so intense that we feel with unwilling relish the floor under her bare feet (214, 186) and the stuff of her belted sleeping-gown (214, 185 – and why must the belt be so tight, and no tighter?), or feel the earth of the grave, which she must scrape out daily with her white hands (62, 51). The presence of the grave, in her cell and as her cell enclosing her,[22] suggested to me a rewriting of Marvell's well-known lines: 'The cell's a fine and private place,/ But none (I wish!) do there embrace.'[23]

In explanation I cite an article by Robertson in which she suggests that the anchoritic cell could be an ideal study-space, and that the anchoress was encouraged to read – to join the world of books. The text of *Ancrene Wisse* undermines its own purpose, of keeping the anchoress passive as reader/recipient, and by its rich and sensual literariness allows her to become a vital, active thinker. Robertson deems that the anchoress is thereby invited to 'eat the apple'.[24] I should like to build an extra reading on to Robertson's, and suggest that the apple might also represent sexual activity – a sensual as well as an imaginative freedom. The most extensive of the passages with which Robertson illustrates her argument is that dealing with the last of the five senses: 'nomeliche i þis leaste. þ is ifelunge' (62–3: 'especially in this last, that is, feeling' (51–2)). It contains two startling images of the young woman's beautiful white hands: she must dig her own grave and she must not stretch them out of the cell window to touch and feel another's.[25] This is one of many passages that are sensational (as it were) rather than bookish or cerebral.

The *Ancrene Wisse* is obsessed with the body, though not in a crudely dualistic

---

ence was by no means uneducated; moreover, many of the examples she adduces are found in texts for men or in Latin (or both).
20 See Bennett, *Middle English Literature*, p. 270. However, the touching picture of the anchoress with a cat as her only pet (213, 185) must be qualified: in the Middle Ages cats were necessary (and the only practical) pest control operatives.
21 See Price, 'Conceptualising', pp. 192–3, on how fabliaux may have arisen.
22 Like Lacan's Antigone, and figures such as Oldcastle and Richard II (see Paul Strohm, *England's Empty Throne* (New Haven, 1998), p. 82 and ch. 4), she is between two deaths.
23 'The grave's a fine and private place,/ But none, I think, do there embrace.' From Marvell's 'To His Coy Mistress', lines 31–2 (Andrew Marvell, *The Complete English Poems*, ed. Elizabeth Story Donno (London, 1974), pp. 50–1).
24 Elizabeth Robertson, ' "This Living Hand": Thirteenth-century Female Literacy, Materialist Immanence, and the Reader of the *Ancrene Wisse*', *Speculum* 78:1 (January 2003), p. 36.
25 'ha schulden schrapien euche dei þe eorðe up of hare put þ ha schulien rotien in' (62: 'They should scrape up earth every day out of the grave in which they shall rot' (51)); 'Haldeþ ower honden inwið ower þurles... nawt ane monglin honden. ah putten hond utward... is wohunge efter grome' (62: 'keep your hands inside your windows... not only touching hands, but the mere putting out of the hand... is to court God's anger' (51)).

way.[26] To be convinced, as I am, of the writer's genuine horror of sin is not to deny his desire for the anchoress nor his fear of her lovers, real or imagined. As Grayson reminds us, writer and reader shared 'religious ideals and attitudes . . . in a manner and to a degree lost to us today'.[27] If he does not wish her to sin (nor to sin with her) in her 'private place', it is yet part of his duty to imagine or envisage what she does in there – in other words, to spy upon her.

It has been noted that in some ways the Rule is less restrictive than it might at first appear. For one thing the writer is giving the anchoress and her sisters a Rule because, as he explains, they have asked him to and not because he thinks they need one (5–12, 1–6). We understand that they entered their cells because they wanted to, insofar as medieval life offered women a choice at all; it is reasonable to assume that they were trying to live their chosen life as well as they could. As with any book of instruction (and as with lyric poetry or complaint, where the writer's object cannot reply), the reader is silenced; it is very difficult to hear the anchoress, as it were. We sometimes hear her voice, in confession or saying prayers, but the words are not her own.[28] Because she has chosen silence, the text is helping her to silence herself.

The writer's indulgent tone at times masks how excruciatingly uncomfortable this stable enclosure was (it is hardly surprising that the text should be obsessed with the body):[29] he urges moderation, but within an extremely harsh regime. The anchoress is told to punish her flesh, but without destroying it completely (73, 61); not to starve herself, at least not *quite* to death (211, 183); not to scourge herself, or not without permission (214, 186). However, as Price explains, the anchoress' inner space is offered an extra dimension to compensate for the physical movement denied her by enclosure.[30] *Ancrene Wisse* is structured so that the first and last parts relate to the so-called Outer Rule; nearly all the dense, dynamic, and colourful imagery appears in Parts II–VII: the Inner Rule. Part I is curiously static: the hours, prayers and postures succeed one another in an endless round like a series of still photographs or a very slow dance.[31] Part II explodes into movement and life: the exploration of inner space is grounded[32] in an exploration of senses and feelings, of temptations and sins with their punishment, and finally of

---

[26] Beckwith, 'Passionate Regulation', pp. 808, 813. On this large subject, see also Caroline Bynum, 'Why All the Fuss about the Body? A Medievalist's Perspective', *Critical Inquiry* 22:1 (Autumn 1995), pp. 1–33, and Price, 'Conceptualising'.

[27] Grayson, *Structure*, p. 228. I make no attempt to psychoanalyse the text.

[28] She is not allowed to sing through the squint, the window into the church (27, 19). One wonders whether, when she is driving out the 'dogge of helle . . . snakerinde wið his blodi flehen' (149–50: 'dog of hell . . . sneaking up to you with . . . bloody fleas' (128–9)), she is supposed to yell at him inwardly, or whether the entire anchorhold resounds to her cries in the middle of the night.

[29] Or that 'as the official conditions of her life are obviously unendurable, she must corrupt them' (Price, 'Conceptualising', p. 195).

[30] Price, 'Conceptualising', pp. 203–4.

[31] Grayson (*Structure*, p. 17) doubts whether Part I is truly 'external': it contains the passage that, in the whole book, most closely approaches the mystical (21, 14).

[32] Because Christian asceticism is a doctrine defined by the body (R. W. Southern, *The Making of the Middle Ages* (1953; repr. London, 1973), ch. 5, discusses the body's importance for both female and male religious) and because the outer world, of which her body is a part, is the only objective correlative she can have (see Georgianna, *Solitary Self*, p. 50).

love. Grayson analyses the anchoress' 'allegorical journey'[33] in terms of structure and imagery; the genre of *Ancrene Wisse* is that of a sermon, incorporating a range of styles: dignified, matter-of-fact, facetious, simple and passionate. It has a wealth of Latin quotations, inset stories, devotional and confessional material, social detail, and rich sensual illustration. It begins with grammar and geometry and ends with the management of servants; mostly written to 'ȝe' or 'þu', it also has long sections in the third person, ranging from patient exegesis to courtly narrative, bestiary and biblical lore to sheer comedy. Her inner adventures include flying like several kinds of bird, encounters with animals (trampling on serpents, catching foxes and bopping bears on the head), wandering with pilgrims and desert saints (who include male and female), crossing the Red Sea with God's people. There are high places: the hill of incense by the mountain of myrrh, the bridge of heaven (which she must not fall off), the high tower buffeted by strong wind, the castle whence she pours scalding water down onto her enemies; she goes up St Bernard's ladder and rides in Elias' fiery chariot. She will feast as a queen, in holiday clothing, sit on green boughs or play in the wide pastures of heaven – wooed and saved by a splendid champion, she is fair even among the angels. These give a general idea of the text's sensuality and liveliness – many others crowd the pages of the Inner Rule (Parts II–VII); Grayson discusses the imagery in detail. It is strange, nevertheless, that the very first exciting escape (at the beginning of Part II) is one that she must *not* do: 'Þe heorte is a ful wilde beast. ꞇ makeð moni liht lupe' (29: 'The heart is a very wild animal and often leaps lightly out' (21)).[34]

I have mentioned that the anchoress, although forbidden to develop her intellect through conversation (35–6, 28–9), is encouraged to read and think actively; what is more, the writer knows how much she values her books.[35] The *Ancrene Wisse* is seen by some scholars as a metaphor for the outer enclosing the inner, but in fact the writer offers escape from the monumental structure of Parts II–VII enclosed by Parts I and VIII: he wants his book to be read in random order (see 221, 192; there are cross-references, too).[36] There is no need to read straight through, for instance, to the mundane Outer of Part VIII after experiencing the marvels of Part VII. A book that can be de/re/constructed at will by its user is a book of almost endlessly variable shape.

The Rule may be less restrictive than at first appears, but not very much less. The freedom offered is in the mind, but I argue that the visual, the earthy and the tactile are springboards for that freedom (in spite of the example of poor Dyna, who leaped out only in order to see but ended up being seen and destroyed (32–3, 23–4)). The writer cannot help reminding the anchoress of the pleasure of her body, if only to tell her she must not enjoy it: references to her youth and beauty, the softness and tenderness of her flesh (which she must not love too much), and

---

33 For a synopsis, see Grayson, *Structure*, pp. 223–9.
34 Perhaps the writer is a little worried about the freedom he is going to offer her.
35 I can't agree with Robertson that the author believed 'the anchoresses were unfamiliar with books' (*Female Audience*, p. 45). Whether he fears or respects his audience's level of education, he clearly recognises it (see e.g. 27, 18–19; 125, 108; 127, 110; 146, 126; 148, 127).
36 E.g. 37, 30; 154, 133; 209, 181. See Elizabeth Robertson, 'Savoring "Scientia": the Medieval Anchoress Reads *Ancrene Wisse*', *A Companion to Ancrene Wisse*, ed. Yoko Wada (Cambridge, 2003), pp. 113–44 (p. 120). I would like to thank the author for sending me a copy of this article.

the danger of her tempting others, are scattered throughout the book in addition to less personal references to the disgusting delights of bodily sin. His fascination with the circumstances of her life, as suggested earlier, is in large part responsible for the startlingly vivid style of the book.[37]

Paradoxically it is because the writer's attention is focused so intensely upon the anchoress and how he envisages her life, and because he gives away so little about his own feelings, that we cannot see what she is really like. In some ways a figure such as Amans' lady, in Gower's *Confessio Amantis*, seems more real because instead of staring at her all the time the lover is talking about her; he is so obsessed with himself that the lady's image, though shadowy and fictional, somehow rings true. The anchoress is further obscured by the fact that the writer sometimes talks through her and at her companions of the now rather larger community (130, 112). It would be naïve, at least for my purposes, to subtract everything that he says is 'not for you, my dear sisters, but. . .', or to analyse the text by 'ȝe' and 'þu'. How can we possibly guess what she is like? Surely not the idealised and slightly over-zealous goody-goody that the writer holds up as mirror or example to the others, though not the unruly and transgressive superwoman, either, who is enclosed and restricted in order to protect men from her.

The list of common sins, near the end of Part V, is the nearest to meeting the anchoress that we are going to get. It is unlike the other lists of sins (and unlike the exemplary pictures of sisterly love) and includes grumbling or looking miserable, spilling stuff or getting the giggles, leaving things out in the rain or not doing the mending (175, 152). Even more than the domestic routine set out in Part VIII, this passage approaches most closely – I dare not say to reality – to you and me.

But there is an appealing picture, very near the end, of her 'playing frivolous games' with her maiden (221, 192; I give Salu's phrase here); this passage also, oddly enough, is not in the later version.[38] She is not, of course, supposed to do this: 'ne ticki to gederes' – it sounds delicious![39] There are a few other passages that may provide clues to the way the writer is thinking, although each in its context is rather abstract or general. 'Of hire ahne suster haueð sum ibeon itemptet' (34: 'an anchoress has sometimes been led into temptation by her own sister' (27)) is apparently about not opening windows, but the writer fails to say what exactly the temptation is. However, the passage where he talks of those who enter the anchorhold in order secretly to defile it is suggestive, in fact, because love between the women seems both more probable and more convenient in the circumstances (it can't have been so easy to smuggle a man in!): 'for hwa haueð mare eise to don hire cweadschipes þen þe false ancre?' (68: 'For who has more opportunity for her iniquities than the false anchoress?' (57–8)). There is a reference to lust – gendered

---

37 Price ('Conceptualising', p. 194) talks of the 'alarming corporeality' of the passage about village gossip, for example; 'physical and spiritual become ... worryingly mixed'.

38 *Ancrene Riwle*, ed. Zettersten, p. 184.

39 *MED* gives only this one illustration of the verb 'ticki' – perhaps from verbs in related languages meaning to pat, touch lightly (as in games). Despite reservations expressed by some scholars (e.g. the editors, in *Medieval English Prose for Women*, ed. Bella Millett and Jocelyn Wogan-Browne (Oxford, 1990), p. 163), I think, given other hints in the text, that Hall's proposed meaning, 'caress each other' (Joseph Hall, ed., *Selections from Early Middle English*, 2 (Oxford, 1920), p. 405), need not be ruled out.

female and attacking, then groping, the lady of chastity – that is missing from our text (which lacks two leaves here). It is supplied by Salu (26); it appears in an earlier version, and it seems reasonable to assume that *Ancrene Wisse* contained something very similar.[40] A whore is by definition female, and if it seems an unusual figure given the circumstances it is nonetheless characteristic of this writer, whose 'unusual interpretations are to some indefinable degree reflections of [his] closeness to the women he wrote for'.[41]

The Scorpion, together with its children, is grammatically neuter ('hit') because it partakes of both genders. My final point here is not a matter of a word or a phrase, but of a whole image. Lucinda Rumsey's article on the Scorpion of Lechery analyses the unusual nature of the scorpion as well as the fact that it is not generally used as a figure for lechery (and *Ancrene Wisse*'s writer draws attention to this). Rumsey stresses the androgynous nature of the beast[42] (it has a woman's face, but a decidedly phallic tail (107–8, 92)) and even, at the end of her argument, mentions the writer's insistence on – and refusal to name – certain sins. I suggest that the androgynous beast, with its unspeakable offspring, is a poetically appropriate image for (medievally demonised) gay or lesbian love.

As to whether the anchoress did or did not: there is no firm evidence either way. Given the writer's anxiety, it seems at least probable that she did; though only her confessor knows (if she tells him). It seems unlikely that the writer confesses her himself: he never talks of visiting, and he advises her about whom she may confess to and whom she must be wary of.[43] Therefore he cannot know either.[44] So I want to leave the question open, in order to allow her the choice – and her privacy.

---

[40] See Salu, p. xxiv, and Mabel Day, ed., *The English Text of the Ancrene Riwle*, EETS OS 225 (London, 1957), p. 26.
[41] Cited in Hasenfratz, ed., *Ancrene Wisse*, note p. 466.
[42] Lucinda Rumsey, 'The Scorpion of Lechery and Ancrene Wisse', *Medium Ævum* LXI (1992), pp. 48–58. Dinshaw mentions a medieval confusion of hermaphrodite with sodomite (*Getting Medieval*, p. 80). For the female use of the word sodomite, see Dinshaw (p. 8), and Lochrie (*Covert Operations*, ch. 5).
[43] See Part V, Confession, passim.
[44] 'The recovery of gay voices from within the medieval period will never be easy or sufficient...' (Kolve, 'Ganymede', p. 1065).

Erotic Historiography:
Writing the Self and History in Twelfth-century Romance and the Renaissance

ALEX DAVIS

THIS VOLUME investigates the presence of the erotic in a certain historical period, the Middle Ages. But eroticism is also a key trope in our attempts to define what is distinctive about historical periods. That is, it is not only an object of study, but also functions in terms of mapping the boundaries of the field of study: it has historiographic value. As an example of the almost gravitational attraction that the erotic can possess for those seeking to draw period distinctions, we might begin with a piece by Hugo Estenssoro that appeared in *The Times Literary Supplement* on the seven hundredth anniversary of the birth of Francesco Petrarca, under the title 'Tell Laura I Love Her':

> It is [Petrarch] who is the initiator of a way of being that, within limits, is still ours today ... the modern Western lyrical tradition begins with Petrarch ... Nothing comparable existed in classical or medieval literature, before Petrarch celebrated the self in each and every one of the poet's fluctuating states of mind and feeling throughout his adult life ... all previous literature (including Petrarch's own Latin writings) lacks the elements we find in his work, for the simple reason that he was the one poet to embody in his poems, a new way of being human, a sensibility that was eventually to become what we see as modern man.[1]

The self being described here is, as the title of the piece suggests, specifically an erotic one, because the new, incomparably richer subjectivity that Estenssoro celebrates is the paradoxical product of unsatisfied desire. The emphasis here is explicitly on Petrarch's vernacular love poetry addressed to Laura. As he longs for her, we are told, so he discovers within himself a complex and unstable inner space undreamt of in medieval times: tortured, self-divided, irreducibly complex and ultimately mysterious. The piece thus maps historical development (from the medieval to the Renaissance, or 'modern' eras – the two are here conflated) on to shifts in forms of literary production (the development of a new style of lyric

---

[1] Hugo Estenssoro, 'Tell Laura I Love Her: Seven-hundred Years After his Birth, Petrarch Remains the First Modern Man', *The Times Literary Supplement* (16/07/04), pp. 12–13.

verse). The erotic is central: Petrarch's frustrated desire for Laura acts as a historical lynchpin, the point of contact between two different eras and the place where the transition between the two emerges with the greatest clarity. Indeed, the emphasis placed on it is so strong as to court hyperbole – we might reasonably wonder whether it is seriously being claimed that the transition into modernity is nothing more than this, one man's self-discovery in the face of his sexual frustration, and how much detailed scrutiny such a claim might withstand – but hyperbole is of course entirely to the point; this is a magnificent eulogy on the occasion of the poet's anniversary, not a detailed historical argument.

But if Estenssoro's piece barely rises beyond the level of assertion, it is nonetheless effective precisely because it praises Petrarch against a background of similar if more developed claims, both about Petrarch himself and about the relationship between the Middle Ages and the Renaissance. Studies of Petrarch routinely argue for his status as 'the first modern man',[2] and the connection between self-awareness and the historical transition that we call 'the Renaissance' is if anything even more strongly established. To take one famous example:

> In the Middle Ages both sides of human consciousness – that which was turned within as that which was turned without – lay dreaming or half awake beneath a common veil. The veil was woven of faith, illusion and childish prepossession, through which the world and history were clad in strange hues. Man was conscious of himself only as a member of a race, people, party, family or corporation – only through some general category.[3]

Thus the Swiss historian Jacob Burckhardt, writing on 'The Development of the Individual' in his famous study of *The Civilization of the Renaissance in Italy*. This idea of a birth into a new form of consciousness is for Burckhardt one of the distinctive features of the Italian Renaissance, and therefore functions as a pivotal moment in Burckhardt's narration of what Lee Patterson has called 'the pervasive and apparently ineradicable *grand récit* that organises Western cultural history, the gigantic master narrative by which modernity identifies itself with the Renaissance and rejects the Middle Ages as by definition premodern'.[4] The leap from the development of the individual to eroticism as one along a series of ever-more-specific tropes that can be used to focalise the theme of historical transition seems clear enough, but the consequences for a study of medieval eroticism seem startling: no individuality, no eroticism. The erotic is for us the perhaps most personal, the most individual aspect of our lives, and it is hard to imagine a state of affairs in which things were ever much different. Could one have an age without individuality or eroticism, or (perhaps even more strangely) with eroticism but without individuality? (Can hive minds be sexy?)

Of course, medievalists have often protested against Burckhardt's idea, mainly on the grounds that it is simply incompatible with a detailed knowledge of the

---

[2] Nicholas Mann, *Petrarch* (Oxford and New York, 1984), p. 113 – a standard introductory guide.
[3] Jacob Burckhardt, *The Civilization of the Renaissance in Italy*, trans. S. G. C. Middlemore, intro. Peter Burke (Harmondsworth, 1990), p. 98.
[4] Lee Patterson, 'On the Margin: Postmodernism, Ironic History and Medieval Studies', *Speculum* 65 (1990), pp. 87–108 (p. 92).

range and variety of medieval selfhoods present in medieval writing.[5] Nor does it sit terribly easily with much contemporary thought on the viability of traditional notions of the subject, which often proceeds, sceptically, regardless of period specificities. One might finally note that Burckhardt's words don't even necessarily describe Renaissance literature particularly well: it is not hard to find Renaissance texts that are intensely concerned with the relationship between the self and general social categories. (Putting the matter in terms of such a crude dichotomy seems over-simplistic, but Burckhardt's formulation of the case seems to more or less oblige one to produce a response on his terms.) The opening scenes of *Hamlet*, for instance – like the *Canzoniere*, a text often taken as the epitome of the new concern for the individual[6] – are about nothing if not the Prince's tortured attempts to renegotiate his relationships with his mother, uncle, family and nation in the wake of his father's death. And what, exactly, would it really mean for an individual to define his or her self *without* reference to some larger, corporate category? Someone whose identity is undetermined by any sense of ties to family, state, nation, church – or whatever – is not just an individual. He is, more likely than not, a psychopath. It must be admitted that many of the Medicis, Sforsas and Borgias who so entertainingly populate *The Civilization of the Renaissance in Italy* seem to have been precisely that, but this (one feels) was not quite what Burckhardt meant when he initiated the debate on Renaissance individualism.[7]

Nevertheless, the deficiencies in Burckhardt's argument have done nothing to stop it becoming something of a cliché in discussions of 'the Renaissance'. (Indeed, insofar as they provide space for debate, those deficiencies may well have helped in this process, since they bestow upon the idea of 'the discovery of the individual' the status of a theme to be argued over – rather than simply killing the notion off.) Over and again, studies of the Renaissance articulate the central perception – however qualified, however contested, however marked up as problematic – that, as one of the most distinguished and influential writers on the period puts it, 'there is in the early modern period a change in the intellectual, social, psychological, and aesthetic structures that govern the generation of identities'.[8] And as long

---

5 See, for example, David Aers, 'A Whisper in the Ear of Early Modernists; or, Reflections on Literary Critics Writing the "History of the Subject" ', *Culture and History, 1350–1600: Essays on English Communities, Identities, and Writing*, ed. David Aers (New York, 1992), pp. 177–202; Patterson, 'On the Margin'; David Wallace, *Chaucerian Polity: Absolutist Lineages and Associational Forms in England and Italy* (Stanford, 1997).
6 For a recent and extreme example of this tendency, see Harold Bloom's discussion of the play in *Shakespeare: The Invention of the Human* (London, 1999). As Patterson and Aers note, other critics produce postmodern variants on this trope which, while attacking and even reversing traditional assumptions about identity in the Renaissance, nonetheless preserve its essential periodising function: see, for example, Catherine Belsey, *The Subject of Tragedy: Identity and Difference in Renaissance Drama* (London and New York, 1985).
7 For a discussion of this issue and its function as a mark of historical distinctiveness, see Norman Nelson, 'Individualism as a Criterion of the Renaissance', *Journal of English and Germanic Philology* 32 (1933), pp. 316–34.
8 Stephen Greenblatt, *Renaissance Self-fashioning from More to Shakespeare* (Chicago and London, 1980), p. 1. Although Greenblatt prefaces this passage by saying that 'one need only think of Chaucer's extraordinarily subtle and wry manipulations of *persona* to grasp that what I propose to examine does not suddenly spring up from nowhere when 1499 becomes 1500', as Patterson

as this is the case, the erotic retains its periodising potential: if identities change as we pass from one historical period to another, then the way they experience desire probably ought to, too; conversely, the study of the expression of desire ought to offer a nice, concise way of emblematising that historical shift.

The aim of the present essay is not to argue that there are *no* differences or discontinuities between the medieval and the Renaissance, or the medieval or the modern. But it does want to suggest that a sometimes rather stale debate might be reinvigorated by paying some detailed attention to the themes and tropes that are so often pressed into service to represent historical change. For example: as an instance of the sheer usefulness of the trope of eroticism in the drawing of period distinctions, we might turn to one of the subtlest and most complex articulations of this theme, Thomas M. Greene's *The Light in Troy*.[9] The point here is that Greene's study is, implicitly at least, a response to the twentieth-century 'revolt of the medievalists'[10] that had argued that the interest in classical culture from which the Renaissance takes its name was actually anticipated by another renaissance of the twelfth century. How, then, to stop the outlines of a familiar and convenient historical narrative dissolving into an amorphous puddle of quarrels over precedent that would seem to leave no way of articulating a sense of historical progress whatsoever? Greene follows Erwin Panofsky in taking a particularly ingenious route out of this interpretative conundrum: the way of saving the uniqueness of 'the' Renaissance is to acknowledge the medieval interest in the ancient world while stressing the different spirit in which this classical material is treated.[11] Formally, *The Light in Troy* is a study of the theory and practice of literary imitation. But what really interests Greene about this theme is the way in which it can be used to draw out historiographical contrasts between the Renaissance and Middle Ages. What he values are 'texts that can be said to have historical self-consciousness, texts that manipulate or dramatise or incorporate their intertextual makeup as a constitutive structural element, texts that reflect an awareness of their own historicity and build upon it'.[12] Historical change – the decisive crux that separates medieval from Renaissance – is located not so much in exterior matters, in wars or politics or inventions or even an interest in the classical past, for all these can be found in other historical periods, but rather in this question of attitude, the stance from which the past is approached: is one aware, how finely is one aware, of the past as the past?

Medieval authors, Greene argues – with their famous anachronisms, their tendency to represent Apollo as a bishop and Mars as a knight[13] – lack this element of historical sensitivity. They are aware of the past, but not as an Other: their natural tendency is to assimilate it within their own cultural frame of reference. All of which seems to place *The Light in Troy* a long way from the theme of

---

notes, this gesture is just and only that: 'less a recognition of history than its suppression' ('On the Margin', p. 99).
9   *The Light in Troy: Imitation and Discovery in Renaissance Poetry* (New Haven and London, 1982).
10 The term is Wallace K. Ferguson's: *The Renaissance in Historical Thought: Five Centuries of Interpretation* (Boston, 1948), pp. 329–85.
11 Erwin Panofsky, *Renaissance and Renascences in Western Art* (London, 1970).
12 Greene, *Light in Troy*, pp. 16–17.
13 Greene, *Light in Troy*, p. 30.

eroticism. Indeed, Greene seems to have selected a new and really rather elegant trope for focalising the theme of historical transition: what distinguishes one period from another – the Middle Ages from the Renaissance – is now the ability to distinguish one period from another. But even here, the pull of the erotic can be felt, because, it is argued, firstly that Petrarch is the key figure in the development of this new historical sensibility, and secondly that it can be discovered not just in his correspondence and scholarly researches, but also in his love poetry. Consider, for example, *Canzoniere* 23. In this poem Petrarch describes the impact of Laura as a series of cruel metamorphoses. Spurned by the youthful poet, Love sought the aid of a 'powerful lady':

> ei duo mi transformaro in quel ch' i' sono,
> facendomi d'uom vivo un lauro verde
> che per fredda stagion foglia non perde.
>
> Qual mi fec'io, quando primier m'accorsi
> de la transfigurata mia persona,
> e i capei vidi far di quella fronde
> di che sperato avea già lor corona,
> e i piedi in ch' io mi stetti e mossi e corsi
> (com'ogni membro a l'anima risponde)
> diventar due radici sovra l'onde
> non di Peneo, ma d'un piú altero fiume,
> e 'n duo rami mutarsi ambe le braccia!
>
> (the two performed this metamorphosis:
> made me, a living man, a laurel tree,
> which sheds no leaves however cold it be.
>
> Oh, what a sight I was when first I noticed
> my wretched person altered utterly;
> and saw my hair had become the very foliage
> I always hoped would make a wreath for me;
> and my two feet on which I stand, move, run,
> (since, as the soul is, so each limb behaves)
> transformed into twin roots besides the waves
> not of Peneus but a prouder river;
> and my two arms converted into branches!)[14]

Plainly, the allusion here is to the metamorphosis of Daphne in Ovid; other sections of the poem allude to Echo, Actaeon and Danae, among others. For Greene, the point is that Petrarch's distinctively 'Renaissance' sense of historical difference is at work even here – more subtly than in his scholarly writings, but also more compellingly, more clearly harnessed to Petrarch's distinctively modern (that is, non-medieval), fractured sense of self. Compare the poem with the passages it alludes to in the *Metamorphoses*: could it be that it is the differences between the two that matter as much as the similarities? Rather than just appropri-

---

[14] Petrarch, *Selected Poems*, ed. T. Gwynfor Griffith and P. R. J. Hainsworth (Manchester, 1979), p. 70; translation by J. G. Nichols, *Petrarch:* Canzoniere (Manchester, 2002), p. 18.

ating Latin culture, might Petrarch not be giving voice, via these differences, to a sense of what was possible then, and what is possible to him, now?

> The poem provides a direction and a version of poetic history that we can intuitively apprehend . . . We are led from the relative wholeness of Roman mythography, with its visual and rhetorical clarity, its calm impersonality, its security within nature, its accommodations with suffering, its refusal of psychological paradoxes, and its capacity for repose – we are led from all these to the turbulent egotism, the problematic divisions and restless intensities of a voice pathetically in quest of its own integrity.[15]

Petrarch's allusions, it is argued, refashion Ovid in accordance with his view of history into the exemplar of a lost serenity (although one might well wonder if the *Metamorphoses* are really as serene as all that).[16] They outline a literary and cultural history predicated upon a discontinuity that is both an echo and the cause of the author's atomised consciousness. Historical self-consciousness – the awareness of the cultural gulf that separates fourteenth-century Italian from classical Roman – can now be equated with a fuller, if more tormented understanding of one's own identity. People in the Middle Ages, therefore, may not have been the depersonalised communal minds imagined by Burckhardt, but they lacked true individuality in a subtler sense: lacking an awareness of genuine cultural alternatives, unattentive to the true nature of their cultural heritage, they could, in a sense, only ever but slenderly know themselves. A complex historical narrative can now again be superimposed on the history of literary forms: within this scheme, it makes perfect sense for Greene to apply a vocabulary of personality and character to literary techniques, as when he refers to forms of allusion that are 'self-conscious'.[17] With the development of Petrarchan lyric, we see that the history of poetic forms is also a history of historical consciousness – which is also the essence of historical development itself. The interpretative circle is complete, almost to the point of overkill. In Greene's dazzlingly complex and nuanced work the idea of the Renaissance in relation to the Middle Ages; a narrative about individualism and self-awareness; issues of literary history; and the tormented, fragmented, erotic Petrarchan lyric model as the vehicle for these innovations – all are tied together into a scarcely extricable knot.

Commonly overlooked by scholars of early modern literature (although not by Thomas Greene, who really seems to be writing in reaction to perceptions of an underlying historical continuity between the Middle Ages and the Renaissance), but also to some extent by those seeking to rebut claims about a distinctive Renaissance individualism (because the pattern seems uncannily to reassert itself even where the overt intention is dissent), is the fact that the medieval period has its own historiographical literature on the discovery of the individual: a literature focused on the 'other', twelfth-century renaissance of European culture, and one

---

[15] Greene, *Light in Troy*, p. 131.
[16] On 'urbane' Ovid versus 'savage' Ovid, see Neil Rhodes, *Shakespeare and the Origins of English* (Oxford and New York, 2004), pp. 120–2; and on the medieval Ovid specifically, see James R. Simpson, *Fantasy, Identity and Misrecognition in Medieval French Literature* (Berne, 2000).
[17] Greene, *Light in Troy*, p. 17.

that shares a disconcerting number of discursive features with its properly 'Renaissance' counterpart. In both cases, a classicising period is defined and given shape through accounts of the way in which it offers opportunities for novel descriptions of individual subjectivities. In each case, too, generically innovative forms of erotic literature are described as offering a significant focal point for these new cultural trends. On the one hand, we have lyric verse derived from Petrarch; on the other, the medieval romance.[18]

We might begin by taking as a case-study another historiographical classic, a work described by Norman Cantor as 'arguably ... the single most widely read and influential book written on the Middle Ages in the twentieth century'.[19] This is R. W. Southern's *The Making of the Middle Ages* (1953), and in particular his final chapter, 'From Epic to Romance'. As Southern describes it, the chapter aims to provide a summation of 'the scattered threads of this book'. Having discussed the various changes he sees at work in European society between 972 and 1204 in their communal aspect, it is now time to 'try to see them, as far as may be, from within, in their effects on individuals'.[20] It quickly becomes clear that these individuals do not simply reflect wider societal changes. They are themselves in a state of flux; even as medieval society evolves more complex forms of social organisation, the individual becomes ever more sharply defined:

> The extension of the boundaries of knowledge was accompanied by, and indeed made possible by, the changing structure of society, by the enlarging of the field of vision beyond the confines of highly localised interests ... And the converse of this extension of the community and the enlarging of the bounds of organised effort was the emergence of the individual from his communal background. This impulse towards individual expression was at work in religious communities, in the enlargement of the opportunities for privacy, in the renewed study of friendship, of conscience and of ethics. In the secular life, it found expression in the theory of love and the literature of the passions.[21]

All these changes find their summation in a generic shift, from epic to romance: from life viewed as an 'exercise in endurance', to life as 'a seeking and a journeying'.[22] Southern at this point is referring to far more than just heroic literature (he speaks for example of 'Christian romance'[23] with reference to the religious thought of St Anselm and St Bernard), but it is significant that he should choose to epitomise it in this way. The theme is underlined when he comes to contrast the *Song of Roland* with the work of Chrétien de Troyes: epic is communal, romance individualistic; one belongs to the past, one to the future. '[Chrétien's] romances

---

[18] Medieval lyric is also implicated in this historiography. See, for example, Sarah Kay, *Subjectivity in Troubadour Poetry* (Cambridge, 1990), and R. Howard Bloch, *Etymologies and Genealogies: A Literary Anthropology of the French Middle Ages* (Chicago, 1983). But the boundaries between genres are rarely completely clear, and in practice it is evident that romance could often serve as a vehicle for these lyric subjectivities (this is the theme of Chapter 5 of Kay's study).

[19] Norman Cantor, *Inventing the Middle Ages: The Lives, Works, and Ideas of the Great Medievalists of the Twentieth Century* (New York, 1991), p. 338.

[20] R. W. Southern, *The Making of the Middle Ages* (London, 1956), p. 219.

[21] Southern, *Making*, p. 221.

[22] Southern, *Making*, p. 222.

[23] Southern, *Making*, p. 240.

are the secular counterpart of the piety of Cîteaux. Of both, love is the theme. Love is an inward thing, and therefore a onely [sic] thing united only to its unique object. So the knight of Chrétien's romances seeks solitude for the exercise of his essential virtue.'[24] Throughout the twelfth century, Southern discerns a movement towards self-disclosure, empathy and inwardness. (Indeed, it is these very qualities that make his study so immediately appealing: as an early reviewer noted, *The Making of the Middle Ages* is distinguished by its ability to understand its subject matter 'from within . . . to survey the problems of European politics, for example, through the eyes of the Counts of Anjou or to consider the relations between Church and State by reference to the Counts of Barcelona'.[25])

Once again, then, we have an investigation of inwardness married to the historiographic theme of period distinctiveness, and once again historical change is seen to be played out through shifts in literary form. According to Norman Cantor, *The Making of the Middle Ages* opened the way for a series of studies that emphasised the theme of the medieval individual. Before Southern, he argues, 'there was lacking a substantial credibility and intellectual dignity in even pursuing the subjects of medieval romance, eroticism, and individualism, as if the people who studied these phenomena were themselves considered marginal, gauche, bohemian, and not genuinely academic'. After Southern, these themes became central.[26] Cantor's is a self-confessedly idiosyncratic and emotive account by a former student of Southern's, but whether this is the case or not, the fact is that there is a substantial literature devoted to the renaissance of the twelfth century, paralleling in almost every point the characteristics attributed to the later one.[27] So we have individualism, in studies such as Colin Morris's *The Discovery of the Individual, 1050–1200*, with its Burckhardtian title, and Robert Hanning's *The Individual in Twelfth-Century Romance*.[28] We have an interest in classical literature. We even have new and innovative forms of historical consciousness: 'it was not the least splendid achievement of Latin Christendom in the twelfth century to awaken in men's minds an active awareness of human history'.[29] And as with 'the' Renaissance, the impulse towards historical definition can be channelled through an analysis of erotic literature, with chivalric romance a particular favourite – as for example in Robert Hanning's study. For Hanning, romance epitomises a new interest in the individual, and it does because of the way it represents desire:

---

[24] Southern, *Making*, p. 244.
[25] 'Medieval Life and Thought', review by David Charles Douglas, *The Times Literary Supplement* (08/05/53), p. 299.
[26] Cantor, *Inventing*, p. 337.
[27] For a useful summary, see Caroline Walker Bynum, 'Did the Twelfth Century Discover the Individual?', in *Jesus as Mother: Studies in the Spirituality of the High Middle Ages* (Berkeley, Los Angeles and London, 1982), pp. 82–109.
[28] *The Discovery of the Individual, 1050–1200* (Toronto, Buffalo and London, 1987); *The Individual in Twelfth-Century Romance* (New Haven and London, 1977). Southern is thanked in the dedication of the first of these volumes, and his work is repeatedly footnoted in the second. Both are mentioned as having been written in the intellectual wake of *The Making of the Middle Ages* in Cantor, *Inventing*, pp. 359–61.
[29] Marie-Dominique Chenu, quoted in Lee Patterson, *Negotiating the Past: The Historical Understanding of Medieval Literature* (Madison, 1987), p. 157. On perceptions of historical change and mutability, see Giles Constable, *The Reformation of the Twelfth Century* (Cambridge, 1996), pp. 161–7, 298–9.

the centrality of love and its literary depiction to a study of the individual in chivalric romance cannot be denied, for love in its very nature is the private relationship par excellence between two human beings whose lives take on a unique configuration ... The lover, by his or her passion for someone singled out from among all other persons in the world, experiences and emblazons the fact of radical individuality in acknowledging love's dominance.[30]

This emphasis on the individual evolves in tandem with a revived appreciation of classical literature: crucially, for Hanning, a text like the *Roman d'Enéas*, so influential on later romance, achieves its effects by marrying 'the outer dynamic of chivalry' to 'an inner dynamic of love' developed from Ovidian themes and narrative techniques.[31] Once again, different historical themes can be coordinated through the study of a particular genre.[32]

The parallels in the historical narratives outlined here are striking. Still, one might contrast Hanning's emphasis on the interpersonal nature of desire with Greene's presentation of a fundamentally solipsistic Petrarch – for whom the past is the really significant Other. Can we find examples of chivalric romances that marry the theme of eroticism to that of historical rupture? Thomas Greene would have us believe not: he specifically singles out Chrétien's *Cligés* by way of suggesting the bankruptcy of the medieval historical imagination, its inability to think about past culture in any meaningful way.[33] And it may be that this romance lacks the awareness of anachronism that Greene prizes in Petrarch (as do plenty of Renaissance texts). On the other hand, though, this is a romance – delicately poised between the recreation of a past world and a flagrant, carefree fictionality; one might question whether Greene is invoking a relevant standard. Closer inspection suggests that, right at the very birth of the chivalric genre, *Cligés* demonstrates its potential as a genre of a kind of historiographic reflection.

Cligés opens with a preface in which the author begins by listing his previous works: *Erec et Enide*; a translation of Ovid on the art of love; something that is probably a retelling of the tale of Pelops; tales of King Mark and Iseult; and various other Ovidian narratives of metamorphosis – a combination, then, of chivalric stories and Ovidian material translated into the vernacular. We are then told that this will be 'un novel conte'

> D'un vaslet qui an Grece fu
> Del lignage le roi Artu.

---

30 Hanning, *Individual*, p. 53.
31 Hanning, *Individual*, p. 58. James Simpson's volume in the New Oxford English Literary History attempts to undermine claims for Petrarchan novelty by stressing the continuity represented by this Ovidian tradition, continuing well into the Renaissance (*Reform and Cultural Revolution* (Oxford, 2002), Chapter Four, 'The Elegiac', pp. 121–90). However, he follows Greene in suggesting that Renaissance literature evinces a greater sense of historical rupture, p. 127.
32 As an indication of the historical weight the chivalric genre is being asked to bear, one might consider the chronological distortions imposed by the 'epic to romance' model of literary history – as Sarah Kay notes, it requires the redescription of the *chansons de geste* (defined as public, communal, formulaic and primitive) as chronologically prior to romances (individualistic, erotic, literary), when in fact they are to a large extent contemporary. Once again, literary history and eroticism are used to buttress a period classification, even at the expense of historical accuracy (*The Chansons de Geste in the Age of Romance* (Oxford, 1995)).
33 Greene, *Light in Troy*, p. 86.

> Meis ainz que de lui rien vos die,
> Orroiz de son pere la vie,
> Don il fu et de quel lignage.
> Tant fu preuz et de fier corage,
> Que por pris et por los conquerre
> Ala de Grece an Angleterre,
> Qui lors estoit Bretaingne dite.

(a new story about a young man who lived in Greece and was a kinsman of King Arthur. But before I tell you anything of him, you shall hear of the life of his father, where he came from and of what family. He was of such noble, spirited temperament that, in order to win a reputation and renown, he went from Greece to England, which was at that time called Britain.)[34]

The source of the tale is mentioned (a book in the library at Beauvais), and then we are told this:

> Par les livres que nos avons
> Les feiz des anciiens savons
> Et del secle qui fu jadis. –
> Ce nos ont nostre livre apris,
> Que Grece ot de chevalerie
> Le premier los et de clergie.
> Puis vint chevalerie a Rome
> Et de la clergie la some,
> Qui or est an France venue.
> Deus doint qu'ele i soit retenue,
> Et que li leus li abelisse
> Tant que ja meis de France n'isse
> L'enors qui s'i est arestee.
> Deus l'avoit as autres prestee:
> Car des Grejois ne des Romains
> Ne dit en meis ne plus ne mains;
> D'aus est la parole remese
> Et estainte la vive brese. (27–44)

(Through the books we possess we learn of the deeds of the people of past times and of the world as it used to be. Our books have taught us how Greece ranked first in chivalry and learning; then chivalry passed to Rome along with that fund of transcendent learning that is now come to France. God grant that it may be kept here and find such a pleasing home that the honour now arrived may never depart from France! The others had received it from God on loan; for no longer do people speak at all of the Greeks and Romans – there is no more to tell of them, and their glowing embers are dead. (p. 93))

Chrétien's preface invokes the theme of *translatio*, of the westward movement of learning and empire from Greece to Rome to Western Christendom.[35] Yet despite

---

34 *Cligés*, ed. Wendelin Foerster (Amsterdam, 1965), lines 9–17; Chrétien de Troyes, *Arthurian Romances*, trans. D. D. R. Owen, Everyman (London, 1991), p. 93.
35 See Michelle A. Freeman, *The Poetics of* Translatio Studii *and* Conjointure: *Chrétien de Troyes's*

its apparent confidence in France's secure possession of that 'fund of transcendent learning' – corresponding to Chrétien's classical translations mentioned at the outset – the preface seems full of anxiety, riddled with fractional displacements and incongruities, which in turn affect our reading of the narrative that follows. Some years ago, Tony Hunt argued for the structural independence of Chrétien's prologues, none of which, he contended, 'functions as a guide to the interpretation or significance of the following *narratio*'.[36] Yet there is a clear parallel implied between the *translatio* theme and the life of Alexandre, Cligés' father, who passes from Greece to England.[37] It would seem on the one hand then that what we are being offered here is a way of reading *Cligés*, almost in allegorical fashion, as a story of the westward movement of the classical heritage. And yet, on the other hand, there is a pervasive sense of uncertainty. What is being translated? Is it 'chevalierie' or is it 'clergie'? Both? And where does it end up – in England (should that be Britain?) – or in France? The prologue seems unclear about the location of the past in the present. And we cannot help but note that, having moved from Greece to Arthur's court, either Cligés or his father must have moved *back* again, since the former is said to have lived in Greece. A bold statement of the *translatio* theme is played off against a nagging sense of elusiveness.

When we reach the narrative proper, our confusion only increases. We begin with a Byzantine Greek – that is, someone who might reasonably claim some sort of purchase on the classical heritage – travelling to Britain, for what are essentially reasons of personal development (Alexandre wants to prove himself and be knighted), thus fixing in our minds a potential parallel between psychic maturity and the possibility of cultural maturity represented by the *translatio* theme. But what Alexandre finds at Arthur's court – after an initial episode that carefully emphasises both his Greekness and his Christianity – is not 'chevalierie' or 'clergie', but rather love, as the narrative unfolds into a series of showpiece Ovidian interior monologues from Alexandre and Gauvain's sister Soredamors. From here on in, questions of love are interwoven with the confusions of post-classical identity. While the prologue may have primed us to expect something like an allegorical correspondence between the narrative and the theme of *translatio*, the pieces stubbornly refuse to fit. Instead, the story happily wanders around the Mediterranean and central Europe, criss-crossing between Athens and Constantinople and England and Saxony, constantly teasing us with what may or may not be intimations of the *translatio* theme as it cleverly reworks classical texts into the vernacular,[38] digressing into further love-narratives, before finally collapsing into a shaggy dog story: Fenice's career, we are told, is the reason why the emperors of Constantinople keep their wives under lock and key.

Cligés (Lexington, 1979), which argues that the narrative celebrates the author's role as a 'translator' of classical culture. The present essay considers the romance to be more ambivalent.

36 Tony Hunt, 'Tradition and Originality in the Prologues of Chrestien de Troyes', *Forum for Modern Language Studies* 8 (1972), pp. 320–37 (p. 336) – although he does note the ambivalent attitude in the prologue to the past (p. 325).

37 As noted by Karl D. Uitti, 'Chrétien de Troyes' *Cligés*: Romance *Translatio* and History', *Conjunctures: Medieval Studies in Honour of Douglas Kelly*, ed. Keith Busby and Norris J. Lacy (Amsterdam, 1994), pp. 545–57 (p. 547).

38 See Freeman, *Poetics*.

So does the prologue relate to what follows it? Yes and no – at any rate, one can safely say that for the prologue to suggest a way of reading the narrative which the narrative then comprehensively frustrates is not quite the same thing as having no relationship at all. The overall impression may be one of the epic, Virgilian potential of the *translatio* theme being frittered away in a series of love-narratives. The generic self-consciousness of romance, its sense of its own digressive, 'errant' potentialities,[39] here exists in a dynamic relationship with, is thematised by – maybe even comes into being by playing off – the theme of *translatio*, the quest to assimilate the heritage of the ancient world. But even that impression may require modification. In his revised thoughts on *Cligés*' prologue, Tony Hunt notes that there is in fact a connection with what follows: 'Chrétien's literary productions, as he lists them, all deal with love rather than chivalry, despite the fact that love is not thematised in the prologue: *Erec* has been described as a "meditation on marriage", the works of Ovid (perhaps just the *Ars Amatoria*) deal with love casuistry, and *Marc et Ysuelt* treats of adultery. It will later be apparent that *Cligés* deals with all of these.' And yet, he adds, our feeling may be that 'this story of a Greek whose legacy to womankind is to cause all subsequent emperors of Byzantium to lock up their wives . . . is hardly the stuff of which "les livres des anciens" are made'.[40] But of course it is that, and Chrétien's subsequent narrative is as Ovidian in tone, in its way, as it is in technique. In the twelfth century, then, at the time of the very birth of the romance genre, one might see a work like *Cligés* as decisive in the way in which it establishes the position of the erotic as both the very essence of the search for the classical heritage and a maddening diversion from it.[41]

---

[39] On which, see Patricia Parker, *Inescapable Romance: Studies in the Poetics of a Mode* (Princeton, 1979).
[40] Tony Hunt, 'Chrétien's Prologues Reconsidered', *Conjunctures*, ed. Busby and Lacy, pp. 154–68 (p. 166).
[41] Lee Patterson also investigates how medieval romance channels its historiographic interests through representations of eroticism ('Virgil and the Historical Consciousness of the Twelfth Century: The *Roman d'Eneas* and *Erec and Enide*', *Negotiating*, pp. 157–95). He argues that while the *Eneas* largely suppresses historicity by privileging subjectivity and eroticism, in *Erec* the concern with the self and its exploration goes hand in hand with the Virgilian theme of *translatio imperii*.

Index

Abelard, Peter, 13, 147
Abu Ghraib, 130–1
adultery, 105–15, 174–5
Aelred (*De Institutione Inclusarum*), 157
Allman, W. W., 10–12
An Alphabet of Tales, 95–100
Ancrene Wisse, 155–63
Andreas Capellanus (*De Amore*), 24–5
Anti-Semitism, see *Jews in Literature*
aphrodisiacs, 22
Aquinas, St. Thomas, 3
Arabic literature, 4, 80
Aranrhod, 105–11
Archibald, Elizabeth, 73 n.8, 86 n.11, 87 n.16, 90–1
aristocracy, 1–2; 88–91, see also *courtly love*
Aristotle, 19
Arundel lyrics, 143–54
Augustine of Hippo, St., 97, 118–19, 126
Avicenna, 20
The Avowyng of Arthur, 30–2
Ayenbite of Inwit, see Dan Michel

Bartlett, Anne Clark, 128
Beckwith, Sarah, 158
Benson, Larry D., 34
Berengar of Tours, 149–51
Bernardus Silvestris, 147
Bersani, Leo, 8–10, 12
Bertilak (Bredbeddle), 32–3, 46–7
bestiality, 106–16
Beves of Hamtoun, 12, 70
Bezzola, R. R., 144
Biblical books
  Genesis, 118–19
  Numbers, 119
  Psalm 102, 115
  Song of Songs, 148, 152
Biddick, Kathleen, 94

Black-Michaud, Jacob, 108–13
Blacman, John, 8
Blamires, Alcuin, 10
Blodeuwedd the Flower Maiden, 112–15
blood, 94–104
Bollard, J. K., 115
Bond, James, 27, 30
Brandles, 36–7
breasts, 7–8, 72–4
Brock, Edmund, 116
Brooke, G. L., 116
Brundage, James A., 3, 5 n.28, 18 n.3
Bullough, Vern L., 6
Burckhardt, Jacob, 165–7
Butler, Judith, 8, 13–14, 94
Byfield, Catherine, 115
Bynum, Caroline Walker, 60
Byzantium, 173–5

Cadden, Joan, 20, 77
Caesarius of Heisterbach (*Dialogus Miraculorum*), 95–100, 102–4
canon law, 2–3, 18–19
Canterbury Tales, see Chaucer
Cantor, Norman, 170
The Carle of Carlisle, 34–5
Cartlidge, Neil, 145
Castelford's Chronicle, 123–4
castration, 127–8
Catullus, 146
Cazelles, Brigitte, 11–12
celibacy, 142–3, 155–63; see also *virginity*
Chaucer, Geoffrey
  Clerk's Tale, 91
  Franklin's Tale, 134, 139
  Knight's Tale, 11, 51
  Merchant's Tale, 7, 11, 22–4, 26, 85 n.8
  Miller's Tale, 10–11, 23, 85 n.8
  Prioress' Tale, 94

Chaucer, Geoffrey (cont.)
  Reeve's Tale, 11
  Shipman's Tale, 2 n.10, 13–14
  Sir Thopas, 11
  Squire's Tale, 28, 37
  Troilus and Criseyde, 37, 51–5, 61–3, 69, 74
  and violent sexuality, 10–14
  Wife of Bath's Prologue and Tale, 1 n.4, 8–10, 18–26, 40, 51–2, 62–3
Chestre, Thomas, 8, 41, 47, 54–6, 65–8, 71–5, 76–81, 87 n.16
  Lybeaus Desconus, 47, 54–6, 60, 67–8
  Sir Launfal, 41, 71–81, 87 n.16
Chevalier à l'épée, 29
Children of the Scorpion, see *lust*
Chrétien de Troyes, 170–75
  Le Chevalier de la Charette, 7 n.43, 43, 121
  Cligés, 172–5
  Yvain, or Le Chevalier au lion, 29
Christ, 72–3, 95, 148
clerics, 1–3, 94–104, 142–52, 155–63
  and Jewish girls, 94–104
clothing, see *eroticism*
Cohen, Jeffrey J., 7, 12, 117, 119, 128
Criseyde, 37, 61–3, 69, 74
De Coitu, see *Constantine the African*
De Curis Mulierum, 20–1
confession, 3, 155–63; see also *penitentials*
Constantine the African (*De Coitu*), 22
courtesy books, 2
courtesy tests, 34–5
courtly love, 4, 28–29, 59–60, 112–13
  Andreas Capellanus, 24–25
Crane, Susan, 7
cuckoldry, 112–14, 173–5
Custom of Logres, 31
Cynferth (Law of Women), 107

Dafydd ap Gwilym, 7 n.45, 105
Davies, Sioned, 112
demons, 13, 49–50, 86 n.12
Dialogus Miraculorum, see *Caesarius of Heisterbach*
Dinshaw, Carolyn, 10
Dobson, E. J., 158
Donaldson, E. Talbot, 7, 10
Dronke, Peter, 144–5, 148

Duby, Georges, 4 n.27

Eisenblicher, Konrad, 6 n.36, 8
Elaine of Astolet, 13, 33–4
Emaré, 13, 53–4
enchantresses, 35–6, 38–52
The Erle of Tolous, 60–1, 68–9
eroticism,
  of breasts, 7–8, 72–4
  of Christ, 148
  and the Church, 1–3, 19–21
  and clothing, 53–70, 82–3, 90–1
  and courtesy tests, 34–5
  definition, 4–6
  of giants, 117–31
  and hagiography, 11–12
  of heat, 71–81
  and historiography, 164–75
  of humiliation, 11–13, 109–11, 130–1
  and imperialism, 129–30
  and the individual, 164–75
  lesbianism, 155–63
  love poetry and the English, 7
  and magic, 38–52
  masochism, 9–10, 12, 60
  masturbation, 6–7, 13, 124, 156
  and medicine, 4 n.26, 19–21, 77–8, 80–1
  and nudity, 60–3, 72–4
  and nuns, 155–63
  and power, 8–10, 129–30, 138–40
  of skin (colour), 71–2, 81
  and submission, 8–10, 59–60, 138–40
  as trope dividing historical periods, 164–75
  violent sexuality, 10–14; see also *rape*
Estenssoro, Hugo, 164–5
Ettarde, 33–6
Eucharist, 149–51
Evans, Ruth, 94
Eve, 100
exempla
  Alphabet of Tales, 95–100
  Caesarius of Heisterbach, 95–100, 102–4

fabliaux, 4, 85–86, 96
fairies; see also *enchantresses*, *Sir Degarré*
  King of Faerie, 50, 71–5, 82–93

Nimue (Nynyve), 35–6, 49
Tryamour, 65–8, 71–5, 78–81
Finke, Laurie, 129
Flashman, Harry, 27–8, 29, 33
foreplay, 19–21, 74
'glossing', as erotic touch, 10, 23–5
Foucault, Michel, 8, 123
four humours, 77–8
Fourth Lateran Council, 3
Freud, Sigmund, 89, 94, 130

Gaddesden, John (*Rosa Anglica*), 21
Galen, 19, 77–8
Gawain, Sir (Gauvain), 14, 27–37, 46–7, 55–7, 174
 in *Sir Gawain and the Green Knight*, 14, 29–30, 32–3, 46–7, 55, 56–7
 as 'Young Man', 28, 37
gaze
 female, 30, 91–2
 male, 10, 31, 64–5
gender transformation, see *magic*
Geoffrey of Monmouth, 117, 119–21
Gerald of Wales, 142
Gerbert de Montreuil, see *Fourth Continuation*
Giant of Mont St. Michel, 116–31
Giddens, Anthony, 7
Gilfaethwy, 106–15
'glossing', see *foreplay*
Goewin, 105–15
goliardic poetry, 146–7
Goodman, Peter, 146, 151–2
Gower, John
 Confessio Amantis (frame), 162
 'Tale of Florent', 57–8
The Greene Knight, 32–3
Greene, Thomas M., 167–72
Gravdal, Kathryn, 2 n.10, 12 n.68, 120
Grayson, Janet, 158, 161
Gregory the Great, 13, 87 n.16
Grendel, 123
Gruffydd, W. J., 111–12
Guinevere, 7, 12, 38, 81, 87 n.16, 120–1
Gwerfel Mechain, 105
Gwydion, 106–15

hagiography, 11–12
Hahn, Thomas, 28
Hanks, D. Thomas, Jr., 10–12
Hanning, Robert, 171–2
Hansen, Elaine Tuttle, 23
Havelock, 54
heat
 and the erotic, 71–81
 and madness, 78–9
heirs, 88–91
Helena, Duchess of Brittany, 13, 116–31
Hellawes, 49
Heloise, 13
Heng, Geraldine, 48
Henry VI (king of England), 7–8
Henryson, Robert
 The Testament of Criseyde, 37
Hoccleve, Thomas, 78–9
homosocial bonding, 30–2, 45–6
Hsia, Ronnie Po-Chia, 95
Hugh of Lincoln, St., 100–2
Hugh Primas, 142, 148
Hunt, Tony, 174–5

iconolagnia, 10
incest, 82–93, 107–8, 156
Isolde (Iseult), 7, 12, 38, 172

Jacobs, Nicholas, 84
Jacob's Well, 21, 102
Jacquart, Danielle, 4, 20, 72–3
The Jeaste of Sir Gawayne, 36–7
Jews in literature, 94–104
 in Caesarius of Heisterbach, 94–104
 in *Jew of Malta*, 95, 99–100, 104
 male menstruation, 94–5
 in *Merchant of Venice*, 94–5, 99–100, 104
 women in the Old Testament, 100

Karras, Ruth Mazo, 1, 4–5, 62 n.32
Kay, Sir, 31–2
Keats, John, 38–40
Keefer, Sarah, 111–12
Kelly, Kathleen Coyne, 98
Kempe, Margery, 75–6, 132, 134
King Arthur, 28–9, 35, 64, 120–1, 125–30, 173–4

King Arthur and King Cornwall, 28–30
Kittredge, George Lyman, 10
Krishna, Valerie, 116
Kruger, Steven, 94

Lampert, Lisa, 94, 100
Lamorak, Sir, 31–2, 87 n.16
Lancelot, Sir, 7 n.43, 13, 28, 33–4, 38, 43, 49
Lanfranc of Canterbury, 149–51
Lanfrank of Milan (*Science of Cirgurie*), 19–20
Lanval (character)
  in Chestre's *Sir Launfal*, 41, 71–7, 78–81, 87 n.16
  in Marie de France's *Lanval*, 40–1, 63–5
  in *Sir Lambewelle*, 66
Lanval (poem), see Lanval (character) and Marie de France
Law of Women (Welsh *Cynferth* text), 107
Layamon, 117–18, 122–3, 129
leprosy, 12
letters, 132–41 (see *Lisle family*, *Paston family*, *Plumpton family*, *Stonor family*)
Lisle family, 133
Lleu, 112–15
Loathly Lady motif, 51–2, 57–60
Lochrie, Karma, 7
lust, 2, 59, 94–104, 162–63
  Children of the Scorpion, 156–63
  and leprosy, 12
Lybeaus Desconus, see Thomas Chestre
Lyrics
  Latin, 143–54
    'Grates ago Veneri', 142–54
    'Licet eger cum egrotis', 145
    'Sevit aure spiritus', 144, 151–2
  Middle English
    'Our Sir John', 25

Mabinogi
  Fourth Branch, 105–15
MacBain, William, 63–4
magic, 38–52
  as metaphor for desire, 38–9
  transformation of appearance, 45–6, 51–2
  transformation of gender in Fourth Branch, 106–7, 108–9
  transformation of species in Fourth Branch, 106–7, 113–15
Magnus, St. Albertus, 3
Malory, Sir Thomas, 8, 12, 13, 31–2, 33–4, 35–6, 47–50, 76–7, 79, 84 n.4, 92 n.31
Mannyng, Robert (*Chronicle*), 124
Marie de France
  Le Fresne, 111
  Guigemar, 42
  Lanval, 40–1, 53, 63–5
Marlowe, Christopher
  Jew of Malta, 94–5, 99–100, 104
marriage, 3, 9–10, 18, 21–2, 58–60, 73–4, 132–41
  marital debt, 2
  marriage group in Chaucer, 10, 59 n.16
  and Wife of Bath, 9–10, 18, 21–2
The Marriage of Sir Gawain, 35
Martial, 146
Marvell, Andrew, 159
Math ap Mathonwy, 106–11
Matthews, William, 117
Melusine, 45–6
Menealfe, 30–2
menstruation
  of Jewish men, 94–5
  reaching puberty, 86–7
Merlin, 49
Metham, John (*Physiognomy*), 25
Michel, Dan (*Ayenbite of Inwit*), 19
misogyny, 1–2
Mordred, 120–1
Morgan le Fay, 32, 46–7, 48–9
Mort Artu, 33–4
Morte Arthure, alliterative, 116–31
Morte Arthure, stanzaic, 34
Morte Darthur, see Thomas Malory
Moser, Thomas C., 146 n.17, 147–9
Murray, Jacqueline, 6 n.36, 8
Myrc, John (*Instructions for Parish Priests*), 19

necrophilia, 49
Nietzsche, Friedrich, 131
Nimue (Nynyve), 35–6, 49
nudity, 7–8, 60–3, 72–4, 124

INDEX

O'Donoghue, Bernard, 7
Ovid, 146, 168–70, 172–5

Pandarus, 61–2
Panofsky, Erwin, 167
Partonope of Blois (Middle English), 41–5
Paston family, 132–41
Patterson, Lee, 117, 165
Patterson, Nerys, 109
Paul, St., 2, 142, 155
Payer, Pierre, 1 n.4
Pelleas, Sir, 33–4, 35–6
Perceval, Sir, 49–50
Perceval Continuations
    First Continuation, 30, 36
    Fourth Continuation (Gerbert de Montreuil), 30
Perlesvaus, 29, 49
Peter of Blois, 142–54
    Epistle 76, 144–5
    'Grates ago Veneri,' 142–54
    'Sevit aure spiritus,' 151
Petrarch, 164–75
phallocentrism, 9
Pitt-Rivers, Julian, 113–14
plastic sexuality, 7, 129–30
Plumpton family, 132, 135, 138
pornography, 5, 11–12, 12 n.68
pregnancy, 2–3, 7, 19–25, 82–93, 94–8
    antisemitic parody of Mary, 94–8
    medical lore, 19–25
    and romance heroines, 7, 35 n. 26, 36, 82–93
Price, Jocelyn, 158
prostitution, 37
Pucelle de lis episode, 30, 36–7
Putter, Ad, 30

Ragnelle, 35
Ramsey, Lee C., 73–4
rape, 2 n.10, 9, 10–12, 30–2, 50–1, 82–93, 105–9, 116–31
    in *alliterative Morte Arthure*, 116–31
    and chivalry, 30–2, 129–30
    custom of Logres, 31–2
    in Welsh Law of Women, 107
Renaissance, 164–75

Robertson, Elizabeth, 158–9
romance (genre), 27–37, 38–52, 53–70, 71–75, 76–81, 82–93, 116–31, 170–5; individual romances are listed under titles
Round Table, 30–2
Rubin, Miri, 95
Rumsey, Lucinda, 163

Sade, Marquis de, 12–13
Sands, Donald, 73
Saunders, Corinne, 88 nn.17–18, 93, 117–18, 126
Schmidt, A. V. C., 84
Schultz, James A., 60
Science of Cirgurie, see Lanfrank of Milan
Scot, Michael (*Physionomia*), 80
Second Lateran Council, 142
sexuality, see *erotic*
Shakespeare, William
    Hamlet, 167
    Merchant of Venice, 94–5, 99–100, 104
    Taming of the Shrew, 30
Sheedy, Charles E., 149, 151
Shichtman, Martin, 129
Simpson, James, 89, 92–3
Sir Degarré, 50–1, 82–93
Sir Gawain and the Green Knight, see Gawain
Sir Lambewelle, see Lanval (character)
Sir Launfal, see Thomas Chestre
Sir Orfeo, 50, 53, 86 n.12, 87
skin (white), 71–2, 81
Southern, R. W., 144, 170–1
Spearing, A. C., 64–5
species transformation, see *magic*
Stonor family, 132, 137–8
Strohm, Paul, 103
submission, see *eroticism*

Taylor, Andrew, 6–7, 10
Thomasset, Claude, 4, 20, 72–3
Tristram (Tristan), 28, 38, 116
Troilus, 61–3, 69, 74
Troilus and Criseyde, see Chaucer
Trojans, 116–31
    in *Troilus and Criseyde* (see Chaucer)
Trotula (Latin), 20

Tryamour, 65–8, 71–5, 78–81

Valente, Roberta, 105
Verdon, Jean, 60
Virgil (Vergil), 119, 145
Virgin Mary, 57, 72–3, 94–8
  antisemitic parody, 94–8
virginity, 5,
  in Welsh foot-holders, 109, 142–3
Vitz, Evelyn Burge, 9
voyeurism, 61–2, 158

The Wedding of Sir Gawain and Dame Ragnelle, 35, 58

Wace, 117–18, 122–3, 129
Walter of Châtillon, 142–6, 148
  'Licet eger cum egrotis,' 142–6

Weiss, Judith, 59
Welsh, Andrew, 111, 115
Welsh literature, 7 n.45, 105–15, 142–3
Winward, Fiona, 109–12

Yalom, Marilyn, 72–3
'Young Man' motif, 28, 37

Ziolkowski, Jan M., 146
Žižek, Slavoj, 129

www.ingramcontent.com/pod-product-compliance
Lightning Source LLC
Chambersburg PA
CBHW070806230426
43665CB00017B/2508